Jan left school at fourteen, married young, producing five spectacular offspring before hearing the siren call of the feminist revolution, at which time she abandoned the kitchen (but not the children!) and headed for the lecture theatre, graduating from Macquarie University with Honours in Political Science and English Literature.

She worked as a political speech writer and stood for a State seat before establishing her own PR consultancy. In more recent times she made her mark as a controversial panellist on the popular daytime TV show, *Beauty & the Beast*. These days she claims to do more writing than talking.

Jan, a sailor, a dreamer, a happy Nonna to fourteen grandchildren lives a secluded life in an offshore community, below an escarpment and below the poverty line, claiming it's a glorious writing life!

www.janmurray.com

Also by Jan Murray

FICTION

Goodbye Lullaby (revised edition 2019)
No Bridge. No Way! (children's novel 2019)

NON-FICTION

Sheer Madness; sex, lies and politics (2010)
Pilgrim Souls (2019)

BRIGHT ECHOES

A novel

JAN MURRAY

Published in 2022 by Ingram Spark
First edition Sydney NSW Australia

Copyright © Jan Murray 2022

The right of Jan Murray to be identified as the author of this work has been asserted by her in accordance with the Copyright Amendment (Moral Rights) Act 2000.

This work is copyright. Apart from any use as permitted under the Copyright Act 1968, no part may be reproduced, copied, scanned, stored in a retrieval system, recorded, or transmitted, in any form or by any means, without the prior written permission of the publisher.

ISBN 978-0-6480002-9-7 (paperback)
ISBN 978-0-6480002-8-0 (hardback)
ISBN 978-0-6480002-7-3 (eBook)

Cover design and internal design by Cathy Campbell, Solas Text and Design (solastextanddesign.com)

Cover images by Travel Dawn / Shutterstock.com / 1641647167 and Peerayot / Shutterstock.com / 401904127

DEDICATON

For Julian, Andrew, Caitlin, Christopher, Jonathon

For Molly, Orlaith, Eli, Connor, Lucien, Honey, Chifley, Tiger, Angel, Tomas, Xanthe, Paddy, Daisy, Ollie

For Noah, Emma, Abbie

ACKNOWLEGEMENT OF COUNTRY

I acknowledge Australia's Aboriginal and Torres Strait Islander peoples as the Traditional Custodians of this ancient land. The Guringai peoples of the Eora Nation have a continuing connection to the land and waters where I live and work. I thank them for protecting this coastline and its ecosystems since time immemorial and pay my respects to Elders past and present.

AUTHOR'S NOTE

What else is there to do if you can't leave your house? Bake bread? I chose to do that in spades. And write the novel I had been promising myself for several years I would write. I began planning it in the early weeks of the first COVID-19 lockdown, March 2020 and amidst the street protests and rioting following the murder of George Floyd in the United States.

In April/May 1992 during my visit to L.A. I experienced the riots and Mayor Bradley's dusk-to-dawn city-wide curfew. And as sure as I'm triple-vaxxed and masked, I've experienced these past two years of full and partial lockdowns amid international riots and social unrest.

Yes, art often reflects life, I hear you say.

I have no crystal ball. I cannot see where we are going but I know where we've been these COVID years and my heart is heavy with thoughts of the devastation the pandemic has visited on so many families around the world who have lost loved ones. May memories of them always be a blessing and might a smile one day replace the tears.

THE ORDERS

Curfew:

An order to stay off the streets. Technically, it requires people to leave public property or vacant private property. Residents must stay inside or face arrest on misdemeanour charges.

State of Emergency:

Issued when a local government is overwhelmed by a crisis. In the case of the riot, it gives the mayor authority to make whatever rules he deems necessary to ensure the public safety. It is issued when officials determine the usual agencies have reached their capacity, and it opens the way for neighbouring departments to assist. Such an order was issued by Mayor Tom Bradley at 12:15 a.m. Thursday.

Martial Law:

A call for greater military powers. Martial Law gives a military commander the authority to make rules or take actions he deems necessary to restore order. Such authority is granted by state or federal governments.

Source: *City Attorney's Office, Los Angeles April 1992*

1

A CITY IN FLAMES: LOS ANGELES, MAY 1992

As instructed, we barred our doors, obeyed the curfew and peered through our TV screens into the hostile night.

Van Jones, 1992

L.A. is burning.

Has been since Wednesday, ever since the all-white jury brought down its shock verdict, giving a free pass to the four white LAPD officers caught on video the previous year dragging Rodney King from his vehicle and mercilessly beating him to a pulp, resulting in a skull fracture, broken bones, broken teeth and permanent brain damage.

And while the baton-wielding quartet are smashing more than fifty savage kicks and blows into the body of the helpless black man before dragging his broken body along the ground face down, seventeen of their fellow officers stand by, approving the violence. Captured on camera and beamed around the world. Horrific to watch. And yet at 3.00pm Wednesday the four assailants walk free from the Simi Valley courthouse.

The arc of the moral universe is long, but it bends towards justice, said the sage. But try telling that to the men and women standing outside the courthouse since sunrise sweating on the verdict. For them, the arc of their moral universe just collapsed. Justice isn't blind, she's racist.

Black rage ignites the angry mob. Its fury erupts, the shock reverberates across the nation. But it's Los Angeles where the brunt of the mob's fury is unleashed.

So fierce the South-Central riots, so out of control, so far beyond the means of the law and even the military to quell that days later buildings are still being torched, shops still being looted, the mob still venting its fury. And now it isn't a Rodney King under the boot. Now it's a white man being dragged out of his truck and savagely beaten by black men wielding tire irons and bricks while their own kind look on, applauding the violence.

According to the archives of the L.A. Fire Department, from the moment of the eruption—3pm on the Wednesday through to 11pm the following Monday—the official death toll will stand at 54 dead and 2,383 injured, of which 228 injuries will be deemed critical. Over 12,000 arrests will have been made and 7,000 fires reduce buildings to cinders. In terms of property damage, the estimate was almost $1 billion, with 3,100 businesses affected by rioting and looting. Significantly, the 1807 Insurrection Act would be invoked to allow the Commander-in-Chief, President George H. Bush, to deploy the United States military against its own citizens.

Many Los Angelenos will never recover from the violence; from their loss of faith in the justice system; the deaths; the personal injuries; the property damage; the sundering of their communities and the failure of the authorities to protect them and their families from the horror of those few terrifying days and nights when an unjust verdict was brought down and their city exploded in a paroxysm of vengeance.

It will be their legacy, the stories they will tell their children and their children's children, the horrors they will never forget. Others who suffered far less than traumatized Los Angelinos but who still found themselves caught up in the events, their personal experiences of the time they spent in 1992 during the L.A. riots will figure in their stories also, be a part of their histories as well.

2

CYNTHIA

Being human is a complicated gig.
So, give that ol' dark night of the soul a hug.
Howl the eternal yes!
Friedrich Nietzsche

Why was I in the City of Angels on that eventful day in the Spring of 1992, America's Spring? Back home it was Autumn. Call it Fall. Why? Because on the eve of my 40th birthday I was desperate for new beginnings. Make that New Beginnings. Worthy of caps. Worthy of a drum roll. Recently, certain issues had unfolded not to my liking, to the point I was prompted to take a hard look at myself. A hard look at my life, an unexamined one being one not worth living.

So, I put my life under the microscope and came away feeling miserable, not liking what I saw. Not liking how things were panning out. Compared myself to Connie. Realized I needed to get a life. Connie had found contentment. Cow-like contentment for sure but Con was doing it her way and good for Con. For me, a single woman, childless woman, woman unhappy in her job it was time to disrupt the stasis, throw inertia to the four winds and ring in the changes. And for that to happen, I needed an action plan, one to herald in a newly minted forty-year-old Cynthia Lorraine Smart.

Do not delegate to Fate, I cautioned during that long night of the soul, the night I lay awake strategizing, panicking about the Big

Four-O flashing in neon up ahead.

With the dawn came certainty. I reckoned I had it mapped. Three bullet points defining the strategy: Item One on my Let's Get Cynthia a Bit of What She Deserves Action Plan would be to turn my back on an admittedly lucrative but personally unsatisfying career as a Group Account Director with Baker & Glassop. Crazy brave? Not if you knew Haydn Glassop. Giving that man the bird was possibly top of my list. Like walking out into sunshine after a colonic irrigation, I opined to Connie.

Everything came at a price.

Walking away from B&G would mean giving up on trying to drag their sorry arses into the new millennium, giving up on having the Neanderthals realize the untapped potential of the young women in their agency. Lien for example, a highly capable young woman. Lien Nguyen was all anyone could desire in a personal assistant but selfish of me to go on limiting Lien's career potential. The agency should be giving Lien Nguyen an opportunity to manage a couple of client accounts. I would have happily mentored her, given half a chance. Even the younger females around the office who toiled with no higher expectation than mail-sorting and coffee runs deserved a chance to shine. But I'd grown weary of the battle. There were other ways to blow up the ramparts.

Item Two was to find a qualifying male, a man to meet my standards if I were to consider the motherhood question. Not Connie's prolific motherhood, naturally. God forbid. No time for that kind of fecundity. Nor the desire. But a son or daughter would ease the emptiness that of late had me staring into the void. Even before the current agonizing and strategizing I'd cleared the way for the man-search, having already treated my mating life to an overdue clean-out.

Truth be told, I had been on a dry paddock for months. I had made some bad choices in the man department over the years, which had left me jaded and, approaching my 40th birthday, childless. During my nubile decades I'd kissed off one husband and many lovers ranging from downright toxic to just plain ineffectual. The last of the live ins to be given his hat and shown the door had not been a bad person. Just that he had nothing much of interest to say after rolling off me, was how I put it to Connie once that door had slammed shut and I'd frisbeed his Nirvana *Nevermind* album out the upstairs window.

Why waste good coffee on losers, was Connie's come-back.

Item Three: Once no longer shackled to the advertising industry treadmill I could set my sights on the successful screenwriting career I had been promising myself. Even with a child in tow, I could write, produce and—dream of dreams—direct. I could kick off the dream by finally accepting David's generous offer of assistance.

Once *Surrender Song* was green-lighted, Lien might even welcome the challenge to work as my production assistant. It would be a Level One entrée into the film industry. God knows, there would be no stopping that girl once she grabbed the bit between her teeth. As auteur, I would insist on a female-heavy cast and crew. The possibilities were unlimited for those with good intentions and mine were good intentions. Eventually I closed my eyes and surrendered to sleep on that seminal night of the soul.

However—and it's a big However—all the midnight-hour angst, all the steely determination to end the torpor and set out to conquer a brave new Cynthia World occurred before Professor Wadsworth's diagnosis landed.

The following week I would hear words that had the power to torpedo dreams, set the clock ticking down to the zero hour. It was the joker, the wild card in the pack. Read: mean, unfair card. But put a pin in it for the moment. For now, I needed to stay resolute about getting a greenlight on *Surrender Song*, which meant forgetting old man Wadsworth's doom and gloom scenarios and hopping on a plane to L.A. Stick a confident Cynthia-smile on my face and shop my project to Hollywood.

Now more than ever, straight to Tinseltown. No messing about on home territory with 10bA tax breaks, cobbling paltry bits of funding together from country dentists and doctors who sought nothing more than to see their names appear in the credits and maybe, if the film bombed, pick up a handy tax break. Or for the pathetic jocks with their hairy chests and gold chains, the promise of hob-knobbing with the red-carpet kids. No, next week I was off to the States on serious movie business. To L.A., where else?

And so, here I am; in the City of Angels in America's Spring of 1992, on the eve of turning Forty on what will be an historic day for the United States of America but no less historic for me, Cynthia Lorraine Smart.

3

CYNTHIA

Rouse, and for shame the goblet bring.

Omar Khayyam

Santa Monica, Los Angeles
Friday 1st May 1992

A sweet Southern California day. You'd think. But from where I sat in the back seat of the 1967 blue Ford Mustang rental, roof down, cruising along Wiltshire towards the luxurious Miramar Hotel on Ocean Avenue—sirens splitting the air and chopper blades whirring overhead—it felt more like a war zone than a California Dreaming kind of day. Surreal. One I hadn't planned on in all that pre-dawn strategizing.

'So, the Samuel Goldwyn guy hasn't given you anything to take to the bank, Cyn? Nothing at all?' Connie saying this from the front passenger seat. I pretended not to hear. Blame the choppers, the sirens.

I landed here last night with the screenplay tucked under my arm, planning to hit the ground running this morning. Have Hollywood eating out of my hand by lunchtime. Or at least coughing up a pre-sale. David had set me up with Myron Spinak, the big acquisitions honcho at Goldwyn and for sure the man would say he was in—Australia was still flavour of the month in Hollywood, hungry for Outback stories—and then Arthur Anderson's people—David's US accountancy colleagues—could confidently go to their investors for funding.

Easy-peasy. What wasn't there to love about being in L.A. today? L.A., the movie capital of the world, the place where a screenwriter's dreams come true. The greenlight. A shooting script. Production meetings. Casting sessions. Catching the dailies, the rushes. The box office takings. The film festival circuit. Credibility among peers, followed by new offers. Media interviews. Explaining how, through your story, you hoped to raise issues affecting women's lives. The reason you quit advertising to pursue a higher purpose.

What wasn't there to love about L.A., a place where the magic begins?

Here's what; the L.A. I'd landed in was otherwise occupied.

I had flown straight into the belly of the beast. Los Angeles, aflame. A conflagration. Whole neighbourhoods torched. Citizens killed. And to top that off, my screenplay had just copped a great big fat Hollywood-type raspberry a few hours ago. Walking out of that meeting this morning in Century City, I'd felt like a beaten down wannabe, someone way out of her depth.

Nevertheless, I wasn't finished with Hollywood. Not yet. Not by a long shot. I would suck it up and get back in the fight. There was still tonight's important meeting with the money men. They would understand in this game a writer has to kiss a lot of frogs before she finds her prince. Myron Spinak was just the first of the frogs. They would give me other leads. There would come a prince, and with Arthur Anderson's financial backing I was in with a great chance. Meanwhile, I had been dropped into the mother of all riots.

'Cyn?' Connie, again.

Ignore her.

This was the third day of rioting. The infernos were still raging unabated. Chaos reigned, looters looted, news broadcasters alarmed the population with their accounts of downtown devastation. But as I was about to find out, the shit storm was no longer confined to South Central. It was spreading out from its molten core, entrapping whole suburbs. So, no, there was not much to love about the situation I found myself in when I stepped off the plane and into a world gone mad. And then to have Samuel Goldwyn's acquisitions guy blurt at me? A sweet day? Go figure.

The station was replaying Rodney King's press conference from earlier in the day. *People, I just want to say, can we all get along? Can we stop making it horrible for the older people and the kids?*

'Give me some volume on that thing, missus,' I ordered Connie. And then, leaning across and tapping Con's shoulder, 'Pump it up a bit.'

We can get along here ... we've just got to ... just got to. I mean ... I think it's just not right ... and ... um ... it's not gonna change anything ... um ... we'll get our justice ... um ... they've won the battle, but they haven't won the war ... we'll have our day in court, and that's all we want ... and, ah ... y'know, I love everyone ... I'm not like they give me out to be ... we've got to quit ... we gotta quit! After all, I mean ....

'Poor man. He sounds so depressed, so nervous.' Connie eyed me in the rear-view mirror. 'He probably—'

'Shush.' King had just said a security guard had been killed.

It's just not right. It's just not right ... because those people will never go home to their families again...

Connie, turning around in her seat: 'How did it go this morning? I mean really go. Half okay, or what?'

Useless to try and hear what King was saying.

Let's try to work it out.... Let's ...

'Was he forthcoming—with anything?'

'Hey, Con?' said David, looking sideways at his wife and indicating the mountain of boutique shopping bags on her lap and at her feet. 'Looks like you cut a decent swathe through Rodeo Drive this afternoon.' He turned from the wheel and over his shoulder, threw a wink. 'Have a good time, you girls?' A second wink. 'Cyn? A good time, hey?'

David would know what a good time I'd had trailing his wife all afternoon. The torment. The tedium. Consumerism gone mad. On and on and on, until had the woman suggested we attack one more lousy boutique, I would have pulled out the old Swiss Army and gone for a major artery. Sticking it out all afternoon, a push-over, a pet poodle trotting along beside the mistress, drooling as mistress plunders Rodeo Drive for outfits, trinkets, handbags, perfumes. Oohing and aahing as middle-aged mistress comes skipping out of fitting rooms all aflutter. Pirouettes for poodle's benefit, checks herself out in mirrors, giddy as any teenager choosing her prom dress. Poor darling, blind to those persistent mother rolls of hers.

I had tried. Lord knows, I'd tried to ignore the condescension oozing out of every pore of those toned-up saleswomen looking down their cosmetically enhanced noses at a pair of scrubbers from Down Under who were wasting their time. The hoity-toity dames weren't so ready to look down their reconstructed snouts once Connie started flashing her platinum.

Haughty to unctuous. A pantomime of human behaviour.

Before Wadsworth dropped the bombshell on me last week, I might have just laughed at the attitude of those Rodeo Drive counter jumpers but now I felt snarky, snarky towards all attractive women confident in their femininity. I resented them. Wished them all to Hell.

Please? We can get along, here ... we all can get along ... we just got to! I mean, we're all stuck here for a while... King, his pleas to his brothers and sisters, black and white, delivered with grace. The man has grace.

The interview over, the announcer began riffing on the violence spreading across a wider area of Los Angeles.

I was glad we'd opted for Santa Monica's Miramar over the famous downtown Biltmore, the lavish thirties-era hotel known for its glamorous Hollywood celebrity clientele, past and present. At least way out in Santa Monica we'd be quarantined from the riots. A good thing, because David had arranged the Arthur Anderson dinner tonight at a restaurant somewhere along Third Street Promenade. David believed in my film. As he promised back in Sydney, he was keen to introduce me to his stateside colleagues, the serious money men. Unlike the lunch today with a bunch of name-dropping self-important industry luvvies who made yours truly feel like a hanger-on, an extra in a B-grade movie, this one tonight would be a working dinner to discuss funding for the project. A dinner for Cynthia's benefit. Ooh la la. Here in Hollywood. Imagine.

I had copped an extra raspberry at the lunch. Somewhere short of my watermelon shaved ice dessert I gave up on trying to get my surly table mate to spark up, offer some conversation about himself and his work, about Hollywood goings-on. About anything. No hope of that. The guy was AWOL. Had he not been, I might have performed a subtle segue, mentioned en passant my own project. That's if the occasion had arisen. It hadn't. And it seemed the legendary indie auteur Nick Cristos had zero interest in Cynthia Smart, or the reason she was in L.A. with the Labelles.

After all these years hearing about Nick Cristos from Connie and Sapphire—not so much from David—I had finally met the guy, Connie's long-ago American lover and Sapphire's biological father. And the introduction had fallen flatter than a fiddler's fart.

Lover boy. Con's Mexican conquest. Sire of Sapphire. Darling of the Toronto and Venice Film Festivals last year. All the above he was but what Nick Cristos was not was the life of the party.

Taciturn is how I would describe the man's personality. Slow to make small talk. Not that taciturn was necessarily a fault in a man. Far from it. Taciturn can work. Holding back can work. So many men go into overdrive to impress a woman on a first meet; indulge an atavistic imperative, make like a peacock fanning his tail feathers, doing the strut to impress the hens. No tail feathers, no strut today. Not from the oh-so-serious, sober-sided Mr Super Cool Nick Cristos. A woman could have had more fun at a Chinese opera.

A stranger in their midst I may have been, but I wasn't exactly a complete outsider. He knew who I was. I was Connie's friend from childhood. Yet we hadn't wandered down that tangled path. He stayed schtum. Aloof. Disinterested. Perhaps he felt uncomfortable traversing that territory. Did he think I blamed him for what happened sixteen years ago—getting my girlfriend knocked-up—he, an older married man, a documentary filmmaker, sweeping young Constance Bray off her feet? All the jazz of a big international conference, a guy in town alone, and an attractive young Australian delegate looking lost on the big stage in Mexico?

No, I had never thought to blame him. Connie hadn't either, so far as I knew. It was a three-day coupling resulting in a pregnancy. Sapphire, the blessing from that intercontinental dalliance being one of the more substantive spin-offs from the 1975 International Year of the Woman Conference. I could still raise goose bumps recalling Connie's homecoming back then, seeing her step off the plane at Mascot with baby Sapphire strapped to her chest.

Nick Cristos. Even though I'd struggled at the lunch to engage him in any kind of meaningful conversation, and awkward in his presence, it struck me that were I casting for a men's cosmetics campaign—promoting a musky he-man deodorant for instance—Cristos would be my guy; confidently mature, owning strong features, a beard worthy of a serious writer, a full mop of steel grey wavy hair just sufficiently unkempt to stir a woman's imagination, and with a Hemmingway-style virility. It was a fact; the man conveyed a certain male mystique that would move product off the shelf.

Connie sat us next to each other at lunch. Connie, the matchmaker. From time to time, I felt her sneaking a sly glance across the table at us. As if the man could give a flying fuck for matchmaking. As if I could. Cristos had come through a second divorce last year, and according to Con, was still bruised.

Good old Con, with her sympathetic meddling Mother Earth complex, probably thought she could hatch a match. But if that were her game, lover boy wasn't buying into it. Me, neither. I had no need of Connie's ministrations. I could still catch and kill my own. As I was certain Mr Cristos could. And I was sure Cristos would have felt more comfortable sitting beside any one of the other guests, any of the locals around the table, rather than the woman from Australia they lobbed on him. Even if I were his daughter's godmother. Surely a talking point. But apart from a cursory enquiry and a couple of anecdotes I offered him about his adorable Sapphire—before he turned back to the rest of the table—no.

Nothing. Zilch.

For all that, I did welcome the attentive way he held the chair back for me when the luncheon party finally rose to leave the restaurant, and how he courteously rested a firm hand beneath my elbow to guide me out the door. Leaning in to kiss my cheek at the curbside during the alohas was a pleasant surprise, as if I were family. But then they are a kissy crowd, the lot of them. L.A., what else? If schmoozing were ever made illegal, their jails couldn't cope.

Asking if I would care to have him look over my screenplay was the real kicker. He held my briefcase until I settled myself into the Mustang. It had come out of nowhere, the request.

Still waters, Mother would have said of this man. Still waters runneth deep, my dear. The arrogant prick had all but ignored me throughout lunch while all the time he knew I'd written a screenplay. Connie would have informed him. Or David. Well, he had finally come good and asked to read it. Out of curtesy to the Labelles, no doubt, and not before the luncheon was over and he was safely out the door. He would have suspected he'd been set up, feared I would be in his ear trying to pitch my project to him over the gazpacho and still going when the macchiatos came around. Hence the stand-off. He must cop it all the time. Didn't need it. This woman from Down Under getting in his lug about her amazing project.

Truth be told, I had been grateful for his lack of interest. Grateful, too, the rest of the table hadn't shown interest. By the way, Cynthia, dahhling; your screenplay, honey? How'd your meeting go? Samuel Goldwyn's guy, wasn't it? Spinak? A good guy, Myron. Big shot. A real comer. He like what you give him, Cynthia? Shouldda mentioned my name, honey.

No, nothing of the kind from the luncheon party. They had left me alone, excluded me from their in-house chatter. And for that, at least, I had been grateful, having suffered enough humiliation for one day. I had a thing about bleeding in public.

With my advertising hat on, I was a hard arse who could leave her ego at the door, pitch campaigns to clients and deal with their qualms and criticisms with equanimity. Not so with my creative writing. Rejection stings, I'd learned this morning. Spinak had kissed me out the door. Not with a flat-out rejection, admittedly, but not by waving a pre-sale agreement at me, either. Maybe think about putting one of our writers on the job, he said to David, ignoring me. Y'know your Outback has appeal ... we're always looking for good Aussie product ... blah, blah, blah.

Just not mine, it seemed; a couple of ballsy sixteen-year-olds with a baby to feed, trying to make it in the Australian outback of the Fifties. Victims of a hypocritical society, forcing an unmarried girl to surrender her baby. And in the Seventies, the girls—now women—finally taking on the establishment. Maybe another writer, he opined.

I'd known before I sat down at the great man's desk this morning that in this town a writer of my lowly status is going to be pushing a barrow uphill, especially with an art house project. No big names attached. I would be given a few minutes to pitch. Take longer and you've lost him. He has his concealed panic button. A perky young assistant sticks her head in the door and reminds her boss about his luncheon engagement, or some other confab. The elevator pitch, the synopsis in twenty-five words. And best if those twenty-five words begin with a What if? And you need a high concept. What if we get Arnold Schwarzenegger and Danny De Vito to play twins? How about a monster shark visits a crowded tourist beach?

We sailed through the introductions, thanks to Spinak and David having mutual friends and connections in Hollywood. And, as Spinak was quick to declare, Down Under has special appeal. Every Aussie is related to Crocodile Dundee. He gushed about how that little Aussie battler had captured the hearts of America's cinema goers. But then, as if a flight from Sydney to Los Angeles were an odyssey of unimaginable travail, he had to marvel at the distance we'd travelled to get to his front door. If he had intended to put me off my game, he scored points for trying. I had brought him a gift from an outer galaxy, a curiosity piece, but superfluous to his planet's requirements.

Kiss, kiss, aloha.

David had warned me that this studio executive, Myron Spinak, was something of a soulless creature. But the guy had clout. Young, brash and intolerant of projects which did not jump out at him, but able to greenlight a project if it took his fancy. It was worth a try. From Detroit's auto industry via a stint at Twentieth Century, he had earned a reputation as a top gun. However, that reputation came with a footnote; the guy could be a total arse-wipe. Spinak had leant back in his chair, put his hands behind his head and his boots up on his desk. Open to the magic.

Nothing to it. I was back at Baker & Glassop. On my feet. Articulate. Confident. A belief in what I was pitching. Owning the room. Closing the deal.

So, you have these two young women who—

Yeah? Young women, hey? He grinned. Seemed to like it.

They're two strong females and what if they—

The grin vanishes. So, strong women, hey? Let me get this; your girls are lesbians, right?

No, no. They're—

So? Feet off the desk. Leans forward on his elbows, grins. When do our gals get their gear off?

By the time we walked out of the Century City office, my tough Aussie girls had morphed into a couple of New York pole dancers, one set upon by a horny gorilla in Central Park Zoo, the other slain by the beast atop the Empire State. Not really. But it felt so. Bean-counters. Dullards who sign the cheques with their dicks and know their balls are on the line if the first weekend's box office returns disappoint. Bozos who care nothing for artistic integrity. So, I was secretly a little jazzed when someone of Cristos's standing, even belatedly, enquired about *Surrender Song*.

Americans are a polite race, however, and if he ever gets around to reading it, he will possibly think less of it than the studio guy. Nevertheless, to knock back the great Nick Cristos' offer would have been not only discourteous, but downright idiotic. The guy was a guru to aspiring writers. Just maybe—just maybe he might find something to love in today's orphan.

The Mustang was approaching the Miramar when I noticed the army helicopters dipping and disappearing out over the Pacific Ocean. The police sirens had also taken a hike.

Connie raised her eyes to the rear-vision mirror. 'What did you think of him?'

'Myron Spinak?' I was playing it dumb.

'Nick! Cute, no?'

'For godsakes, Connie. The man was your—' I stopped myself from saying the word 'lover'. David was in the car and while I knew he worshipped Sapphire and apparently got on well with the biological father on the rare occasions they met, how he felt about the old romance who could say? Sophisticated enough and madly in love with his wife, as I discovered last week, there was probably some residual rivalry there.

Connie turned off the car radio and spun around full-on to face me. 'Okay, missus, let's change the subject. Back to your meeting. Good in parts? Or totally otherwise?'

'Jesus, Con.' I yanked her sunnies off and stared into the glare of Los Angeles, its air fouled by rising plumes of black smoke off in the distance. All afternoon together, traipsing from one boutique to the next while the woman hoovered up every size twelve on Rodeo Drive and now—when all I wanted was to get upstairs, kick off my shoes, undo my belt, pour a drink and forget about the miserable lunch, forget about the poor souls down in South-Central and most of all forget about the god-awful supercilious Myron Spinak—the woman wants to grill me about the meeting. 'Good, or otherwise? Otherwise, I guess you could say, Con. Yeah, decidedly otherwise.'

'Hey, that's a bummer, love. He really didn't go for it then, hey? But don't worry. Y'know what I've been telling you; you needed to spice it up a bit for Hollywood.'

'Spice it up, you reckon? Spice it up, hey?' Oh, blithe spirit.

'Yeah, babe. Give it a bit more ... y'know, a bit more oomph.'

'Con, let it go,' said David.

'Only saying.'

He patted his wife's knee. 'Don't you worry. She's still in the game.'

The Mustang hung a right and we drove in through the Miramar's big iron gates and up the driveway past the mighty fig, a long-ago gift from Australia.

We pulled in under the porche cochere. A uniformed valet snapped to it, opening David's door and relieving him of the keys. I jammed my Aviators back on and climbed out, wriggling to adjust the cream linen skirt that had ridden up around my thighs. I turned to Connie, put a hand on her shoulder and eyeballed her. 'You know what, Con? You and that studio prick are on the same page.' I reached into the car's back seat and grabbed the briefcase then straightened up again. 'Yep. He pretty much said the same thing. A bit more oomph.'

'Well, there you go.'

I left the Labelles to sort out Connie's forest of boutique bags tumbling out of the Mustang and headed inside. Thank the lord this day would soon end.

Until it did, however, it would take a nip or two of the duty-free Glenfiddich sitting in my carry-on bag upstairs to smooth the way to anything like a tolerable evening.

4

SAPPHIRE

First love is only a little foolishness and a lot of curiosity.

George Bernard Shaw

Santa Monica, Los Angeles
Friday 1st May 1992

She sat on the soft grass alongside the busted bicycle feeling uneasy.

Not because she had come a cropper off the bike—which she had—but because of the buckled wheel, which wasn't her fault. And she was feeling uneasy because her mother would be lobbing at the babysitter's and freaking out because she wasn't there. She should be heading back to Goldman's bungalow instead of sitting Shiva on a hired bike while she waited for a sweet boy to go get a plaster for her grazed knee.

Not all the boys around the grounds of the hotel were as sweet as Mateo Lopez. Particularly the nut-job who had just tried playing chicken with her by forcing her off the path at full speed. A creep who hadn't come off that well, himself.

Mateo had left his treasured boombox in her safe keeping. Tuned to KFWB, it was broadcasting a steady stream of Mexican music. Good for him, but she could only take so much of the clanging noise and started searching the dial for something more to her liking. Movies, they agreed on, for sure. Music, no. She stopped twiddling the dial when a news item caught her attention; police wanted Los Angeles city beaches closed.

No, not happening. This is Santa Monica. She was promised a day out tomorrow.

A man, short, old and probably famous—because this was L.A.—smiled at her, turning his head as he hurried past, still gawking at her.

'Rubber neck,' she said, loud enough that he heard because he laughed as he waved back at her with a grin and walked off.

She knew what he'd been thinking. After all, this was the Miramar Hotel and in her flea market gear she could easily be mistaken for Jody Foster. Plenty said it, she was Jody's double. Complexion creamy, face heart-shaped, chin dimpled, streaky blonde hair and green eyes flashing their No Trespassing warning at passers-by like him. Only difference, unlike Jody, she didn't see her future in movies. She was set on becoming a foreign correspondent.

With one hand, she held her hair back and leant forward to check out the graze, doing her best with chewed nails to ease away shreds of torn skin. It hurt like Hell when she blew on the raw wound. Worse, the fall had damaged her purple tights and left grass stains on her yellow mini. Her favourites, the tights. But now a massive ladder running up her thigh. Bummer.

The graze was deep enough to scar. No sweat. Personal history. She would be marked for life and for all her life she would only need to touch the ridge of tough skin to remember being here. Los Angeles. In America's Spring of 1992. Always remembering she had met a fabulously gorgeous boy called Mateo Lopez.

Years from now she pictured herself sitting in the lecture hall—UCLA, of course, School of Communications—the Fiat Lux Freshman seminar—and slipping her hand down to her knee, rubbing her finger over the ridge of skin and smiling to herself. Her scar. Her secret. The memory of this magic Miramar day. They would ask her about it. It is what it is, is all she would say. Let it be part of the mystery that was and always would be Sapphire Cristos-Labelle. Kids at school already thought her a freak because she had two surnames.

Two dads. Her Bi-Coastals. Her Adorables; David and Nick.

Come on, Mateo, where the heck are you? How long can it take to drag up a First Aid kit. Rita Goldman would be wetting her pants. The woman was so boring. Mateo wasn't. And Rita Goldman was a Republican.

She drew her leg up tight into to her chest. Stretching the skin increased the pain and made the graze weep blood and clear stuff but made it easier to study the damage. Several layers of skin had been left behind on the pavement. Layers of epidermis. She learned about the epidermis in Biology, the medical term for the seven layers. And learned skin was the largest organ of the human body. She adored Biology. And Miss Carpenter. Cutting up a dead frog was way cool. Or maybe not so much.

Studying the graze with forensic intensity, she noted the shards of embedded pavement, minuscule clumps of sharp gravel and dirt. Already it was scabbing with dried blood and other muck. Where was that boy? She knew about gangrene, had once read about a plane crash victim lost in wilderness in the Gold Coast hinterland. He let flies blow his wound so maggots could go to work healing it. This place was too posh for maggots. Gangrene preferred.

She straightened her legs out, leant back against the tree and closed her eyes. Was this to be the moment in history when she changed her name? She often played around with the idea. Fanaticised about ditching Sapphire. She preferred to be called Piper. Piper Cristos-Labelle, reporting from Patagonia. Her by-line. She might try Piper out this week, here in freaksville, where else? The Hollywood stars improve on the names they're given at birth. Nick told her Leaf Phoenix was born Joaquin Rafael and his favourite, Elton John, was christened Reginald Dwight.

She spat a glob of frothy saliva on two fingers and patted the wound. Animals heal their babies with their spit. She'd read about the natural healing chemicals in saliva. Mrs Goldman told her this morning there'd been a drive-by shooting in the riots downtown. Gangland stuff. It sounded tragic. Four people killed. You couldn't imagine a thing like that ever happening in sleepy Katoomba. Not up in the boring Blue Mountains. She still couldn't believe what had happened today. Certainly not boring. She and this boy, Mateo Lopez. It was as if they'd known each other from birth. Not like he was this Mexican kid from L.A. and she, a girl from Katoomba. He felt as comfortable as her old Reeboks.

Mateo had never seen *Thelma and Louise.* Lots of other movies they both agreed were awesome. Just not T and L., which was uncool of him. But he promised he would get the video out. Providing she promised to get *Die Hard* and watch it. *Die Hard?* God! But the excellence of *My Own Private Idaho* was the thing they most agreed on. That, and *Edward Scissorhands.* Keanu Reeves and Johnny Depp were legend. Mateo reckoned, too.

Affirmative.

He went for *Fast Times at Ridgemont High* just as much as she did. Didn't everyone. He laughed when she told him she had kind of the same feelings when he said hello to her earlier today as Geena Davis had when Brad Pitt—blue jeans and big white hat—walks up to their convertible and says Hi to the girls. He owns his own bike, Mateo. By comparison to the hotel's hired one, his is a classic so she was glad she hadn't been riding his when the nutcase took her on.

Made up from bits and pieces scavenged around his neighbourhood, he said when she complimented him on his awesome speedster. He was clever. The Miramar should put him in one of their *really* smart uniforms Like his big brother, a proper waiter. They should give him a better job. Not just gathering up people's dirty plates all day, scraping their slops into bins and running messages.

At last! From around the corner of the building, peddling furiously, she saw him heading towards her.

With the sun at his back, his crazy dreadlocks flying in the wind, he reminded her of a warrior riding into battle. Wild black corkscrews they made him tie up under his cap. At work, he told her he wore white coat and black trousers but now he was in faded blue jeans, a white tee and a soft black leather jacket. He wore all kinds of leather and bands on his tanned wrists. Nothing like any other boy she knew.

'Got it,' said the rider, screeching to a splintering halt, painting rubber on the pavement. 'Plasters and—'ow you say—i-o-deen?' A satisfied grin. He docked the bike and knelt before her and screwed the lid off the iodine bottle. When he took hold of her leg she winced and pulled away.

'Hey, you have to wash the dirt away first!' She struggled to her feet and looked around for a tap. 'Water? Where can we get water round here?'

'No. Please. Sit. I should 'ave brought water. Clean water. Stay. I will go for it. Sterile water. And tissues. I will cleanse you.'

It sounded ceremonial. I will cleanse you. Cleansed, like a sacrifice to be offered at the altar. She smiled at the sweet naiveté of the boy 'You will? You'll do that for me? Ride all the way back to the kitchen just for sterile water?'

'Si.' He shrugged. Embarrassed. 'Of course. Only is the kitchen. Not—' He hesitated then grinned, '—not Oss-strahlia, okay? No kan-ga-roos. Cock-a-toos.'

Lame. Anyone else, she would have groaned. Instead, she grinned and waved him off again, blowing a kiss and staring after him as he disappeared around the corner of the building again. Already, she missed him. A Mexican boy. Mateo Lopez. She whispered his name. Softly. But not so soft she couldn't hear herself say the words. Or feel her body catch a thrill she had yet to name.

Relaxing against the tree trunk, she gave the brush-off to a couple of concerned guests strolling towards her looking as if they were about to put on that kind of adult worried act that bugged her. She turned off the radio, preferring to be left alone with her thoughts of the boy; his husky musical voice with its ups and downs in unexpected places, his golden skin, his hairy limbs. Half boy, half man. Sixteen to her fifteen. She pictured the kids back at Katoomba High. That doofus tribe. Craters of acne and bouncing Adam's Apples that alarmed her. Where had they been before they popped out, those bony throat corks? She compared Mateo to her classmates back home. Not only did they not measure up to Mateo Lopez's native beauty, but none of those boys were nearly half so clued-up. No clue about American politics, for a start. Or movies. *Home Alone* was about as good as it got in Katoomba. God, *Home Alone?*

She just hoped he would return before her leg turned gangrenous, that was all. She turned the radio on again to kill time but just as quickly turned it off. What did she care that some clown had just phoned 9-1-1 threatening to blow up a police station?

A woman pulled up on her bike, planting her espadrilles firmly on the path either side of the bar. A concerned look contorted her sun-damaged face. 'Are you okay, dear?'

'I'm good, thanks.'

'What happened, darling?'

'Ran over a dog.'

'My god!' the woman gasped, her hand flying to her chest as her jaw dropped. 'You ran over a dog?'

The befuddled woman's eyes were bulging so far out of her head Sapphire was ready to duck.

'What kind of a dog?'

'Big one. Buckled the wheel.' She shrugged and turned back to her wounded knee while the dumbstruck rider peeled away from her.

5

CYNTHIA

Keep calm and carry on.

Winston Churchill

Santa Monica, Los Angeles

Friday 1st May 1992

It came as a blow. No sooner in the foyer than the hotel's man came across to us from Reception. 'Ah, Mr and Mrs Labelle, Suite 746. And Ms Smart, Room 708, right?' All apologies on behalf of management, he launched into a spiel about the 'escalating tensions', the rioting heading this way. The authorities had just announced they were extending the curfew city-wide. Santa Monica, included.

'Santa Monica?'

'Confined to barracks. Dusk to dawn, I'm afraid, Ms Smart.'

Kill me now! This was not good news. Not at all. Where were Arthur Anderson's money men in all this? Caught up in the curfew? Here for only another twenty-four hours before I fly to New York and dinner tonight now cancelled? This was not what I wanted to hear. 'Precisely what does it mean? Dusk? A disappearing sun? Darkness descending across the earth?' I was livid.

'Dusk, Ms Smart?' He smiled, raised an elegant eyebrow. 'I guess you could define it as the undark that heralds in the night.'

Nice comeback! 'Ah, ha. The undark that heralds the night? Pretty. I like it.' Lexical flexibility, a choice of words to create something greater than the sum of its parts. A natural-born copywriter. Or poet.

He preened. The clever man. Vain man. And, truth be told, a man not hard to look at. While he shone his light on the Labelles, I checked him out, top to toe, the Miramar's guy; a flustered matinee idol challenged by events beyond his control, poor dear. Plain to see he was uncomfortable delivering these messages to his swell guests.

Rudolph Valentino. Tall, slim-as. And slightly south of thirty, I'd wager. Slick-backed Brylcreemed hair. Black as jet, a la the pharmacy bottle. And a pencil-thin moustache which did wonders to highlight sensual wine-dark lips. He may as well have been standing there in a robe and turban beside an oasis, a scimitar in his belt, camel at his back and a reclining maiden strumming a dulcimer somewhere down stage. A studied throwback to the Hollywood Golden age and more appropriate to the Spanish Mission-style Biltmore Hotel than this palmy balmy more modern up-market pub. Good for you, Rudi. Everyone needs a persona. Especially in Hollywood. Mandatory in Hollywood. No doubt he made time in his busy schedule to fit in auditions.

'Officially, they say it's just before night fall when the daylight dims' He was putting it out for the Labelles as well now—the not so cynical guests—but it still came across as good copy or poetry.

'Okay, then; the undark. The gloaming. The curfew tolls the knell of parting day. But what happens if I had plans for this evening, an important industry dinner up the road for instance? Suppose I give the bird to their undark?' I caught and held his gaze. 'Do they shoot me?'

'Mayor Bradley said lawbreakers will be arrested. And while I do not think our mayor would line you up to a firing squad, Ms Smart—' he said, lifting one finely arched eyebrow and his head to the side '—I would suggest you not put your supposition to the test.' There was the hint of a grin. 'It is expected to be rough on the streets tonight. The National Guard and the military reinforcements are taking their time getting here and that's making everyone nervous. Ergo: The police are not coping. Tensions are running high. Danger on the streets.' He held my gaze. Lowered his voice. His words for me, alone. 'I would not run afoul of their guns, were I you.'

'Dangerous,' said David with a chuckle, as if this whole rotten lockdown business were nothing more than a deck chair in the Bahamas. 'Shoot first, ask questions later, Cyn.' He two-finger shot me, blew down his barrel and holstered his Glock.

You can't help loving David.

And then came the real kicker. Totally unexpected: Due to the curfew, the Miramar needed to accommodate its staff throughout the hotel tonight and, said Rudi with sincere apologies, as a single female guest Ms Smart's room has been designated as able to accommodate two female staff members. Two folding beds would be set up in Room 708. Two housemaids would be sharing her cell. Total strangers!

'Mexican ladies,' said the management's spunky messenger.

'Mexican ladies? Or Mexican women?'

The epitome of suave was momentarily caught off guard. 'The Hotel's female domestic staff, Ms Smart.' With his clipboard tucked underarm and fingertips in steeple mode, he continued, 'Their homes, unfortunately, are in South Central. The epicentre. Even without the curfew restrictions they would have no way of getting home tonight. Not with the streets the way they are and all public transport systems down.'

Two total strangers bunking down with me.

Two Mexican housemaids, for godsakes.

But ethnicity or job descriptions are not at issue. I wouldn't care if they were Hydra-headed Martian royalty, it was just too weird. Like the fractured reality of dreams. The school bus and you realize you're naked, save for your Bonds singlet and you're desperately pulling the singlet down to cover your bits. All wrong. Out of place. A weird kind of public intimacy. Discombobulating. Two strangers sharing the privacy of my bedroom.

No one would be going anywhere tonight, no money men dinners. And as if that weren't bad enough, for me there would also be the privilege of accommodating a couple of random Latinos. Too bad if Nick Cristos had made a move on me over lunch this afternoon. Too bad. Unless a group grope was on the cards and with a pair of Mexicans in the mix.

One thing was for sure; it wasn't going to be an ordinary L.A. night, tonight.

'Not a problem, is it, Cyn?' said Connie, dropping a load of boutique bags and reaching an arm out to wrap around my shoulder. 'We all need to get along together if we're stuck here, right? Like Rodney King just said. God knows, we've all done it haven't we? In our student days. Been housemaids. Waitresses. Remember when we took off down the South Coast and—'

'Sure, we've done it.' Please God deliver me from this woman.

'Let's face it,' Connie continued for young Valentino's sake, 'I do it every day, anyway. An unpaid housemaid. Run around after a parcel of brats and His Lordship, here.' Connie tweaked David's ear. 'Pick up their shitty undies and wet towels all day. Right, lover boy?'

Poor man. He must feel like the lad whose mum has just told a woman on the bus her little Davey had recently sprouted pubes. I felt for him, but then again, he married Connie Bray. He was used to it. He deserved it.

'Guests will need to remain within the hotel precinct until the curfew is lifted.' Rudi V was all business again. Speaking from the script. No sign of what I'd taken to be a mild flirtation. The verbal jousting over and done with. 'Only those with authority to do so will be allowed on the streets. The police will arrest on sight anyone caught out after curfew.'

The sound I heard was Arthur Anderson's funding dollars flying out the window. Item Number Three of my turning-forty-strategy had just copped another kick in the teeth. Now more than ever, all I wanted from this dramatic day was to get to my room and tally up my losses. Alone. With a drink. Before the coming of the maids. The Mexican Invasion.

'It's all quite dramatic, actually.' Connie, flashing her dimpled smile for the guy.

'I really do wish to apologize for the inconvenience, ladies. We must deal with it the best we can, I guess. I sincerely apologise on behalf of management.'

'It's fine,' Connie insisted. 'Don't apologize. Not of your doing. Cynthia, here, doesn't mind sharing her room. Do you, love? The poor sods down in South Central are the ones we have to worry about.'

Sure, but this is Santa Monica, I felt like screaming in their stupid, smug faces. Not a dollar-a-night youth hostel. Santa Bloody Monica, that's what it is. Okay for Connie. Hubby was picking up their tab.

I, on the other hand was responsible for my own expenses, an unemployed advertising executive. Having gambled everything on Hollywood's open arms, I'd put out for Business Class and the Miramar, only to cop the swanky Miramar Hotel giving me grief. Didn't I have every right to be upset about their high-handed arrangements? The Miramar was pricey. I'd been happy to pay. Knew I had to cough up for the hefty room rate. A smart address in L.A. is mandatory. When you do deals in this town and expect to have your calls returned then your address is everything. The gorgeous Miramar with all its gorgeous people, glamorous guests and professional staff like Rudi, brought in from Central Casting. Not your Biltmore, but a luxury pub, none the less. And they would all be confined inside the place, at least until the sun came up tomorrow. Guests and staff.

I looked around at the polished marble floors, at the ornate columns and the elaborate ceiling, the gold trimmings everywhere, the ritzy brown leather lounges scattered about the huge reception area, the profusion of rainforest palms and the cascading waterfall by the sun-drenched courtyard café and pool. All awash in dappled afternoon sunlight. 'These women? What time should I expect them?' The question I should be asking however was, 'What's my discount on the room rate for going quietly?' Instead, I silently fumed and waited.

'I'm sorry, Ms Smart. I will check on times for you.'

The accent detectable behind the Californian drawl added to the Sheik of Araby mystique. Had the star of the silent screen ever lived long enough, the real Rudolph Valentino would have sounded just like his doppelgänger here at the Miramar. I watched him walk away, feeling Connie watching me watching him walk away.

So, what? Unlike Connie, I was a free agent. I could admire beauty. Even get horny over it. Even act on basic impulses, reap the privileges of travelling solo, a single woman with no baggage. There had to be an upside to the downside. I moved off a little way from the Labelles.

Scoping the place while Connie and David confabbed, I spotted two spike-heeled starlets returning from the Women's Room, wiggling towards their stools at the bar. We all did it at that age. When we looked that spunky; sashayed back and forth from the loos desperate to be noticed. This pair was doing the full Marilyn Monroe routine; one stiletto planted directly in front of the other to make the hips swing.

Not only were they doing it for the cool jocks at the bar, but also for the benefit of the various Hollywood executive types huddled in leather lounges negotiating deals over lychee martinis and lashings of B.S. The young femmes presented a sight for the eyes as they perched back on their stools. Neat tushes wiggling into place. Curvy butts, tiny waists and long lustrous hair. This was Hollywood and they were all Lana Turners, only they didn't know it, of course. Way too young. Aren't they all?

It hit me that while all this movietown palaver was going on in the hotel foyers and bars of L.A., outside, the flames were rising higher and higher, the violence spreading out further and further across the besieged city. A security guard lay dead in a gutter. Rodney King's voice rang in my ear. The radio jock's, too. Not far from where I stood, in this oasis of calm, Korean shop owners were trying to save what was left of their premises by shooting everything that moved. Mothers were shielding their young from flying bullets. Mobs of angry black men were dragging white drivers from their vehicles and beating them senseless.

And now it was coming for us, this riot.

I'd seen the images of carnage on cable news. Now I was slap-bang in the middle of it, not just sitting back in Paddington with the remote in my hand feeling grateful to be on the other side of the Pacific. It was a fact; L.A. had gone berserk and it was mean of me to quibble about dossing down tonight with a couple of strangers. Still, it was weird by anyone's reckoning. Grant me that. It was an unfair universe.

I noticed our herald of bad news had gone up to Reception and was speaking with another liveried staffer. On my behalf, I presumed.

They had given him the tough job, alright. I felt sorry for the guy. Sorry for his hotel. Sorry for the whole of Los Angeles. For the whole of the United States of America. It wasn't pretty what had happened since Wednesday's verdict came down. To quote Yeats, as I often did—Yeats or any poet writing before modernism sounded the death knell—a terrible beauty was born. And now the Miramar was going into lock-down because neither the LAPD, the county sheriff's men, the fire fighters, the National Guard, and if they could ever get their act together, Bush's military guys, were equal to the level of violence in this town. None were coping with the scale of passions unleashed in the face of injustice. The avenging mob slashing and burning its way through South Central and now, apparently ready to take on the ritzier precincts, its rage and rampaging about to lob on our doorstep.

Don't panic, Cynthia.

David turned around to check I was still with them. He left Connie talking to the hapless guy she had waylaid and came across. 'You, okay?' Touching my forearm, bringing me back from riot territory to their present palmy sanctuary. I marvelled that after the way I'd carried on in Katoomba last week David could still find it in his soul to act gentlemanly towards me. I certainly hadn't acted ladylike.

'You think Bush will extract his digit any time soon? Get his big guns here so we can all sleep easy tonight?'

'He's sure taking his time.'

'It's only them, though, isn't it, Davey? The hoi polio, the poor buggers doing it tough down in South Central. So, what does Bush the Republican care?'

For all Connie's faults, she was true to the cause. They had kept the faith, she and Con. Burnt their bras, donned their Che Guevara t-shirts. Plastered the Shame, Fraser, Shame buttons all over our chests. A pair of Whitlam groupies back then. Still idolized the man and kept true to the Party. In the world of advertising and marketing that hadn't always gone down well. Easier for Con up there on her mountain-top, populated by leftie creative types. All beanies and chunky hand-knits living on arts grants. However, I had a sneaking suspicion David, with his CBD life these days, could be a Republican sympathizer.

'I guess L.A. feels a long way off if you're sitting in the Oval Office way over in DC,' said David, cutting POTUS some slack. Confirming my suspicions.

'I wonder what Clinton thinks of these riots. The Arkansas Gov's solid with black America. And Latinos.'

'Y'know the great man's in town, tonight, right? Clinton?'

'No. Did not know that.'

'Here to campaign, so I heard from the Anderson boys. A big bash Sunday night at the Biltmore. Diane Warwick and the like.'

I grinned. 'Sapphie been briefed?'

'Don't think so.'

'The man's her idol.'

'Fair enough. Good guy.' David, with a two-finger salute as he moved off to rejoin his wife.

Maybe not Republican.

6

SAPPHIRE

Almost everything that is great has been done by youth.

Benjamin Disraeli

Santa Monica, Los Angeles
Friday 1st May 1992

They had talked for so long this afternoon, she and Mateo.

Cool, swapping serious stuff with an American kid, a boy who knew nearly as much as she did about the elections. She knew everything about US politics. After all, she was an American citizen. She couldn't wait to vote. Couldn't wait for the first Tuesday in November.

Poor Mateo. Not for him, American citizenship. He had been vague about how he and his family had come to the States but she understood it had been hard. Legal, maybe not so much. His mother and his older brother had been first to cross the border. Years later they sent for Mateo and his little sister. Four years without a mother. Just an old grandmother and a few cranky aunties who didn't care much what he got up to.

God, she should be making for Rita Goldman's bungalow down the path behind her. If she didn't, she would also have a cranky woman to deal with.

She twisted her body around to take in the view of the white-washed bungalows. Part-buried behind lavish banks of palm trees and exotic colourful shrubbery, the bungalows appealed to her romantic nature. Magic. Exotic Hollywood of yesterday. Way cool and she wished they'd chosen a bungalow instead of their boring suite on the Seventh floor of the main building. Imagine such an exotic name as Mateo Lopez up on the mountains. She had explained to Mateo her American dad sent her clippings from the Los Angeles Times and the Washington Post. Everything about Bill Clinton's campaign. Mateo felt the same way they all did about George Bush and his stupid war in Kuwait. Shock and Awe. Mateo wished he could vote. Told her he had a bumper sticker on his locker, *No blood for oil.*

'Last year's sticker.'

'Si. But good, no?'

Why hadn't Nick sent her one? She pictured old Muldoon's face if she rocked up to school with that sticker plastered across her textbooks. Apoplectic, the old boy. No one got off on Anzac Day as much as Muldoon. Rapturous about the Fallen. She had Clinton campaign stickers pasted all over her books. Buttons pinned across her backpack as well. *Clinton—Gore, '92.* And another, *Sons of the New South '92.* And *Rebuild America for Our Children.* Her favourite, though, was the button with both their faces in the 3" circle; *Bill and Hillary Clinton Inaugural, January 20th·* President Bill Clinton. First Lady, Hillary Rodham-Clinton. Awesome.

Muldoon had tried to make her remove the stickers and badges from her backpack, saying Katoomba High students couldn't politicize the school. Caused offence to adults on the trains and buses, he reckoned. Children promoting political parties was just not on. American ones, especially.

Especially American ones, because it told their community they were not only too politicized but very un-Australian. No true daughter of ANZAC. She proposed to Principal Muldoon that the seniors debate the issue. The Question: Should students be allowed to advertise their political preferences in public while in school uniform? Yes, or No?

Enough pestering and he finally agreed. The positive and negative cases. She led on the Yes and her team blitzed it. Kids in Years Eleven and Twelve weren't children, she'd said to loud applause. Some, thanks to Gough Whitlam's 1972 government, would be voting at the next election and so it was their duty to be informed. And if being informed led to strong political commitments, then society should applaud it. Not discourage it. In the States they have a constitution saying you can't stop free speech, she said. Their First Amendment. Even without a constitution or a Bill of Rights, Australian kids should be entitled to a free opinion. Their birthright. That got applause.

Some in the assembly hall would soon be old enough to be sent to war, she reminded her audience in her closing remarks. And old enough to be responsible for their own debts. Old enough to marry without consent. Even to engage in consensual sex without breaking the law.

She hadn't been so sure of the last point, but no one challenged her. It won their team loud cheers, whistles and catcalls from the kids at the back of the hall. To say they couldn't state a preference for one political party over another was constitutionally wrong. David had helped her prepare her case. He knew things when it came to civil rights. And of course, she'd run her speech past Nick.

The last time she had her two weeks with Nick it was in New York. New York city was awesome, but nothing matched Los Angeles this week. It was wild. She had to write home about it. The riots. How close they were to the burning buildings and all the lootings. They reckoned the big library downtown was on fire. She looked about, at the garden with its fountains and palm trees, the lush colours of the flower beds, all typical L.A. Heaven. Pure Heaven.

She put her hand to her forehead and squinting, scanned the path up ahead.

And there he was, Mateo, her divine water carrier, overtaking two other cyclists and pelting towards her as if his tail were on fire.

7

CYNTHIA

If goodness is its own reward, shouldn't we get a little something for being naughty?

Lauren Bacall

Santa Monica, Los Angeles
Friday 1st May 1992

Across the other side of the lobby, I noticed Connie's victim had extricated himself and walked off, leaving Con scanning the room for the next pair of ears. David shot a knowing glance my way, which I returned with a palms-up shrug. We are both old hands when it comes to appreciating Connie's gregarious personality.

'Ms Smart?' announced Rudi, breaking into my thoughts, standing so close his powerful musky cologne rushed at my senses.

'Yes?'

'They tell me the—women—come off duty at six thirty. Reception will phone you in advance.'

'No one back home would believe this was happening' Connie chipped in as she came across the room, arms akimbo. 'Locked up overnight—'

'And thrown together with two Latino housemaids?' said David to Rudi V, as if to plead on his client's behalf for a reprise.

'Management really does apologize for the inconvenience, sir but—well—that's just how it is, I'm afraid.' He seemed saddened not to present as the charmer his job description detailed.

'No sweat, my friend,' I assured him. 'We're living in interesting times. L.A.'s a shit-storm.' While ever we have military tanks and Humvees rolling along the Santa Monica promenades, I might have said, but didn't. And helicopters whizzing overhead. And armed guards standing at the ready to shoot civilians. 'Have you heard if the cavalry is on its way, yet?'

'The President is aware Mayor Bradley and the Governor called for urgent assistance during the small hours of this morning. Not just to cover the downtown area, but here and the whole city. Places like Brentwood, Westwood. Santa Monica. We need the military right here, right now.'

'So? Where are they?'

No reply from Rudi other than an insouciant shrug, accompanied by one perfect raised eyebrow. For an instant, I wondered if I would receive the same response were I to drop the hard word on him. The charming shrug. The eyebrow.

Whatever happens, one thing's for sure, these riots were stymieing my mission. 'I put out big time to get here. To pitch my project to one of Hollywood's major players,' I moaned. 'Dinner tonight to lock it in. Great. But now they've stolen Christmas from me, told me to go to my room and stay there. It's no longer about black, brown and yellow killing each other and incinerating their communities, is it? Now it's party time all round. They're coming for us, too.'

With a polite bow, Mr V turned his attention to David and Connie. 'Mr Labelle. Mrs Labelle, the emergency sleeping arrangements, of course do not apply to married couples and families.'

'Only to losers like me.' Mumbled, but audible enough for Connie's ears.

'Cyn, honey. Look at you. You're no loser.'

Rudi made a temple of his fingers, bowed his head. A formal gesture of dismissal. Disappointing. I'd hoped for more from the matinee idol. Nothing approaching Item Two of the strategy but simply a little something to kick off the quest. Back in the saddle, so to speak. But then, from beneath a canopy of black lashes young Rudi looked directly up at me. A penetrating gaze, which I read as desire. And naughty boy, he let that look linger a milli-second longer than professionally necessary, enough that it caused a pleasant jab, a wee frisson, which lit up the sex in me.

'Let me say, Ms Smart, I do hope we can make it up to you.' Still formal. 'Somehow.' A lower, cheekier, register.

'No, no, don't worry. It's fine.' Connie, interrupting the Rudi-wants-Cynthia, Cynthia-wants-Rudi moment. Connie reached out with a gentle hand to the side of my face and with cow eyes that bespoke the question, drooled, 'You're cool with all this, aren't you, love?'

'Of course. Why wouldn't I be?' I snapped back. And then a shrug. 'It's a war zone out there.'

'Thank you for your understanding Ms Smart. Now you all have a great day,' said Mr V as he turned to leave. But not before he shot me another suggestive glance, one my libido took to the bank.

'You too,' I whispered, grinning as I feasted on the tight buns his retreating figure presented to my hungry eyes. Really, when had I last swung my leg over? Or felt this hot desire. No panic. No hurry. Dr Wadsworth, you with your probing speculum and Jeremiah words. I do not wish to hear what you have to say. Be gone. I am still young. Still irresistibly attractive to the male of the species. I am thirty-nine—and fuckable. I dare you to gainsay me, man.

'By the way'—said Rudi, doubling back—'meals during curfew will be a little different. Buffets. We're issuing tickets. You collect them from Reception. Guests will present their tickets in any of our restaurants.' He aimed a crease of a smile at Connie. 'All guests, Mrs Labelle.'

Good on you, Rudi. He'd caught the drift. With studied dignity, he bestowed a professional smile on the three of us and walked away. It was over; the possibility of pleasures to come. I had held out for a further sign, a promise, but apparently what I had just been given was all I would be given from the Miramar's Sheik of Araby. Jeremiah vindicated. Not so fuckable after all. Pity. Exotic lovers are hard to come by even at the best of times, and this was certainly not the best of times. Not for me. Not since Wadsworth brought down his verdict on my ebbing oestrogen.

Connie took off for Reception. 'I'll grab your tickets, too,' she said. 'Hold the lift.'

I wasn't holding any lift for anyone. I stayed where I was, no rush.

'Cyn? You okay, mate?' said David.

'Sure. Why?' I had forgotten he was there.

'You looked ... I don't know ... kind of worried?'

'Dinner's off. The project's going nowhere.' I scanned the room before looking back at him. 'Tomorrow I fly out, David. What's there to smile about, you tell me.'

'Let's not panic. Not yet. Okay? Let's not panic. I can arrange something.'

'You're a good man, David. You really are.'

He held my gaze. 'A good friend.'

The word packed a punch. I turned from him so he would not catch the rising flood as my face coloured. Oh, David, forgive me.

My life was one big clusterfuck right now, I realized. All my 3a.m. strategizing out the window. And this good man standing next to me, no doubt feeling uncomfortable in my presence, given what happened last week. We stood together in silence for several minutes, watching Connie. What was there to say?

'It's rough on you, Cyn. The meeting,' said David, finally breaking the silence. 'This bloody curfew. Missing the dinner. Having to share your room with the Mexican women.'

'Could be interesting, I suppose. Even me, without any Spanish beyond ... what? Tequila.? Siesta? Mañana?' I raised an eyebrow. 'Marijuana?'

'Cyn! Marijuana? My god, the place is crawling with cops. Or soon will be.'

Ignore the woman, turning my attention to Mr Valentino—now working the rest of the room—dispensing his hotel's bivouacking arrangements among other unfairly targeted guests. It did not escape my notice that one of the young stunners propped at the bar kept looking over her shoulder, shooting seductive glances Rudi's way. He certainly was pretty. Eye candy, as my cheeky goddaughter would say. And youthful. But the minor flirtation had lifted my spirits, at least for the short time it took for me to delude myself. Then, just as I thought about heading around to the elevators, he turned and caught my eye.

And there you had it, the universal hunger.

In that moment, I knew Rudi was more than a herald of inconvenient riot news. The gloom I had been dealing with, ever since the diagnosis, took a hike. For the moment, at least, I could feel good about myself. Feel desirable. Sex will do that. Flirtation's an aphrodisiac. A Class-A anti-depressant. Big Pharma should bottle it. Adorable, that's me. I feel pretty, oh so—

Rudi's suggestive glance made me wet. A soothing balm to my damaged ego, which thought made me blush. Get stuffed Myron Spinak. And Nick Cristos. And you, Professor Wadsworth with your early-onset menopause. Me? You're kidding, buster. Prime of life, this gal. Stick your cold silver speculum up—wherever. Watching the hotel's man across the room, I wondered which of us would make the next move.

But the Mexicans. Where did they fit in?

David saying, 'You gonna be okay, Cyn, with the arrangements? These maids?'

'What choice do I have? I'm just a bit worried they might—'

'You'll be okay,' Connie piped up. 'Of course, you will. I reckon the poor buggers come off those shifts dog-tired and just want—'

'Worried they might cramp my style, is what I was about to say—had you allowed me to finish.'

'Okay, okay. Keep your knickers on, girlfriend.'

Connie took off again, this time to speak with someone she had spotted leaving the café. Over her shoulder she added, 'Just think of it as an experience, Cyn. Something to laugh about at your next dinner party.'

David winced. He knew how much I detested dinner parties.

'Yeah, okay Con. At my next dinner party.'

I did not do dinner parties, mine or other peoples. Like dog turds, if you're smart you avoid them. I ate frozen or ate out. Or went without. But never the suburban dinner party if I could help it. Jolly married couples sorry for poor single Cynthia Smart. But not sympathetic or sensitive enough in the presence of a childless woman to put a sock in their cross-table chatter. Measles vaccinations, orthodontist recommendations, their dyslexic/autistic/genius kid. The host who sticks you next to his best mate with the bad breath, or the recovering divorcee hungry for a sympathetic ear. They weren't all Nick Cristos.

'I'll go call the Arthur Anderson boys. See if they can get here for drinks, at least,' said David, walking off.

MEDIA REPORT

LOS ANGELES TIMES *May 01, 1992*

MILES CORWIN: TIMES STAFF WRITER

Everyday Life Shattered in Many Ways: Closures:

The curfew is taking a heavy toll on merchants downtown, with some reporting $40,000 to $50,000 in losses per day.

Bus service are canceled citywide. Many employers have told workers to stay home—or go home early. Mail deliveries are halted throughout South Los Angeles. Professional baseball and basketball games are canceled. Schools have closed throughout the city—and in Inglewood, Compton and Lynwood, shopping centers as well, are shuttered early ...

This state of disruption is likely to continue today. Business leaders and government officials say they have no intention of resuming normal activities until they are persuaded that employees will be safe.

As the violence spreads, Los Angeles Unified School District officials decide to close every school and child-care center in the district today. Officials say a decision on when to resume classes will not be made until Sunday. All but nine of the two hundred and sixty-one Catholic elementary and secondary schools in Los Angeles County will remain closed today. At USC, final examinations were to begin yesterday, but they are being postponed until at least Monday, officials say.

Cal State Los Angeles officials closed the campus yesterday afternoon and plan for the campus to remain shut today. Runners announce the closure in every classroom so students can catch buses before the service shuts down ...

The Civic Center suffered significant damage Wednesday night, and on Thursday, firms in nearby parts of downtown Los Angeles were in turmoil. Downtown businesses let thousands of employees leave work early today so they can get home before darkness falls.

Wells Fargo officials told employees in downtown Los Angeles this morning that they have the option of staying or returning home. By mid-afternoon, the company decides to close all its ninety bank branches in Los Angeles County ... Bank of America closed about one-third of its Los Angeles-area branches yesterday.

The fear of violence and looting precipitates the closure of shops and businesses far from the riot zone. The Beverly Center in the Fairfax District, and the nearby Pacific Design Center, and Westside Pavilion are among the major Westside businesses that decided to close early yesterday as a precaution. In Pasadena, the Plaza Pasadena mall closed about 1 p.m.

Bus services were canceled citywide at 4 p.m. yesterday—but the RTD says it plans to resume bus and Blue Line train service in most areas of the city today, limited only by the orders of Mayor Tom Bradley and the police.

If buses roll in the morning, a spokesman adds, the RTD is dedicated to keeping them running throughout the day to avoid stranding passengers. Throughout the county, major Southland companies announce cancellation of their afternoon and evening shifts. Hughes Aircraft closes its facilities. All major Hollywood studios send employees home by mid-afternoon.

The eight hundred downtown employees of the Arthur Anderson accounting firm were told by an emergency message system to stay home Thursday morning if they believed their safety was at risk.

8

CYNTHIA

People who think they know everything are an annoyance to those of us who do.

Isaac Asimov

Santa Monica, Los Angeles
Friday 1st May 1992

'There was a message for me,' said David, returning from Reception. 'Bad luck, mate.'

'What now? Out with it.'

'You're going to hate this, Cyn but the AA guys are a no-show. Not even for drinks. I'd hoped we could sneak in a beer at least, before the curfew kicked in.'

'So, we've got no money men to schmooze?'

'I'm sorry. Really needed you to meet them. They're good value, those blokes. But they'd already left their office. Sent home at three. Ordered to hot tail it for the suburbs. Downtown's not going to be safe for white men in suits after dark, they reckon. But hey, Spinak said this morning he's definitely in the market for stories set in the Outback, didn't he? That's what he said and that's a start.'

'Stop apologizing, David. I gave Spinak a lousy script. And it's not your fault there's a curfew, either. You've been brilliant. Honestly. Just getting me here was so generous of you.' I felt the light touch of David's hand on my arm.

'Listen, Nick took the script.'

'I'm sure the mighty Nick Cristos has better things to do than waste his precious time helping the likes of me. I wouldn't even expect him to read it. He must get gazillions of scripts across his desk, wannabes shoving their screenplays under his nose, poor guy.' I offered David a forlorn look. 'Best I'd stayed home, really.'

'You and Nick could've put your heads together tonight.'

'Good God, what makes you say that? The man hardly moved his lips at lunch.'

'That's Nick. A deep thinker. He was sizing you up. Saving you for later,' he said with his familiar Labelle grin. 'That was the reason for getting you two together. A preliminary.' He winked. 'You passed the test, mate. With flying colours.'

'I bet.'

'Oh, ye of little faith! You impressed him, my friend. The fact you didn't try to bend his ear about your project. He gets enough of that.'

I looked over to where the garrulous Wife of the Mountain was still engaged with a small group near the café entrance. 'One of a kind, isn't she?'

'One of a kind, for sure.'

'What about meal tickets, hey? And queueing up for our tucker? Like summer camp.'

He was still observing Connie. 'That's going to be an experience for madam.'

'She'll cope. Gloriously.'

No doubt the gregarious Connie would milk tonight for all it was worth, up and down the buffet line, going at it full tilt, working the tables, yapping to all and sundry. It was how Con operated; hope to spot someone she could corral and proceed to bend their ear. Connie took no prisoners, hardly came up for air once she cornered her quarry. Cocktail parties were her specialty. If she caught you, you staid caught. Grown men had been known to weep under a Connie Labelle assault. Her children's orthodontic history, a recent movie's moral ambiguities, the prevalence of STDs on campuses, Pol Pot, the Hubble telescope. It made no difference to Con. The woman was across it all. And there was no one who could hold their audience with more élan, or pivot faster when losing it. A genius with a segue, was our Connie. Why hadn't I sent her in to do the pitch this morning? The woman would have grabbed Myron Spinak by his skinny balls and not let go until she'd screwed a pre-sale from him.

'Nice people, that lot over there,' said Connie, from halfway across the room as she toddled back towards us on her too-high heels. 'What a night it's going to be. Everyone in it together, under crisis conditions. Could throw up some interesting moments. You never know.'

'Lining up and holding out our food bowls for our grub like the prisoners we are? Going back to a room you're sharing with two strangers?'

'Summer camp,' David reminded me.

Connie chuckled. 'Liven up, Cyn. Think Romance and Intrigue. We're all thrown in together, confined in a luxury hotel for a dusk-to-dawn curfew and a body turns up. The perfect Agatha Christie set-up, no?'

'Make sure to lock your door then, Con.'

'You know what, Cynthia darling? I reckon a decent scriptwriter could actually have a lot of fun with this scenario. There's probably a few here, tonight.'

'A few what?'

'A few scriptwriters.' So, saying, she threw her arms out wide to embrace the likelihood of such creatures hiding behind the palms

'I thought I was a scriptwriter, Con.'

'Of course, you're a scriptwriter, honey. A dammed good one. I didn't mean that. You know what I was trying to say.' Connie, grinning, put her finger into her cheek and pulled it out, making a popping noise. 'That was the sound of yours truly pulling her Size Nines out of her ugly big mush. I'm an idiot.'

David was conversing with a man who had drawn him aside. When he beckoned us to join him Connie touched my arm. 'Stay here, love. I'll just say a quick hello to this one. I've got to get upstairs and express.' She touched her breasts. 'And listen, I know what happened this morning was shitty but don't worry, love. We can fix it.'

I watched Connie toddle off to join David. Sweet smile. Sweet woman.

Surveying the lobby in the wake of the Labelle's company, I managed to catch Mr Valentino standing at Reception. Me and my Sheik. I still harboured a modicum of hope. Envisaged the steamy sex scene: He enters her room, throws her on the bed and ignores the obligatory coyness, rips off her shirt, lifts her skirt and tears off her black lace panties before going down on her, those voluptuous lips creating the magic.

It was all I could do not to groan in ecstasy. And then, over by the bar, I saw the starlet slide off her stool and make a b-line for Rudi, throwing her arms around his neck in a gesture of familiarity, kissing him with intent to corrupt. Twenty versus Forty? Who was I kidding!

I turned away from the love-in and scanned the lobby. The Hollywood types. Backsides on leather couches pow-wowing among the palms. A festival of arrogance. Only they belonged here. Someone of my calibre had Loser branded across her forehead, a blow-in who didn't belong. I resented their smugness. Nothing but well-dressed hustlers all of them. Fast talkers peddling horse shit, buying into each other's fantasies and lies.

The Labelles were still engaged in conversation. One of David's American contacts, I presumed. Connie signaled me to join them. I signaled a pass. The Glenfiddich was calling from greener pastures.

I headed across the lobby and around to the bank of elevators, looking forward to time away from the Labelles. I needed to get my head together, re-strategize in the wake of today's rejection. And I sure as Hell needed that drink.

'He's a lovely bloke, that one I was just talking to.' Connie, surprising me, coming up behind me as I stood stabbing the row of Up buttons and cursing the slowness of the cars.

'I've made pals with a great couple I met at breakfast this morning, too. You'll love 'em, Cyn. And another woman, a friend of theirs from New York, an agent. She handles some of the biggest names in Hollywood. And New York, of course. It's going to be fun, even without the Arthur Anderson guys.' She paused to draw breath. 'What's with these bloody elevators? Slow, aren't they.'

'What's going to be fun?'

'Drinks, of course. Six o'clock. Our suite. I've invited them all to join us before we go down to dinner.'

'Mmm,' was all I said. Good old Con with her prêt-à-porter guest list. The crème de la crème of tonight's Miramar prisoners, harvested to furnish her salon. I walked the line of elevators, continuing to stab at the arrows with renewed vigour. I wasn't normally thinking of booze this early in the afternoon but some days are diamonds and some are dogs. This one was a growling Rottweiler.

I hissed at the elevator lights. Come on, for Chrissakes. Bring 'em down. Good luck to Connie. All I knew was I would not be a part of any six o'clock soiree. I had no desire for a social drink or for making small talk with Con's new best friends.

'Thought I'd lost m'girls,' said David, coming up between us and putting an arm around both our waists to pull us in to him, notwithstanding Connie's motherload of boutique bags jagging her shins.

We eventually stepped into the crowded car and rode in silence to the seventh floor.

From the corner of my eye, I studied Connie. The woman was busting to be out and at it. Two kids to pick up from a babysitter. Theo needing a feed. Then bath, bed and story time before the fun and games. Or maybe not. Maybe the baby would be kept up. A feature of the event. I had to admire Connie. It wouldn't be easy being so fabulous. Earth Mother and Hostess with the Mostest, all rolled into one. Personally, all I wanted was to hang out the Do Not Disturb and get plastered. Maybe torture myself by envisioning the child-of-light from the bar stool downstairs with her scarlet claws digging into young Mr Valentino's beautiful bod. The naked pair going at it, hot and sweaty, abandoning all shame as they yelp and yawp their thrusting way to a Richter scale climax.

Once the doors slid open Connie shot out of the box like a Melbourne Cup champion, galloping down the corridor at full stretch, despite the weight handicap and the heels too high for the distance. The new outfits were never going to sit properly on that frame. At least not until those breasts returned to human proportions.

David stood aside, held the door open while I stepped out of the lift. A true gentleman. Always. Under all conditions.

I felt his warm palm press against the small of my back as we walked the corridor to my room. An affectionate gesture. Nothing more suggested. No reference to last week. Just David's gentle way of comforting me, showing he understood I'd had a rough morning and was disappointed about tonight's missed dinner opportunity. While Connie was a human bulldozer, David's way was to be sensitive to other's feelings. She had nabbed herself a keeper in David Jacob Labelle. Despite carrying the double burden of being an accountant and a lawyer, he had empathy. Buckets of it. He waited while I dug into my blazer pocket for my key card. Could I invite him in to share a nip of the Glenfiddich?

God, no! Wake up to yourself, Cynthia Lorraine. Not in the pathetic mood you're in. Feeling sorry for yourself. As well as just a wee bit randy, thanks to the cameo played out downstairs. You would be jumping the poor man's bones the minute the door slammed. I was paused at my door, David about to leave when Connie called out.

'Hey, Cyn,' Connie had pulled up halfway down the stretch, fussing in her Hermes, head down, talking into the bag.

'Don't be too downhearted about your meeting today, love. Bugger, where is it?' Finally, she produced the key card and waved it in the air triumphantly, as though we'd all been rooting for her.

Now she decided to head back to us and was talking on the trot. 'I made a few notes for you, by the way. A few suggestions. Remember what I said, more action, less angst and you've got a great script.'

Did Connie ever take stock of herself, ever wonder when too much was too much? Then again, I should cut the old girl some slack, I suppose. David's not here in L.A. promoting his wife's project.

He's here promoting mine. And Connie, as far as I can tell, hasn't complained that he's neglecting hers, some historical story, set in Dutch Bali.

Still on the trot, coming our way. Thank God for empty corridors. 'I can't see why your Miki and Jude need to be so dour, so bloody worthy. Know what I mean?'

'No, I don't, actually.' I shot David a look. He shrugged.

Connie pulled up, breathless. 'They're a pair of wet blankets. Needs lightening up a little. When you come in, I'll go through it with you, okay?'

'C'mon, Con. The kids are waiting. Let's go,' said David, taking his wife's arm and attempting to drag her off me.

'And you need a new director.' Connie looked at her husband, David the Sphinx. 'David? Tell her. I've been saying this all along, haven't I? I can't for the life of me see why she's so stuck on—what's the woman's—'

'Angela. Angela Godwin,' I said.

'Yes, Godwin. Uh-uh, you need one with screen credits, love. You could help her, David. You know them all.'

David was doing a sterling job of holding back his annoyance. He tugged on Connie's arm but she shook him off, determined to have her say. No doubt head of the meeting of the well-connected she was convening this evening.

'I know you feel loyal to the woman but what's she ever done? I mean, really? This lot here have never heard of her, Cynthia love. You need a Campion or a Beresford. Marquee attachments.'

David started to walk off without her.

'Shop around, you reckon? Waste another year or two?'

Connie considered my words, but only for a moment. 'Anyway,' said as she caught up with David, '... get freshened up and come in for a drink. We can toss a few ideas around before they arrive. And I reckon they'll have suggestions, too.'

I caught the apologetic look David shot back at me, his eye-roll. It's okay, I mouthed, knowing he understood. Let Connie be Connie.

I could take it. Had taken it for a long time. Long before David came on the scene. David knew I loved Connie to death, Con my almost-sister. Just couldn't take the in-your-face assertiveness and meddling, that's all. The woman is like anchovies; eat too many and you'll gag on them, but in small doses they make things come alive.

'If nothing else, sister,' Connie, with her dimpled smile persisted, '... we can all kick back with our champers and watch the riots on TV before we go downstairs for our bowl of grits. Looks like it's going to be a hot one in the old town, tonight. After I change these bloody shoes and go get the kids, I'm ordering up the Moet and nibbles. Let's party and forget about their bloody curfews, I say. Why not? Right, Davey boy? We send down for the bubbly and get with a little jailhouse rock?'

'I'm taking a guess room service is cancelled, Con?' I held up the envelope containing meal tickets.

'Cyn's right, honey. They'd have sent as many staff home early as they could spare before the curfew kicks in. Room service'd be the first casualty of the night.'

'Then I'll just have to go down and rustle us up some goodies from the fucking bar my fucking self, won't I, dearies?' She brushed away our reservations with a gesture. 'Wet blankets!' she added with a laugh as she took off again down the hall with a wiggle that would have knocked Marilyn out of the audition.

David laughed. 'Reckon I'll ever make a lady of her, Cyn?"

'You want to?'

'Guess not.'

I watched until David caught up with his wife and the pair disappeared around the corner to their suite. Envy, like a bitter cocktail, left a sour after-taste. But before I had time to litigate the mixed emotions of jealousy, loneliness and regrets, Connie stuck her head back around the corner.

'Don't be long, okay?' she yelled down the corridor, surprising a man who had just stepped out from his room.

The woman could be as annoying as a tangle of wire coat-hangers.

I was grateful to be flying out tomorrow night. God willing.

Connie, unfazed by the lack of any response, tapped on her wristwatch. 'I've got to get over to the bungalows to pick up the kids,' she yelled. 'You wanna come help me?'

David came up behind Connie and tugged at her elbow. 'Let's go, kiddo.'

'The walk'd do you good,' Con insisted. 'Chase away the cobwebs.'

'No thanks,' I whispered, finally sliding my key card into the lock. My star ship was ready for take-off. I was due to leave the planet. Unscrew the top of the Glenfiddich and be on my way.

Connie heaved her breasts up and laughed. 'The old Jersey cow needs milking. Need to empty these. See you later.'

I laughed. David laughed. Even the poor bugger now striding down the hallway and trying to ignore us, laughed. That was the effect my crazy Connie had on the world.

I entered Room 708 shaking my head in amusement. Her colourful language. A 'Fuck' or 'Fucking' dropped from Connie Labelle-nee-Bray's lips was not like a Fuck or Fucking shot from my own. When Connie cursed, she did it with a certain grace, her posh private school voice. Not like me. Mine were authentic Fucks, those of a girl with a chip on her shoulder, a working-class daughter on a Commonwealth Government scholarship. My schoolgirl Fucks were usually in answer to their cattiness. Connie Bray, the daughter of a District Court magistrate and a Mosman GP was never catty but could certainly let fly with gutter talk, enough to make a sailor blush. Con had relished being a schoolgirl enigma, I recalled as I tossed my bag on the bed and kicked off my shoes. You're crazy, I'd said to her the first time we met.

I try, she'd replied. And I can still remember the grin that went with it. Connie Bray's pretty face, the mischief in those bright blue eyes, the dimples when she smiled. The lippy Connie Bray.

I try, she'd said.

9

CYNTHIA

The friend who holds your hand and says the wrong thing
is made of dearer stuff than the one who stays away.

Barbara Kingsolver

Mosman, New South Wales, Australia
February 1965

The stranger, coming up behind me. Tapping my shoulder.

'You've had a show,' said the girl.

'What?' I had been caught bending over, tying up a sandshoe lace and congratulating myself on my game. Bleeding? A show? First kill the messenger, then let me die! I yanked at the hem of my tennis skirt. Turned and faced the stranger. 'I'm not.'

'You are. You're bleeding, love. Sorry to tell you.'

'So?' I glared at this girl. Two more days till I menstruated. Sports day. Tennis. White skirt and sandshoes. Two whole days early. Unfair. I tried to stem the massive blush. Felt pressure behind my eyeballs. A popping sound in my ears. Flight? Or fight? Common sense told me to run from the mortification, flee from this rotten schoolyard and never stop running. Instinct told me I must stay.

'Don't worry. I've got pads and belts in my sports bag,' the stranger called over her shoulder as she sprinted off across the quadrangle towards the gym. 'Stay there! I'll be back in a sec.'

It was true. I was feeling the leakage. Warm and sticky. I cursed my body for betraying me. And I waited. Because ... be honest ... where could a person go, anyway? It wasn't fair.

Standing out in the open on such a scorcher of a day was suicide. I knew I was buying freckles. My Melbourne skin wasn't designed for Sydney summers. I backed towards the giant stringy bark gum and leant against its trunk, welcoming the shade it offered, feeling the dry hanging bark crackle against my back. I kicked at the parched gum leaves, grinding a black beetle into the dust with the heel of my tennis shoe. The smell, like dead ants, rose to meet me. Worse smells coming, I knew. How could I get through the rest of the afternoon and then eventually, to my bedroom? On a sweaty day like this?

Ants, from the tree at my back, found me. Ouch. I jumped away, brushing frantically at the busy insects. My hair, my neck, my arms, crawling with the hideous things. I hated this school.

'Duffer. Don't look so worried,' said the girl. She had doubled back and was standing way too close for comfort. 'Oh, shite!' She noticed the ants on me and started swiping at them until, as if called to a higher purpose, the kingdom of ants suddenly retreated in formation, across the hard ground to disappear below a mound of dry gum leaves.

'Thank you.'

'Forget it. You know the earth's population of ants is four-times the weight of the human population?'

'No. I did not.'

'Here, take this. It'll cover your backside.' The school's summer blazer. Dark pink and white stripes. 'Tie it round your waist. It's okay. It's going to be okay. Honestly, love.'

'It's not okay. Everyone's—'

'Everyone what? So, it's blood, okay? So, we bleed. We bleed for the sake of mankind. Over and over. Every month. We're the moon goddesses. Goddesses of the Moon, all of us.'

'You're kidding me. Periods are hideous!'

'Our moon fluxes. That's what they are.'

'Moon fluxes?'

'It's for real. Stay there, don't move!' And the crazy girl was off again, leaving me processing the dumb notion: We bleed for the sake of mankind. Moon fluxes.

It was a skewered way of looking at the curse. Who was this freak who just lobbed that idiocy at me? Pollyanna? Cramps that flatten you for three or four days out of every month. Uncomfortable belts. Stained bloomers. Pads to dispose of in secret because it's so disgusting, so shameful their very existence is unmentionable. No-swim days. No-fun days. Flood days. Days like this to make you a laughingstock. If we were bleeding for the whole of bloody mankind, then why did we have to hide our periods?

Why was it so shameful to bleed?

I hadn't thought about it till now. The strange girl might have some whacky notion about menstruation but at least she had me thinking. For instance, no one was ashamed to bleed if they were stupid enough to cut their finger. It was only menstrual blood that offended, still blood coming from the body but from the part my mother called 'down there'.

Who else had seen it? I'd been on the court moments ago, running up and down, bending over for balls, teachers and girls watching the game. Why hadn't someone said something? Why hadn't I noticed the stickiness till now? I was aware enough now of the warm gummy feeling between my legs. At thirteen a person can die of shame.

Eventually, the stranger came pelting back down the hill. 'Got it!' she yelled.

Grabbed by a moist and determined hand, I was being dragged across to the lavatory block. Once inside, I watched the stranger bend over at the waist, hands on hips and gasp for breath.

'Phew! Out of condition,' said the girl.

'You, okay?' It was the least I could say, I supposed. Too rude if I pointed out this one needed to lose a bit of weight if she were going to run up and down hills on hot sweaty days.

'Give us a sec. Too bloody fat, that's the trouble.' The girl straightened up and from a tapestry toiletry bag, produced a Kotex pad and held the offering above her head. 'Behold, the Blessed

Object!' She ripped off reams of toilet paper, bunched it up and after wetting it, said, 'There. In you go. Wash your messy bits. And grab heaps and wrap your bloomers up. Pass 'em out to me when you're done. Here's the bag. There's a spare pair of knickers in here.' She pulled out navy cotton bloomers and held them to her hips. 'What ya reckon? Fuck, they're way too big for you, aren't they? Look at you, you Skinny-Minnie!'

'They'll do, I guess.' The swearing from this dimpled one, at this posh school, was a shock. The strange girl laughed, swaying her hips in an imaginary Hula hoop move.

'There's talc in there, too. And spray a bit of this around your fanny. Revlon's Bluegrass. One stink covers the other. You wanna hear a joke?'

'Go on.'

'Only two things smell like fish and fish is one of them!' She cracked up.

A weirdo for sure. We both noticed the spot of blood on the left tennis shoe.

'Give it here. I'll fix it,' said the girl.

I handed the shoe across and entered the cubicle. This is one Hell of a lousy beginning. Forever would I hate this hideous school. First week in the place. I bolted the door and launched the messy business of harnessing up for the curse. This will be who you are around here now, I told the me who was having a lousy day of it. This will define you, Cynthia Loraine.

'By the way,' came the call from the other side of the door, 'I'm Connie.'

I could hear the girl at the basin scrubbing the offending tennis shoe under the running tap. I appreciated her help but right now I just wanted to be a million miles from here. Did I really need to know the girl's name?

'Connie Bray. Bray. Like the donkey. Hee, haw. You?'

Go on, give it a try. 'Cynthia. Cynthia Smart. As in not very—obviously.'

'I'm in 10A, Cyn. You?'

What's with the 'Cyn' thing? It was too familiar, coming from this girl I didn't even know till a few moments ago. It was reserved for family and friends, and this person was neither. They warned me Sydney would be like this. '10C,' I called out. 'Until they assess me. I was in A at my old school.'

'Which was?'

'Glen Iris High. Victoria.' I could still hear the water gushing into the basin. 'Don't worry cleaning them,' I called out. Never, ever again would those sandshoes see the light of day. They were destined for the big dumpster out front of the house down the road from ours. A building works dumpster. They would soon be buried beneath a pile of old bricks and plaster and I would be lying to Moira that a classmate had nicked them.

A minute passed. I fussed with belt, pins and pad.

'How's it going in there? Everything hunky dory?'

'As good-as, thanks.' Jesus, hunky dory?

'Sure? You got all you need?'

'Yes, thank you. Be out in a jiff.' I put the girl's belt on. Clipped the front and back tag of the pad. Tried adjusting the bulkiness. Night and day, one of these jammed up between my legs, chafing me, restricting me. Feeling gross for the rest of the week. And all for the sake of mankind, according to the weirdo out at the basins.

But the girl was certainly the friendly type. And beyond pretty. I could gladly hate her for those dimples and rosy cheeks. Botticelli. The print hanging in our Art Room at Glen Iris. Long brown curls and soft creamy features. All plump and angelic looking. Never in its life had a mean thought ever entered its pretty little skull, I wagered, only too aware of my own shortcomings. Too tall. Too skinny. Too pale. And too bright. I alienated other girls.

That, at least, was Moira's take. A mother, wishing her daughter was a dolt. Easier on her nerves. Her conscience. Maybe if they stood still long enough, settled somewhere long enough, chose a State and put down roots, maybe then they'd see I could attract a friend or two.

A pang of envy stung me, an awareness of everything I wasn't, and everything this girl outside was. Chubby, for sure but only puppy fat, as Mum would say. The shiny forehead, the big blue eyes, the heart-shaped face and the pert little nose. A pretty face dipped in a box of freckles, leaving a sprinkle sticking to her nose.

My own nose. No freckles, but by no means pert. It was as long and straight as the road out of Victoria. I knew I had ordinary kind of eyes that went unremarked. Not blue. Not green. Somewhere in between. Grey, they said, if they said anything at all about my eyes. Anyone who didn't fall in love with those powder blues out there would be soft in the head. They were about the first thing you noticed.

Done with harnessing myself into the goddess pad, I swaddled my soiled knickers in toilet paper, as instructed and left the cubicle.

'What bus?' Connie Bray confronted me.

'The 140.'

'Which stop?'

'Baxter and Carling.' I was about to drop the mummified parcel into the bin.

'Hey, wait! Hold it! Don't ditch them. Here, give 'em to me.'

'What? No way!'

'Yeah. Gimme 'em. They're white. We can bleach 'em.'

The girl loosened the drawstrings on the sponge bag and upended it, spreading its contents across the bench. She jammed the knickers in. 'I'll come home with you,' she said as she piled her personal items back in on top, including a couple of pencils, a sharpener and an art gum rubber. Unexpected items among Kotex pads, combs, lip balm and talc.

'You an artist?'

'Does the Trojan horse have a wooden dick? Hell, yeah. Got pencils planted everywhere. Can't help it. I get the urge when something takes m'fancy. You?'

'Uh-uh.' The tummy cramps had arrived. I was in no mood for any of this. I would have to hang around for the next two hours for the school bell to go and then ride on a public bus with this putrid package. I'd read somewhere that desert people bury their dead within hours of death. For good reason.

I finished drying my hands. 'I'll take that, thanks.' I held out my hand for the toiletries bag with its toxic payload. 'I'll get it back to you in the morning.'

'It's okay. I got it. Which end?'

'Of what?' God, the questions!

'Carling Street, of course, dummy.'

'The north end—I guess—but—'

'You're kidding me! Go on! I don't believe it. That's me, too. You must be the new people who moved into the old house on the corner.'

'Must be.'

The old house. That was about the kindest thing the girl could have said about the dump we were renting. Worst house in the street. Paddy reckoned he and his brothers would get stuck in and clean it up, throw some paint around, fix the fences. Said it would be a corker of a house when they'd finished. I didn't believe my father. Not if some of the other houses we'd lived in were anything to go by. The work would never get done. Their backyard would fill up with junk no matter how much Moira nagged about the rubbish he dragged home. Promise I'll repair it love, get it working, he would say of his council tip treasures. As if? To Protestant Moira, such a lady, my father was nothing but a bog Irish no-good gypsy. All Paddy did was just grin and whack her backside, grab her and spin her around above the ground, saying that's what she loved about him, why she'd fallen head over heels for him. Her raggle-taggle gypsy, oh.

'I'll go home with you,' said Connie Bray. 'We can find out about each other on the way.'

Oh, goody, goody!

The Samaritan thing was wearing me down. I was uncomfortable with instant intimacy. A little of Connie Bray would go a long way I had already decided. Someone to be taken in small doses. Like Vegemite. Spread thinly.

'We'll get Miss Stewart to give us both an early mark. Get the rest of the afternoon off. You're new. You've got a personal hygiene problem. I bet you've got cramps. Am I right or am I wrong, huh?'

'Right. I guess.'

'Headache?'

I nodded.

'Then Stewy'll let us go early, for sure. You won't have come across Stewy yet, probably. Teaches Drama and Art. You'll love her. She goes on about all us girls being in this 'sorority' thing. We're all sisters, in it together.'

'Whatever 'It' is.'

'We have to stick together, us moon goddesses, Stewy reckons. We've got to 'inspire' one another. Come on. Let's go see her and get us some inspiration. You ready?'

'As I'll ever be, I suppose.'

We passed two seniors coming into the washrooms as we were leaving. I leant in and whispered to the girl, 'Won't it …y'know?' I indicated the sponge bag now tucked under Connie Bray's arm. 'Won't it pong a bit … like, by the time we're on the bus? People are going to smell it.'

'Let 'em bloodywell deal with it. It's our gift to mankind. Well, isn't it?'

'Guess so.' Not able to help myself, I finally cracked a smile. 'You know what?'

'What?'

'I think you're shocking!'

'Shocking who.'

'Whom.'

'Yeah, okay. Whom. Is that better, Miss La-dee-da from Glenn fucking Iris?'

'You know what?'

'What?'

'You're crazy.'

'I try.'

10

CYNTHIA

Let us drink, gentlemen. Let us drink,
till we roll under the table in vomit and oblivion.

King Henry II: William Shakespeare

Santa Monica, Los Angeles
Friday 1st May 1992

After hanging the Do Not Disturb card outside the door and bolting the chain, I lunged for my carry-on bag and retrieved the Glenfiddich.

I poured and drank.

And poured and drank some more, my eyes closed, the better to savour the liberating, glorious, soul-comforting malty moment.

Hugging the glass, I crossed to the French doors, opened them and looked down at the street below. They would soon arrive, the Humvees. And the big men with their big guns. The National Guard. The same bozos who gunned down four kids at Kent State. America thrives on riots and it was truly a war zone out there. Clouds of black smoke rose in the distance. I could hear the sirens. This was how it would be all the long night.

I already had a sense of the walls closing in on me.

What a lame word, curfew. Cur-few. The curse of the few. And I was one of them. Cursed. Locked in. Until the sun came up tomorrow morning. I took another sip, a more measured one this time and felt the fire spread magnificently through my entire body. Even unto its extremities. Blessed be the Scots!

After resting the old-fashioned on the nightstand, I switched on the TV, disrobed down to panties and bra and flopped backwards onto the bed, welcoming the satisfying bounce of the springs.

An expensive bed in an expensive hotel. For what, though? What could this L.A. trip produce now?

I lay there balancing the old-fashioned on my bare midriff and after admiring the amber liquid sloshing about, let my mind drift back to this morning's meeting. Poor Miki and Jude. My characters had taken a hiding at the hands of the studio beast Spinak. Zero interest. Low on oomph. A pity. Done with Spinak and his ilk, I rolled over onto my side, hugged the pillow between my legs and turned my thoughts to the Miramar's man downstairs.

Men. The way they make it so easy for young females to betray their older sisters, every time. Not intentionally. Simply youth's privilege and a man's never-sated appetite for firm young flesh. What would I look like this time next year? The year after—and the years after that? Cronehood at forty. I tossed down the remainder of the blessed fire water. Even up here on the seventh floor, I sensed the danger.

Nightfall in Crazy Town.

Darkness. Curfew.

I should maybe smarten myself up. Try being sociable. David had put himself out to get me to L.A. this week. Not his fault the curfew. Or my shitty meeting this morning. Or the fact there would be no working dinner tonight with the Arthur Anderson guys.

CNN announced they were crossing to the White House. I settled myself against the pillows and pumped up the volume. California was three hours behind Washington. Already evening in DC. The anchor said Bush needed to convince the electorate he cared. There was a real challenge to the President's leadership, he said, especially in the middle of an election year. When the President's address ended, they would play an interview with the Democrats' presumptive presidential nominee, Governor Bill Clinton.

George Bush seemed a troubled man; civil war on the west coast and his political future riding on how well he handles this crisis.

Tonight, I want to talk to you about violence in our cities, and justice for our citizens, two big issues that have collided on the streets of Los Angeles. First, an update ... I spoke with both Governor Wilson and Mayor Tom Bradley ... there were still incidents of random terror and lawlessness this afternoon... what followed Wednesday's jury verdict ... a tragic series of events for the city of Los Angeles ... fires ... staggering property damage, hundreds of injuries and the senseless death of over thirty people. First, this morning I ordered the Justice Department to dispatch one thousand riot-trained federal law enforcement officials to help restore order in Los Angeles, beginning tonight ... FBI, swat teams, special riot control units of the US Marshals Service, Border Patrol, and other federal ...

According to the Commander-in-Chief, another one thousand federal law enforcement officials were on stand-by alert should they be needed. He was telling America that earlier today he had directed three thousand members of the Second Infantry and fifteen hundred marines to stand by at the El Toro Air Station outside L.A. Further, he was federalizing the National Guard, placing six thousand troops under federal control.

I noted the man's furrowed brow. Staged or genuine, I wondered. The 41st President of the United States was speaking about the judicial outcome, once his Department of Justice got itself into high gear *...five federal prosecutors are on their way to Los Angeles. ... we will investigate ... our Justice Department has consistently demonstrated its ability to investigate fully, a matter like this ... since 1988 the Justice Department has successfully prosecuted over one hundred law officials for excessive violence ... subpoenas are being issued ... evidence is being reviewed ... expeditious, and it will be fair ... It will not be driven by mob violence ...*

Bush pivoted to a plea to understand that while the images on screen of the Rodney King beating were, admittedly, horrifying, ... *something Americans will never forget, almost beyond belief, there was a need to appreciate there were other acts among all this ... small but significant acts in all this ugliness, that give us hope.*

And then his ode to the police: ... *they help kids, they don't make a lot of money, but they care about their community and their country ... officers and firefighters are risking their lives right now on the streets of L.A. And finally, there are the citizens who showed great personal responsibility, who ignored the mob, who at great personal danger helped the victims of violence, regardless of race.*

In his groove now, POTUS spoke of a special incident he witnessed which stuck in his mind ... *the story of one savagely beaten white truck driver, alive tonight because strangers, four black strangers, came to his aid ... the injured driver was able to get behind the wheel of his truck and drive away, but his eyes were swollen shut, and the woman asked him if he could see. He answered no, and she said, "Then I will be your eyes." Together, those four people braved the mob and drove that driver to the hospital. He is alive today, only because they stepped in to help.*

Then came a sound bite from the likely Democratic presidential nominee, Governor Bill Clinton of Arkansas who, according to the anchor, was in Los Angeles to inspect what was happening in the beleaguered city. ... *Mr Bush is under considerable political pressure to prove his leadership on the issue ... the riots show the need for a new President who can bind up and reunify a nation drifting apart along lines of race and income.* After deploring the violence in Los Angeles and elsewhere across the nation, Clinton speared the Vice President, Dan Quayle; *I'm tired of people on trust funds telling people on food stamps how to live.*

Wow, cop that, guys!

The handsome baby-boomer presidential candidate. The elegance of the man. Sex appeal yoked to a burning intelligence. Romancing the camera, knowing the effect he had on both men and women. Bill Clinton, the man with an overspill of charismatic charm. Lucky Hillary. If the States were going to vote in November on grandad George or spunky baby boomer Bill—The Face they might get to see nightly on their screens—then poor old George was up against it.

Had Sapphire caught the clip? The girl was besotted with the telegenic Governor. I reached for my cigarettes. Shook the empty packet. Remembered I was quitting. Renewed my vows and crushed the packet in disgust. No need to encourage the wrinkles itching to get at my mouth. Early onset menopause. A sick joke. Not hers. Not yet. Please, please, please. It couldn't be happening. But true, it was; a thirty-nine-year-old body acting like a fifty-year-old one. The tests had proved it.

Thirty-nine-years-old. Fit and healthy. It seemed no time since all the folderols had started. The blood. The leaks. The pads. The pimples. The cramps. The moods. And soon it would all be over. Maybe time to rejoice.

I screwed the lid back on the Glenfiddich. Hid it under her pillow. Out of the way of the Latinos.

And then I brought the bottle out again and headed for the bathroom where I washed the glass and then back in the bedroom, putting two old-fashions alongside the whiskey.

It would be mean to hide the bottle. Better to leave it out for the women. Make myself scarce. Go downstairs and do weights, fifty laps of the pool. Skip the food line-up. Grab an apple and a bottle of mineral water and find a hidden corner of the glamorous Miramar to sit alone and contemplate a dark universe. No way was I fronting up to Connie's gig. You had to be in the right mood for Con. The right frame of mind. Tonight, I wasn't. Not in the right frame of mind for all the bossiness. Not up for all the sweet bonhomie it rode in on, either.

I lay back on the bed and surrendered to a pure Glenfiddich glow.

11

SAPPHIRE

What is it else? A madness most discreet,
a choking gall, and a preserving sweet.
Romeo (Act 1, Scene 1): William Shakespeare

Santa Monica, Los Angeles
Friday 1st May 1992

No rubber spent this time. A more measured arrival. 'Here is our water. We boil it.'

Mateo leant his bike against the tree and signaled her not to get up. 'Our kitchen—they did it. Boil it for us. For you.' He looked around, as if being followed, and bent down to whisper in her ear. 'You don't know who is 'ere tonight. I just get the drum.'

'Out with it.'

Mateo hesitated.

'Come on. Don't keep me guessing, you numb skull. Who?'

He cast his eyes around the grounds again. His voice was soft, 'A secret. My brudder's friend. Security guy, 'e tell my brudder this when they step outside to smoke. I am telling you, but you must not tell nobody.'

'Anybody.' She pinched his ear. 'Out with it, Mateo. The suspense is killing me. Who?'

Mateo, finally confident they were not being surveilled, stood to his full height, feet apart, hands on hips. 'Governor. Bill. Clinton! Mr Candidate Clinton, 'imself.'

She leapt in the air and let out a high-pitched squeal. 'Governor Bill Clinton!'

As she started to spin around, he jammed his hand across her mouth. 'Ssh,' he whispered. 'You will get me into much trouble.'

'Candidate Clinton, here? Bill Clinton—in this very hotel? No way! Get out!'

'Get out? You don't like me to tell you this?'

'You've got to be kidding me, Mateo.' She grabbed the font of his shirt. 'Tell me you're not kidding. You are telling me we might see Bill Clinton. Here at the Miramar? The man scooped Super Tuesday. You know that, right? And he's just won New York. He's on fire. He's so hot, Bill Clinton. He plays a trumpet. Played it on TV wearing dark sunnies. So cool.' She cast her eyes to the heavens.' Oh, my God, Mateo, the next President of the United States. Wait till I tell Nick. This is awesome. They'll never believe me back home. Never.' She took a breath. 'You overheard your brother and the security guy saying this, for real? You're sure?'

'For real,' he said with a grin, pushing a flop of spiky curls away from his face, pride in his superior knowledge shining radiantly out of black-as-coal eyes. 'Like I say, you 'ear things like this when you scrape dishes. They forget you. And now, my mudder's friend, Juana? She say she made up his room. He talks nice to her.'

'Oh, my god. Bill Clinton. Of course, he would talk nice. He is nice. He's a Democrat, Mateo!' She spun her head around to check the bungalows. 'The bungalows or main block? The bungalows, for sure. What number?'

He shrugged.

'We have to find out. That's definite. You simply must find out the room number for me from—what's her name? Juana?

'Si. Juana.'

'Oh, my God, the Clintons!' She tossed her hair back with a savagery that emphasised her excitement. 'Bill Clinton. I do not believe this!'

'Governor Clinton comes to see what is 'appening in South Central. He sneaks into L.A. and comes 'ere. Mrs Hillary, no, but 'e 'as a campaign dinner—tomorrow night—with big movie stars. At the Biltmore.'

'The Biltmore?'

'Is downtown. They land 'elicopters on the roof.'

'I know where the Biltmore is, dopey. I'm more American than you are. Let's go!'

'To Biltmore?' Mateo looked stunned.

'To get intel from this Juana woman, silly boy.' She pushed her hair back from her face and straightened the paisley vest. On her feet now and the pain of injury forgotten. 'C'mon, Mateo. What are you waiting for? Haircuts? This is huge. She'll tell us. Let's go.'

Mateo looked hesitant. His eyes shot around the grounds. She could see he must be thinking he had just made his life a little more dangerous by giving out this state secret. 'You must clue me in, Mateo. You must! I'm going to interview him for our paper. I am, you know.'

'Governor Clinton, he will 'ave 'is own security men. Aids. Lots of people to protect him.'

'No, he won't. Not yet. Not until July. The convention. After his nomination when he really is the chosen candidate. Then he gets a security detail.'

'Mr Clinton, 'he was governor and will 'ave security, for sure.'

'Maybe his campaign manager came with him. And I suppose when he goes out onto those dangerous streets tomorrow the cops'll protect him. Not here in the hotel, I don't reckon. Whatever.' She indicated the rows of bungalows behind her, buried among the tropical shrubbery. 'It'll just be him in there, Mateo. Betcha. He won't want anyone crowding him out. Not Bill Clinton! Hey, this is wicked! Come on, we need to find out which bungalow. I can't believe you took this long to tell me something this awesome, Mateo.'

'Last night, they shot a man dead in downtown. He drive a white Tunderbird, the dead man. The man they shoot. A white Tunderbird.'

'Yeah, terrible. Tell me about it. But we're talking Bill Clinton, here. I've been sitting a breath away from the bungalows nursing my stupid knee and any moment the next President of the United States of America could be walking past. He'd stop. I know he'd stop, Mateo. Reckon he'd stop? He'd ask me what happened and ask if he could help me. That's how things happen, how you get your break. How many movies you see that, hey? *A Star is Born*? C'mon, let's go.' She reached for the busted bicycle and started hobbling along the path, pushing it.

Mateo grabbed the back wheel to stop her. 'Is no good. Broken. Leave it. You 'ave a bad knee, right? Sit.'

As unaccustomed as she was to taking orders from boys, this was different. Mateo was right. The wound needed to be cleaned before it festered. She surrendered the bike and watched while he wheeled it back to lean it against the trunk of the big tree again.

'They will come for it,' the boy assured her. 'Later, they will come.' He eased her back down onto the grass. 'Doctor Lopez,' he said with a grin, showing her his row of perfect white teeth as well as the water bottle and a First-Aid kit.

Boy and girl; they faced an awkward moment, Mateo kneeling beside her outstretched legs, his eyes focused on the left leg of her damaged tights. She knew that he either had to tear away fabric from the wound to clean the area thoroughly or get her to drag her tights down and give him free access. At least that way, she might save them for Connie's darning needle. No shame in a repair. She was not about to make it easy for him, however. She locked eyes with him, aware of the power of her gender. To the boy, at this very moment, she was a prized object.

Something strange happened as she held his gaze: She felt her nipples harden, felt tingles that made her whole body take notice of the boy like it hadn't done before. She felt bold. Adventurous. Was this grown-up sex? If it was, it was awesome. And Mateo would be thinking the same thing, she knew.

He continued to stare at her, waiting for his instructions. Doctor. Patient.

'You know which bungalow, don't you, Mateo?'

'Please? I should not be saying. Juana tells me. My brudder too, but he says—'

'Mateo? I intend to write a brilliant article—about all the good things he wants to do.' She continued to stare him down. 'For people like you, for one thing. Okay?'

She lifted her backside, lowering her eyes to indicate the tights. She saw sweat break out on his upper lip, dark fluff glistening. She savoured her role as temptress, her moment of supremacy.

'The number, Mateo?' she said in her best Lauren Bacall voice. 'You do know how to whistle don't you, Steve?' He looked puzzled but there was no need to tell him how she and Nick watched all-night Bogart specials. She spread her legs, just enough, feeling her legs push against the hem of her yellow mini. 'Which bungalow?'

Mateo took hold of the elastic top of the tights and still, he waited for permission.

She cocked her head to the side. There was a bargain, here. She wanted an answer.

A studied silence hung between them, until finally, 'It is not any bungalow. Is the Tenth,' said the boy.

'The Tenth Floor?'

'Si.'

'Three above ours?' A VIP suite?'

'Of course.' Still kneeling. Still with his hands on the elastic top.

'Is Ten a security floor?'

'Si, but there is the service lift for kitchen staff.'

She smiled at him and nodded, leaving him in no doubt when she raised her backside off the grass that he had her permission to pull down her leggings.

'So, how do I get my interview?' she said, reaching out and taking hold of his hand to slow him down. She needed to be the one in charge of things. The foxy heroine in Hollywood's golden oldies who glides a finger across her lips as she holds her man with a steamy gaze before she lowers her eyelids, only to slowly open them again and look up at him. Challenging him. She covered Mateo's hand with her own. Saw in his eyes the excitement she knew she could use to bend him to her will.

'How, Mateo?'

'I use service elevator. Take your note. Put it under 'is door. Okay?'

'Okay,' she whispered, smiling her Jody Foster smile as she raised her bum off the ground and watched him gently tug at the stretch fabric, approving the way he took extra care when he pulled the purple tights over her grazed knee. She lowered her backside to the ground, the tights around her ankles, her legs bared and her knees slightly bent and apart.

She felt a sudden urge to show him what was under her mini. And an urge to see his penis. Would it look like David's, his penis? Or like Nick's, the only ones she'd ever seen. And only then because she had rushed unannounced into bedrooms over the years. Unless you counted Kenny Pittman's the night the whole class camped out and they held him down for a dare, she recalled with a shudder. It was too hideous. A disgusting sight, Kenny Pittman's slug.

Mateo reached for his First Aid kit and, raising her injured leg off the ground, said softly, 'I am sorry. It will 'urt.'

She thought about that. One of the older girls at school had warned them. It hurt. But only the first time, the girl had added with a grin, while not prepared to elaborate. She watched him dig into the kit for plasters while keeping a firm hand under her wounded knee. He was enjoying the touch of her flesh as much as she was enjoying the thought of him wanting to touch her.

'Did kids play doctors and nurses in Mexico?'

Mateo shook his head. He was busy being her saviour, assessing the damage. 'Doctors and nurses? No. Why?'

He was playing dumb, but she bet he would kill to see her vagina, doctor or no doctor. Boys had been asking her to drop her knickers since she was five. Just a look. Down in the orchard, behind the old wooden shed. A dollar if you'll show it. Let's touch it and we'll give you five. Ten, if you open your legs and let us look in there.

Gross.

As he went about his ministrations, she noted he averted his eyes from the mauve lace panties she knew would be visible beneath her mini because she had just wiggled her backside on the grass to make it ride up. No way her mother knew this would happen when she brought home the new underwear for the L.A. trip last week.

'This will sting,' he said, pouring the sterile water over her bare knee.

'Ouch! God, Mateo!'

Struck by the sudden pain, cold water hitting the raw wound, she tried not to pull away. It hurt. So much for the great feelings. The body is a weird thing. So much going on in there that's good and, also bad.

Mateo screwed up the end of a tissue and carefully dug the shrapnel from the gash. Ignoring her protests, he poured the last of the water across the injury and dabbed at it, drying the area around the wound enough that he could apply the iodine and plasters.

The iodine stung like the worst punishment from Hell. She called a halt before he got busy with the crepe bandage. She had milked the injury past the point of interest. She yanked up her tights.

'So, my interview?' she said as Mateo sat himself back beside her, both leaning against the tree trunk. She reached for his hand. 'In the note,' she said, 'I'll tell him who I am and request an interview. And you're sure you'll deliver it?' This was the moment when her fate hung in the balance. An interview with Governor Bill Clinton this close to the first Tuesday in November. Such a scoop would make her a star reporter. All she ever wanted in life.

'Mateo?'

'Si.' He turned and beamed his white-teeth grin at her. 'Too easy. For me,' he said with a shrug.

'They'll let you use the service lift and you'll push my note under his door?'

Mateo looked up at the top floor of the hotel building. He looked back at her as he slid his hand up her thigh. She made no move to push it away.

'I will make it 'appen.' His voice was deeper than it had been when they discussed movies this afternoon, deep and husky. 'For you,' he added. 'Just for you, Sapphire.'

She made no resistance when he slid his hand higher. Under her mini. Gasped when his hand reached inside the leg of her mauve panties.

Mateo held her gaze.

Covering his hand with her own, she surveyed the grounds before turning back to him with a smile. All the permission he needed. She closed her eyes as his fingers touched her yony. She shuddered. She was flying fast down the wild water slide back home. On a swing, hooking the wind with her feet to make her swing go higher, faster, faster. It was thrilling, the sensation. Big girl sensations. Better even than when she touched herself.

Three giggling young girls on pushbikes peddled past. Mateo hastily withdrew his hand and stood up. She straightened her skirt.

He reached for his bike. 'Okay? Good to go?' he said, flustered and looking as if he expected Border Control to swoop down on him, poor boy.

She stayed seated, propped against the tree, wondering what had just happened to her. Then Mateo was helping her to her feet.

'Okay, good to go,' she said, smiling a coy smile at the boy. 'Maybe you will become a doctor, Mateo. Do they let the Mexican kids go to college? I couldn't bear to think of you scraping rich people's dishes for the rest of your life.'

Mateo kept his body turned away from her as she wriggled fully back into the tights, tugging the band up to her waist and pulled her skirt down as far as it would go. 'Done.' She went up to him and planted a kiss on his cheek. 'Thank you.'

She had caught him using the last drops of water from the bottle to wash his hands. He tossed the empty bottle into the wire basket of the damaged bike, laughing when his aim found its mark. 'The city 'as run out of prisons—for the prisoners? The riots? They release many today. Many. I 'ear it from my brudder.'

'Meaning?'

'Mr Clinton must 'ave much security protection.'

'God, Mateo! You have to have the last word, don't you, smart guy?' She laughed. 'But listen, I'm just a kid, a school kid who wants to interview the man for her school paper. He'll be cool with that. Clinton plays a sax; did you know that?'

'You told me, already. A trumpet.'

'Trumpet. Sax. Whatever.'

'You should be getting over there, no? Your mudder comes?' He pointed over her shoulder to the bungalows.

'It's cool. We're good. I need to check with the commissionaire for where's the nearest library. I reckon there must be one around here, somewhere. Santa Monica Library? Let's go.' She pinned him with soulful eyes, her voice low and theatrically breathy. 'It has to happen, Mateo, this interview. If you don't understand that, then you don't understand anything about me.' She turned from him and indicated the rental bike over by the tree. 'Okay to dump it there?'

'Si.'

'Let's go.'

'There is one on 6th. Santa Monica Boulevard,' he said with a certainty that surprised her.

'You're the best, Mateo. Absolutely you are.' She hugged him, much to his obvious discomfort and saw him check his watch.

'This bike? You can ride to the library with it, okay?' said Mateo, indicating his speedster.

'For sure? You're certain of that?'

'Sure, I am sure. For you only. No one else must touch it, okay?'

'I gotta race upstairs. Tell them I'm going. My godmother, she's so into Clinton. She might run me to the library. Worth a try.'

Mateo shrugged. 'Jump up.' He moved forward on his bike and indicated she take the seat behind him. 'Arms go 'ere.' He pulled both her arms around his waist and patted her clasped hands. 'You must hold on. Tight. Hold me tight, okay?'

'If you insist.' She grinned and tightened her grip.

'Or you fall off.'

'Who's arguing. Let's go. Start peddling, hero.'

Mateo pressed down on his peddles and they raced towards the kitchens. She hugged his waist and leant in. Pressed her head into his back. Smelled him. His blacker than black corkscrews tickled her face. She could stay locked onto him like this forever, just the two of them. This was as thrilling as it could get, she imagined.

On a whim, she stuck her tongue out and licked his neck. Pulled his curls away and nibbled his ear lobe until she felt him shudder and then she did it all again. What was going through his head right now, she wondered?

And what on earth was she thinking, being this slutty? Like the girls in their bum-freezer uniforms, smoking cigarettes and hanging off their boyfriends at Katoomba station. He would be Catholic. A Mexican kid. She suppressed a giggle. Wait till she tells them back home about what she let him do. But then remembered she wasn't going to spill the beans to a bunch of immature girls.

'I want to kiss you,' he said, turning his head to shine his grin on her, his rascal eyes alight with mischief.

She ruffled his hair. 'Cheeky fella. Maybe tomorrow.'

'Deal?'

'Providing you can get my note up to Ten.'

She heard the sigh. The silence was freighted with Mateo's concerns. His job and his duty to his employer. His desire for her.

'Promise, Mateo?' She snuggled even closer into his warmth. Shut her eyes and took a deep breath. 'Promise,' she whispered, trying to control the tremor in her voice, the tiny give-away that said she was not quite the woman of the world she was playing at, but instead, a dumb, almost sixteen-year-old virgin who had just let a boy go too far.

'Okay,' he said softly, reaching back to touch her cheek. 'Is good.'

'Is good,' she echoed, all thoughts vanished of Connie being mad at her. Like any good journalist, she needed to research the candidate's policies. After all, it's what her mother did for her morning shows. She could see the look on their faces when she presented her scoop to Mrs Corrigan's class. Social Studies Y-10? She would cream it! So, even if it would have her mother yelling like a banshee, she had a responsibility to her profession to get to the library.

12

CONNIE

We are not here only to demolish discrimination but to envision the benefits to the human race of integrating this forgotten half of humanity in development.

Prime Minister Bandaranaike,
World Conference on Women, Mexico 1975

Santa Monica, Los Angeles
Friday 1st May 1992

She finished tying up her laces and strapped on Theo's Baby Björn, all the while worrying about Cynthia, sad because the meeting this morning had dished her a pie in the face. Cyn's moods were her deep concern. More reason the budding screenwriter should front up for the get-together, she figured. Jolly her up a bit. The New York guys were industry heavies who could prove handy contacts.

'Want me to walk across with you?' David, calling from the bathroom.

'I'm good. Thanks, hon.'

'He's heavy,' he said from the bathroom where he stood by the mirror zipping his fly and checking on his expanding bald spot.

'I'll share the burden with Sapphie. Anyway, the harness is good for the posture. Hope he's awake when I get there. We want him to sleep tonight.' She ran a comb through her hair, glossed her lips, checked her breasts and exchanged soaked pads for dry ones. Anticipation had her breasts gushing like geysers. Mammary exuberance. Welcome to lactation Hell.

David came from the bathroom, drying his hands and planted a kiss on her forehead. 'Then have fun, old girl.' He slapped her backside.

'Fun, you reckon?' Over her shoulder as she exited the suite.

In her runners she made it down their corridor and around into the main stretch in half the time it would have taken in heels. The stilettos were Lady Lunchalot essentials. Her worn-down Nikes were serious motherwear. The heels turned David on, although she rarely got to doll up in Katoomba. A shame. She'd felt his eyes on her this afternoon. As she pressed the bank of elevator buttons, she made a mental note to give spike heels more opportunities, even if only in the privacy of their own bedroom. She owed it to her man to make the effort. Be a little more Cynthia, a little less Constance. But Life was a trade-off.

With a sigh, she checked her engorged breasts again, aware she was humping at least six or seven kilos over the limit to be considered an ice goddess.

The elevator doors split. A sporty young couple stepped out. She greeted them with a smile as she moved past them to take her place in the crowded lift.

Waiting for the sluggish seven floors descent and the multiple stops along the way, she had time to go over the details of what she would need this evening: Guests at six o'clock. She would send Sapphie downstairs for the early buffet, set out the drinks and nibbles, feed Little Man, bath him, read his story and settle him down, then make herself presentable. Sapphire might like to go around to Cyn's room and watch TV as she did last night.

It was a stretch, but she'd manage. She always did. The industry guests were sure to agree with her that *Surrender Song* was good but flawed. Nothing a rewrite couldn't fix. Hollywood wasn't ready for women to take over the world. Not while ever the old boys were in charge. Hollywood was no place to stage your revolution. Cyn needed to play their game if she wanted their money. For a start, her Fifties girls—not enough fight in them. A teenage mum and her girlfriend battling hardships in the Outback. All very dour. Although they say to write what you know, Cyn's story is not the stuff celluloid dreams are made of. When the characters' story shifts into the Seventies, Cyn has written them as women too tough, too driven, feminists out to change the world.

Like the writer, herself, thought Connie, remembering their days as activists when she was as radical as her soul sister.

International Women's Year, the beginning of the Decade of Women and the arrival of the Feminist Bookshop in Glebe, and because she was to be a delegate, they'd asked for a Constance Labelle contribution to their new anthology.

A bright sunny Saturday morning in the inner west. She and Cynthia, their Doc Martens chewing up the macadam as they trudged with their pushbikes up the hill towards the old Balmain Town Hall and joined a crowd of irate women blocking Darling Street.

'It's sad,' she said as they came closer and could hear the racket. 'Poor old Stewy should be around to witness all this.' Had their long-ago mentor been alive, Miss Stewart would have been shouting as loud as any of them, heart-warmed at the sight of so much sororal solidarity. Her moon goddesses on the march.

The women of the inner west had come together to protest the miserable allocation of special funding the Whitlam government was contributing to their district under its International Women's Year grants—and to a woman, they intended to be seen and heard. Noisy termagants. Shrewish females. At least that was how she knew the commercial TV commentators airing coverage of the protest during prime time tonight would portray them. A bunch of nasty, bad-tempered rabble-rousers determined to upset the natural order of things. Women who should have been at home ironing their husband's shirts and looking after his kids.

'You know the networks are going to sensationalize this demo, don't you?' said Cynthia as they approached the town hall and parked their bikes. 'They'll have a field day.' Cyn, always reading her mind.

'Naturally. It's 1975—a new dawn—female power. Bring it on!'

'They'll trivialize our demands, belittle us, ridicule our clothing, the cut of our hair, our 'unladylike' behaviour. Conservatives are terrified of what's coming, Con.'

Confrontations with the police had already begun. They grinned at each other, held up their banners—high and proud— and threw themselves into the melee, blending in with demonstrators still pouring onto Darling Street, blocking traffic and waving placards at the TV cameras.

Balmain's Finest bullied the crowd of hostile women, attempting to push them back onto the sidewalk, until eventually the word went around that the Canberra bureaucrats were about to commence proceedings inside and there was no further need for police to control the street. Like a school of startled fish, the sisterhood ceased resisting, turned and rushed indoors, ready to do battle of a different kind, a fight for funding.

To the disappointment of every woman in the hall, particularly to those like her and Cyn—both having been involved in researching and writing the submission—not a word in the committee's report mentioned a grant for an inner west women's community health centre or refuge. The collective was furious about the knock-back. As Cynthia made clear when she rose to speak, they had made a forceful case to Whitlam's people in their application.

'And now it seems, Liz Reid couldn't even be bothered turning up to hear our grievances. Instead, she sends her representative! Shame! Shame on Canberra!' yelled Cynthia, continuing to excoriate the committee members up on stage for ignoring the needs of a working-class district like theirs, so desperate for a women's community health facility.

The hall exploded in loud booing and angry calls, the crowd punching the air and giving the speaker a standing ovation. Ms Reid's National Advisory Committee had not heard the last of them, vowed the inner west sisterhood as its members filed out of the hall and incensed women stood around in clusters discussing the meeting's outcome. They were strong. And yes; they were noisy women who would go on fighting the Reid committee and the power elites in Canberra.

'Teenage pregnancies, botched abortions, abused wives. What does that lot inside care? They live in their ivory towers, all of them.'

'That lot couldn't give a stuff, Con. All we're asking is for a female-friendly medical environment.'

Theirs was a righteous cause and it would be the basis of her article for the Glebe Bookshop's anthology. They were within their rights to push back on the Committee's ideas of what were and weren't proper feminist initiatives. 'If a centre for dealing with female health issues—including a refuge for abused women and kids—isn't a proper 'feminist initiative'—'

'Under Canberra's own stated guidelines, mind you.'

'And therefore, entitled to be funded under the IWY Commonwealth grants, then what feminist fucking initiatives are acceptable?'

Later that evening, with the aid of the notes she had taken and visions of the day's events burned into her brain—plus being well fortified by the bottle of shiraz on the table and Cyn by her side—she sat down and wrote her piece for Glebe. 'Hopefully Cyn, someday our daughters are going to appreciate how it was for the women of our era,' she said as she ripped the last page from her typewriter and stacked it on the pile. 'Things ought to have changed for the better by then.'

Cynthia raised her glass. 'Let's hope,' she said, draining the last of her wine. 'And no more, the walk of shame,' she added softly.

Such a simple line but coming from Cyn, it packed a punch. As she stacked the typed pages and put away her journal notes, Connie remembered how wretched she felt the day she trudged up Curlewis Road after leaving poor Cynthia behind in that wretched clinic. Four years ago. It felt like it happened last week. The Curlewis Road Clinic, Bondi. At break of day, practically.

By devious means—and by what she'd hoped would pass for casual conversation—she had managed to prize the name of an abortionist's clinics from her mother. Rosemary being a family GP, and the Brays' Sunday evening conversations usually turning to social issues, it had not taken a genius to swing the table talk to the right-to-life versus women's rights hot topic. Curlewis in Bondi was one of the more respectable abortion clinics, said Rosemary, a pro-choice advocate. For just the briefest moment, she had considered confiding in her mother. But Cyn, with a Roman Catholic father like Paddy and the prudish Moira for a mother had insisted no one know. Not even Jesse.

The next day, she booked Cyn into the clinic. Two days later, before the commuter traffic started swamping Bondi, all of eighteen-years-old and petrified, they stepped off the bus and walked down the hill towards the small grey weatherboard cottage with the white picket fence, having drained their student bank accounts to raise the funds.

At the gate, Cyn had taken the overnight bag from her and planted a kiss on her cheek. 'This is it. I want you to leave me now, Con. I can do this. You shouldn't come in. I'll be okay. Promise. I'll get them to call a cab for me.'

For a moment, she had contemplated a physical approach; just drag her away but Cyn was determined to go through with it. She understood but she wasn't happy, particularly that Cynthia hadn't written to Jesse. Reluctantly, she hugged her friend, whispered comforting words and trudged back up the hill to catch the bus.

Several women at the rally had approached Cynthia after her fiery Town Hall speech, insisting she put her hand up as a delegate. The International Women's Year Tribune in Mexico City in June would be a defining moment, one that would shake things up. But so much depended on Cyn's state of mind. Nothing had ever been the same for her since that day in Bondi.

'No way could I address an international conference,' Cynthia said as they left the rally and strolled down to the William Wallace in East Balmain. 'Jolly Cynthia Smart from sunny Oz. No. I couldn't, Con. But you could. You'd be great. You've got to stick your hand up for it. I'm nominating you, anyway.'

She had always known, that for Cyn, some days were darker for her than others. At the meeting she had begun well enough, her mood feisty and up-beat as they mixed it with the sisterhood. But something happened later. Her mood dipped. Maybe the protest meeting had brought back too many memories she associated with Jesse and the Vietnam war. Maybe all the commotion had reminded her of the moratorium marches; the banners, the cops, the chanting, the TV cameras, all before they got the news about Jesse. The soldier boy to the war is gone, in the ranks of death you will find him.

Who said war was purely men's business? So many women's lives had turned to tragedy because of the Vietnam war. How did you get over the horror of kissing the boy you loved off to war—the boy you were planning to marry when you were both older—and have him come home to you in a coffin? Life can be cruel.

The Balmain rally hadn't been fruitful and it had been a long day but the fight wasn't over. As the grandfather clock in the Bray hall struck midnight, she looked across to the other single bed. Her darling Cyn.

'Years from now, it's going to be interesting to look back on all this,' she whispered as she bent over and kissed her soul sister goodnight and turned out the bed lamp. 'Sleep tight, beautiful goddess.'

The descending elevator jerked to a stop on the Second Floor.

Two elderly ladies crowded into the car, blessing everyone with smiles summoned from a more gracious era. As people shuffled and moved grudgingly to adjust to the squeeze, Connie found herself slammed against the mirrored wall, pinned in by a large sweaty individual who insisted on pressing his body hard up against her. She tried resisting the spoon, holding back from jabbing her elbow in his ribs. In a superfluous move, he reached over the heads of other passengers and pressed the ground floor button, releasing toxic body odour into the cramped car.

She appraised the old girls' outfits. Obviously dressed for a big night out, even if the pair could strut their stuff no further than the buffet queue tonight. One wore a flouncy mauve blouse, silver cummerbund and long black skirt. The other had chosen a calf-length maroon chenille dress with cross-over bodice, circa 1940. While Chenille had tight grey curls, Mauve Blouse sported a bleached bouffant; teased, tamed and sprayed to within an inch of its life. Good for the old girls. She was ready to throw them a smile when Mauve Blouse, attempting to save her bouffant from the ravages of an over-crowded lift, accidently elbowed her in the eye. She let it pass without mention. They were all victims locked up in a cattle truck tonight.

No sooner had she accommodated to the punishing conditions than the elevator came to another jarring halt and the mass of humanity around her began jostling its impatient way past, spilling into the lobby. About to step out into blessed fresh air and sunlight, she suddenly buckled at the knees and had to grab for the rail to steady herself. She had been shoved out of the way by a youth who accidentally or on purpose, had just swung his sports bag like a ram rod at the back of her legs. Something heavier than a tennis racquet inside the bag, she thought as she watched him throw the hood of his black sweatshirt over his head and race off.

No apology.

'Hey, you mate?' she called after him.

He turned, frowned and kept going. A master of the universe. Ignorant little prick. She tagged it for a discussion tonight on good manners. Elevator etiquette. It should break the ice. Everyone has a story. She checked her watch. Must get a move on.

She elbowed her way through, excusing herself to people standing around in clusters in the lobby.

The place was buzzing. Curfews and food lines will do that. Obviously, their guy with the clipboard had done a great job of strafing the lobby's landscape with his jabber about curfews, cops, Mexicans, mayhem and meal tickets. The staff at Reception looked to be flat out, no doubt assuaging the concerns of anxious guests. Who knew where it would end before the night was over. Certainly, it was not going to be the night they had planned.

She made her way out onto the sunny outdoor café beside the pool where she was hailed by one of the New Yorkers. She checked her watch. Maybe she could grab a coffee with them and still make it across to the Goldman's by five or thereabouts. A few minutes late and Mrs Goldman ... Goldstein ... could cope, she was sure. Theo might be hollering for his tucker and Sapphie glued to the TV and cursing her for being late but in any case, her kids were safe. That was the main thing.

POLICE REPORT

L.A.P.D. REPORT *Friday May 1, 1992*

Library on Santa Monica Blvd. was reported to be on fire. Additional reports stated that the Vermont Square Library' was also on- fire; and. that the Felipe De Neve Library had been broken into with reported damage.

Revolutionary Communist Party attempted to incite a riot at Pico and Alvarado Street.TWO squads are requested at Rodeo and L.A. Brea to protect the boys Market (only building left in the area), citizens are guarding it and would like help. -

UCL.A. students will be demonstrating against police abuse at the Federal Building at Wilshire/Veteran. Willborn, EOC, advised of this demonstration, In addition, per Lt.—, Captain —-, L.A. City Life Guards, stated he is requesting that L.A. City beaches (Will Rogers, WL.A.) be closed.

.At present, Santa Monica City beaches are closed. Ofcr. Wilshire, advised that approximately 3,000 to 5,000 peOple are massed at the post office at Washington and L.A. Brea waiting for their Social Security .and welfare checks. Willborn, EOC, advised. Advised by EOC that sometime this evening an anti- Cuban demonstration will take pL.A.ce at the Federal Building in West L.A. WL.A. was notified.

359 National Guard enroute to Wilshire from Long Beach; they are due to arrive at 1330 hours and will bivouac at Los Angeles High School.

post offices-in Wilshire- which do not appear to be open to issue welfare checks-were drawing large crowds which are becoming agitated. Department Commander advised.

Hollywood and Wilshire Areas were advised to provide security at above radio stations at the direction of Department Commander.

Det. —, advised that KFWB has been broadcasting in its newscasts that L.A.PD requested closure of L.A. City beaches.

Sergeant ——, EOC, notified OWB of a threat ?to President Bush's life reported by the Secre't' Service. WLS is sending a unit to meet Secret Service Agent at the Four Seasons Motel (Doheny and Burton Way) to assist in taking the suspect into custody.

The curfew, combined.with the significant deployment of personnel appeared to have a positive effect on curbing problems The majority Of burglary incidents resulted in arrests and recovery of property. The indication from arrestees was surprise at the quick response time and number of officers since they anticipated the majority of officers would be deployed downtown.

A bomb threat was received' by Communications Division which targeted Foothill Station. The suspect used the 9-1-1 line to deliver his threat. Communications Division was able to determine his home address and telephOne number...

13

SAPPHIRE

Believe you can and you're halfway there.

Theodore Roosevelt

Santa Monica, Los Angeles
Friday 1st May 1992

She jigged, waiting impatiently for the doors to split. 'C'mon, c'mon!' They shoot men to the moon. How come it takes forever to shoot this thing up to Seven?

At last! Thanks for nothing, guys, she muttered, bursting from the elevator and racing at full pelt down the corridor in a manner her mother would have chastised her for being un-ladylike. Taking only a second to catch her breath, she checked her watch for the millionth time, the tiny silver Cartier with the maroon crocodile leather strap Nick had given her last birthday and which was the absolute love of her life. Better even than her new Walkman. But possibly not the Aviators Goddy presented her with on the way over. An early birthday present.

Mateo said the library closed its doors at five, although they let you stay there till half-past, he reckoned. She had no time to waste. She did a neat side-step, pushing past the couple blocking her way. Nice people. But dawdlers.

'Hey, kid, where's the fire?' the man called after her.

She turned long enough to shoot him a hundred-watt smile, threw a wave over her shoulder and kept going. Adults! She skidded to a halt in front of Room 708 only to find it had a Do Not Disturb sign out. Bummer!

No way was she going to her own room. If they were in there, they'd bar her from going to the library. Goddy would approve. She was into Clinton, big time. She knew this because they'd talked so much about the elections in the plane on the way over. She'd be covered if she'd at least told one of the hovering adults where she was, once they discovered she wasn't at the Goldbergs. Goldmans? Old Rita's bungalow.

For a moment she stood, her ear pressed to the door. What did she expect to hear? Snoring? No way. Her godmother was probably just jet lagged. Resting. Like old people do. Could she ignore the sign and disturb her? Hesitantly, she tapped. No response. She was wasting precious time. Turning on her heels and about to beat it back down the corridor, she suddenly had a change of heart. If Goddy could give her a lift in the Mustang, she'd have more time to swot. And for sure, she would want to know about Clinton. She had to tell someone about him or she would burst. And she had to tell one of them, at least, that she was off to the library. Goddy wouldn't mind being disturbed. It was the middle of the day, practically.

She doubled back. Her knocking this time was a rhythmical knuckle pounding.

'Go away.' Through the heavy door, a slurring of words. Sleepy tones.

'Goddy, it's me,' she yelled. I've got awesome news!' She waited. Did her voice carry through the thick doors? She dropped to the floor, lay on her tummy and yelled through the crack, 'Clinton's here, Goddy!'

The seconds ticked away while the theory was tested. Silence. It was useless. She stood up and checked her watch again. She would have to race around the back, to the kitchens. Catch Mateo. Grab his speedster and fly like the wind. God, could she make it to 6th Avenue?

'Come on, Goddy!' She banged again with the flat of her hand. Who needs to sleep just because they sit in a plane for a few hours?

Not like she had to flap her wings to get here. She would run out of time and it would all be her godmother's fault. One last attempt. Her hand poised to knock as the door opened.

'What's up?'

She took in the fact her tall, tanned and fit godmother was standing in the doorway stripped to her pants and bra. Old, and yet she looked so young, especially her body. 'Goddy, Goddy. What do you reckon?'

'No idea. Out with it, sweetheart before you self-combust.'

'Bill Clinton. He's upstairs! Here! On the Tenth. Can you believe it? In a VIP suite just three floors up from us. It's unreal!'

'Come in and sit. You need to get your heart rate down or you'll explode.'

She hesitated at the door for a moment then stepped into the room. She smelled the booze on Cynthia's breath and propped. 'Uh, uh. I shouldn't have … disturbed you.'

'Crazy girl, of course it was okay to knock. Didn't disturb me.'

She was being ushered further into the room by a gentle hand around her waist.

'This sorry case you're looking at, Sapph was just about to step into the shower. But come in, sweetie, sit down. I won't be long. You can tell me all about your big news while I shower.'

She didn't want to be rude but as Cynthia reached for a glass and retrieved a bottle of Coke from the fridge, she stole another glance at her watch.

'Bill Clinton, hey?' said her godmother, offering her the glass of Coke. 'Mr Sexy, himself. Wow.'

'Yeah, wow alright.' She gulped a helping of the Coke and replaced the glass on the countertop. 'Hey, I need to get around to the library on 6th … before it closes and I just thought … well, I thought maybe you might give me a lift?'

'Hey, what's with the upward inflexion Miss Katoomba High? Of course, I can give you a lift … but right now, though? You need to go now?'

Over Cynthia's shoulder, she saw the whiskey bottle on the night table and the two upturned glasses. She realized she'd be peddling to the library. 'Honestly, don't worry, Goddy. Actually, the bike's fine. It's a speedster, anyway. This boy I know, his bike.'

Cynthia saw that she had noted the bottle and glasses. 'Listen, Sapphie, maybe I—'

'Yeah. Best you have your shower. I'll get a ride another time.'

'Sapph, it was a rough day, hon. But no excuses. Your evil godmother has had a nip or two too many to get behind a wheel. Bad me.'

'Honestly, it's fine. But I've gotta fly. Before it closes. Have to research Clinton stuff so I can interview him. Mateo's getting me an interview, can you believe? For our school paper.'

Cynthia placed a hand on her arm and looked into her eyes. 'I'm a disappointment. I'm so sorry, darling girl. I really am.'

'Don't worry.' She kissed her godmother and hugged her. 'I love you.'

'Love you more.'

'Goddy?'

'Sweetie?'

'This boy I met today? One with the bike? Oops, there I go again, upward—'

'Inflection. Tut, tut. But the boy, what of him?'

'He's so—'

'Mateo?'

'Yeah, Mateo. Well ... he's so awesome, Goddy.' For a moment she almost blurted out how she had wanted to do it with him, right there on the lawn, under the tree. She shook off the crazy idea. Even though Cyn was okay about things like that, or so she said last week, she would probably not want her going to the library if she let on, even to Goddy, what a little tart she was. She dropped another kiss on her godmother's cheek. 'You'll love him. I know you will!'

'Mateo?'

'Yeah, Mateo Lopez. Mexican. Sixteen, like me.'

'You're fifteen. Still.'

'Yeah, right!' She was off out the door with a wave over her shoulder, hurtling back down the corridor, aware her godmother had stepped into the hallway to stare at her. In pants and bra. Intoxicated. Adults, she whispered in despair as she just managed to squeeze through the elevator doors.

14

CYNTHIA

I believe alien life is quite common in the universe,
although intelligent life is less so.
Stephen Hawking

Santa Monica, Los Angeles
Friday 1st May 1992

I shut the door, still smiling in the afterglow of my excitable goddaughter's visit—if a visit one could call that breathless appearance a few moments ago.

The fabulous Mateo?

What was that about? Poor child, she had it all ahead of her, the ecstasy and the agony. And the sheer ordinariness once the glow fades; the mating game's biggest disappointment.

I reclined across the bed, my feet on the floor, balancing the old-fashioned on my tummy. How many years had passed since I'd thought a man even slightly 'awesome'? It was easy to envy Sapphie the naiveté of youth, her ability to drool over a boy. I felt the same way once but it was so long ago. So many disappointments since, sadly so many bruises and thick lips since that glorious, meaningful time in my life when love felt real.

Careful not to spill any liquor on my chest, I raised my head, tilted the glass to my lips and sipped. Tiny, tiny sips but enough to blur Wadsworth's prognosis, that's what I needed. For a while, at least. Such was the glory of alcohol. I fought off the urge to fall asleep.

Instead, I sat up, reached for my handbag at the side of the bed and fossicked for a cigarette. Finding and lighting the last of them, I drew in the nicotine and exhaled floating smoke rings into the air, following their slow passage as they drifted to the ceiling and faded away.

There were three at the funeral I had slept with, including the corpse. Rub-a-dub-dub, three men in a tub. Ormond and Glassop and David Labelle. Three Ex's at a Funeral. An interesting concept to work with. A new script. Scrap *Surrender* and write something shocking. Serve up some oomph to Mr Spinak. Young love. Flaming desire. Dreams, dreams and more dreams A lost war. A lost love. Tragedy. Heartache and longing. Aimlessness of sex, ever after … to fill an emotional void … to forget.

The student flings that went nowhere. A congo line of cheating lovers. A bad marriage. Busted lips and bruises. Betrayal. Broken promises. Roll credits on a sour note: The older woman's desperation. A barren woman in a world full of fecund females. Yes, Myron Spinak, I can give you oomph. How much would be too much, old sport?

Point of View: The woman at the graveside. Scene opens on a cemetery perched on a wet and windy clifftop as we see black limos cruise into the grounds. Mourners gathered at the graveside—camera pans—pulls in tight on the woman's face—a mystery beneath the veil—two men stand behind her as coffin is lowered into the ground—one's a young lawyerly student type—the other silver haired in expensive suit—something catches her eye and we see her hurry past mourners with hands outstretched towards the shadowy figure standing off to the side—cue violins as camera pans in on youth in army jungle fatigues—it slowly pulls back as his image dissolves —the woman's distraught—she's failed to reach him before the apparition fades.

Two with a pulse, one fresh corpse and yesterday's ghost. So, four at the funeral.

Forget it. Pure melodrama. I'm operating on malt. Glenfiddich eighteen-year-old single malt. Pricey. So, what? Alcohol's alcohol and the good ones are the best. Forget the price tag. It's the lift that matters. I would drink piss from Gandhi's loin cloth if it gave me comfort. Nevertheless, I screwed the lid back on and slid the bottle under the night table. I was no lush.

I reached for the remote and surfed the channels. Cable news was all over it, the rioting. From an excited commentator: Police Commission President Stanley K. Sheinbaum said that even the National Guard and the California Highway Patrol will not be enough to quiet the unrest. It was spreading throughout the city. The problem is widening, intensifying. You have a whole social upheaval, cried S.K. Sheinbaum.

Riots on their doorstep, here at the Miramar. Every station showing alarming images; horrific shots of flaming buildings; echoes of gunfire; women and kids running off with armfuls of loot; gangs of black youths vandalizing shops; Korean shopkeepers fighting off marauders with guns; youths smashing windows with bricks and fire extinguishers and jumping on car bonnets; and in one gruesome picture, a freshly slain body lying on the ground beneath a bloodied sheet. The ABC showed a Catholic cardinal reading a message from Pope John Paul 11. The Holy Father was deeply saddened and offered his prayers for the restoration of civil harmony and a renewed spirit for solidarity.

Good for the old boy. A decent chap, Pope John Paul II. Paddy idolized the man. Saint John Paul the Great, according to Paddy Smart, a died-in-the-wool Roman Catholic. Not a Roman Catholic who bothered much about turning up regularly for Mass. Except for the showy ones. A sucker for a Christmas Eve Midnight Mass. Easter Sundays.

And he had a penchant for dropping in on random funeral services. No one knew him but who queries the man in the back row with the sad countenance.

Paddy loved the whole panoply of these rituals. He was especially a sucker for a nuptial mass. Brides in white satin made him weep.

My wedding to Noel Ormond had made him weep, for sure. But

not for sentimental reasons. My father had seen what it would take me countless black eyes, split lips, a broken wrist and truckloads of forged cheques to see. I stayed on the ABC news, propped against the pillows. Forty people had already been killed since the rioting broke out on Wednesday afternoon, and this was Friday, coming on sunset. Eleven of the dead were killed by law enforcement officers, said the anchor. Well done guys. Let's raise a glass to LAPD's finest.

Three police officers were among the 1,899 reported injuries. It was estimated over five thousand people had been arrested across the nation since rioting began. And still the anchor went on spewing out these statistics. Prisons, said the man, weren't coping. Non-violent prisoners were being released to make room in the jails for those arrested in the riots. Colleges and universities were staying closed. Schools closed in Beverly Hills, Compton, Inglewood, Long Beach, Lynwood, Paramount and Torrance. Office workers had been sent home this afternoon.

Some clean-up efforts had begun along heavily hit Vermont Avenue and other areas, including the Mid-City, Mid-Wilshire and Hollywood sections the commentator reported, adding it seemed a fruitless exercise in the face of the destructive fury still wreaking havoc. Image after image of violence. I killed the volume but stayed with the images.

The large white envelope sat at the foot of the bed.

I had feared it arriving in the mail while I was in L.A. and asked that the surgery courier it, express to me at home. It wasn't something for Imelda Cartwright's prying eyes. The stickybeak. Amazing what the woman thought she could get away with so long as she kept a feather duster in her hand. Rifling through closets on the pretence of dusting shelves. Even to trying on my shoes, dear Imelda of the Blessed Agency for Domestic Help.

Mrs C was supposed to collect the mail when she arrived in the morning and stick it, unopened, in my in-tray. But the big white radiologist's envelope slid under the door by our postie would have been a temptation for Mrs Nosey Parker. A little steam, a little peak-a-boo. God forbid the woman should see those images and read the report. Cartwright would take one look and fly out the door bellowing like a banshee, never to return.

I reached for the envelope and studied the way my name had been inscribed in copperplate handwriting.

A woman's handwriting. His receptionist. The words Private and Confidential sitting above the name, a command to not trespass unless you were Ms Cynthia L. Smart. I pictured the woman who had addressed the envelope. Corset-erect in the colonial-era Macquarie Street surgery. Brown panelled walls, dark floorboards, brown leather Chesterfields. A brown waiting-room where even the air had seemed a shade of brown. Miss Craig's domain.

Miss Craig, maybe an Ursula, maybe a Harriet or a Joan, in her late sixties, grey-hair tightly coiffed, conservatively dressed, probably a moggy or three waiting for her at home. An album of sepia photographs tucked away in a draw under lavender-perfumed scarves and cream sateen petticoats lovingly hand-sewn for a honeymoon that never happened. Miss Craig seemed perfectly matched to her mahogany reception desk with its green leathered writing top, its antique banker's lamp, its onyx and marble pen holder. Prof Wadsworth's receptionist had been with him for thirty years and counting. So said the great man himself. Their relationship no doubt a formal one. Old-fashioned loyalty and respect, the key to its longevity.

I fussed about for the cigarettes again but remembered I'd quit and laid back.

Miss Craig's graceful handwriting was of a woman who still corresponded with family and friends by letter and post. The personalised stationary, buff coloured. Or perhaps pale lavender. Her address details inscribed on the letterheads and the note cards. The personal touch. A dinner invitation enjoyed would deserve of a thank you note. A congratulatory note on the birth of an old friend's grandson. A niece's graduation. A note of condolence to the newly widowed. Etiquette in a time of barbarianism.

I picked up the envelope and frisbeed it at the desk. It missed the mark and finished somewhere under the pale blue couch. Of course, it did. Hopeless at sport. And the whiskey was never going to oil the shot.

Oh, my god. It hit me. I put the glass aside and sat up, staring into space. Some godmother. Poor little Sapphie. I'd left the child to get herself around to that damned library. On an afternoon as dangerous as this. But it was done now. I lay my head back on the pillows. Too late to do the right thing.

I returned to Miss Craig and her good manners. No spinster aunt had ever written to me on my birthday. Nor had anyone dropped me a polite condolence note following Ormond's death. Accidental. Pure slapstick. Death by swinging yacht boom, for godsakes. How Laurel and Hardy was that? No, no one had penned a condolence for the widow Ormond, the wronged woman, the one who was stuck at home on the day of the swinging boom, attempting to balance her cheque book and pay their credit card bills and unlike the rest of the world, ignorant of the adulterous affair her spouse was carrying on with his young mistress.

Anyway, I was grateful they hadn't followed up the funeral farce with their condolence notes. It had been all anyone could do that day to even look me in the eye. The mourners, whispering about me behind their hands, asking each other how one acknowledged both the legitimate wife—the barren one, that is—and the sweet young thing who was carrying poor Noel's baby. Carrying their own kith 'n kin, no less. Some doughty old Ormond dowager had sidled up to me after the ceremony, dropping her voice to a conspiratorial whisper to level the young darling's name at me in an aged croak. The name of my nemesis. I stabbed the old biddy with such an icy glare the gossipmonger slunk off, muttering to herself, possibly some ancient Ormond curse.

With a name to it, I'd made a point of observing Miss Anna-Maria Ricci that day, giving myself permission, from beneath dark glasses, to absorb every detail, appearing to look at one group of mourners, while all the while focusing on the bimbo. Sizing her up, mentally placing her beneath the over-weight, dead weight, boom-fucked weight of lover boy the day of the accident. I learned that my adulterous spouse had fallen either dead or near enough dead, backwards on the deck, right on top of the sweet young thing who had to be dragged out from under the corpse and resuscitated.

Pity not to have been there to catch the fun and games. Noel Ormond was a man who, baselessly, had taken himself seriously. He would not have appreciated the slapstick nature of his demise. I copped for the funeral expenses but somewhere deep in this black heart I'd cursed that they hadn't just dumped the body at sea.

Anna-Maria Ricci. The creature had certainly dressed well for the occasion; a cream linen pants suit with a long-tailed soft white silk shirt hanging beneath the jacket to hide—or advertise—the bulge. No sombre black. It would have been a bridge too far. She wasn't the grieving widow, just the incubating whore. Tan lace-up brogues. Black Chloe handbag. An ornate silver bracelet with an inset of lapis lazuli stones. No doubt the whole package a gift from Ormond, which was ironic because to pay for the Vogue look, he nicked and forged my signature on my Amex.

All of twenty-six and drop-dead gorgeous—if one had a hankering for terroni. No doubt Sicilian. Pale, plump and pregnant. Probably not too bright. Peasant hands, short thick digits with large knuckles, a legacy from generations of serf ancestors who dug up potatoes or pulled in nets for a living. Seven-and-a-half-months gone at the time of the funeral, apparently. The bulging mummy-to-be and Ormond, prior to the fatal swinging boom, had picked out names for their bastard, according to another ancient Ormond hanger-on who approached me as I was leaving the boneyard.

I'd made a valiant attempt to keep the rictus grin in place during the crone's gibbering. And during the whole of the ritual socializing that went on outside the church, post-ceremony. Grinding my teeth. Tightening and loosening clenched fists. Holding back from king-hitting them in their smug faces, those relatives of my dead and abusive spouse who had attempted to negotiate their way through their personal etiquette Hell by making just the right number of polite noises, while relieved they were seeing the last of me.

The clichés that day! Spewing from Ormond lips like twice regurgitated vomit. Pure cud. Some, by contrast, had simply pretended I wasn't there, pretend that as the spurned wife I'd opted to stay away. Opted to leave the gig to Clan Ormond and sweet Anna-Maria's mob. Hoped that as the selfish career-driven barren woman who had denied poor Noel a child during five years of wedlock I might have had the good grace not to show up.

I showed up, alright! Showed up still with my black eye and strangulation marks on my throat, the scooped-out neckline specially chosen for the occasion. All from the drunken fool's attentions the week he died. I turned up to make sure the Ormonds knew how I felt about their boxed Ormond. David and Connie had sat either side of me, holding my hand during the solemn service. Especially when the celebrant started lavishing fulsome praise on the dearly departed. Did the Labelles expect I'd jump up and make a lunge at the celebrant's throat, fling open my shirt to show the rest of the bruises? They knew how murderous I felt about the corpse. Connie and David had always tried their best to hide their own low opinion of Noel Ormond. Only there at the funeral to support me.

I left the bed and went across to the bar where I pulled out a bottle of Evian from the fridge and downed half of it in one go. Evian. Spelt backwards, naïve. So much for bald faced marketing; go ahead, ridicule your customer, signal that you're playing to their snobbery while ripping them off.

God, how Connie had wanted to take on the Ormond clan that day. David, luckily, was a steadying influence, bustling the two of us into the limo before going across to do his lawyer thing; speak to the chief Ormonds to make certain they and their lawyers understood who was and who wasn't the legitimate widow; who would and who wouldn't be at the reading of the will. After all, it was my money. Fool that I was, the drunken wastrel had conned me into running a joint bank account. Champaign Charlie was what his racing buddies jokingly called the flash gambler, referring to his penchant for expensive suits and boats and cars.

But why was I thinking about Noel Ormond today, I wondered as I opened the French doors and stood out on the balcony? So long ago and planted these past few years. And the Ricci woman? She had probably gone on to produce whole litters to other married men since then.

I remembered what had happened after the funeral. No sooner rid of Noel Ormond than I tangled with his sailing buddy, Haydn Glassop. And here, my life got stuck. Even up until last week when I finally threw in the towel and walked away from his crumby agency. I looked at my watch. Saturday back home. Haydn would be out on the harbour. Or maybe not. Maybe he was in a hotel somewhere fucking Miss Japan. It would take the promise of a quickie to keep the fool off his ugly yacht on a Saturday.

Coming onto me at the funeral back then. 1985? Yes. Seven years ago. A class act, dropping in on the widow the week after she'd buried her spouse. Promises. Promises. Leave what you're doing, come work for me. Join the agency. Stick with me and you can go far. A partnership. Come to think of it, he was probably doing both things this sunny Saturday back home in Sydney; out on the harbour and fucking Mr Yakima's translator. And who knew, maybe promising her a partnership in his agency. Images of myself flat on my back below deck, Haydn on top of me. Both laughing when he sat up, post-coitally, and hit his head on an overhead beam. The low-ceilinged double birth not commodious. Squeezed into a triangle in the yacht's sharp prow and a reef anchor tucked in there somewhere.

I came back inside and walked over to the small bureau against the far wall and grabbed the black Chanel, the ridiculously luxurious and totally extravagant purchase I made at the duty-free in Sydney. Was it only yesterday? Over-the-top expensive for a mere handbag, but what the Hell. Splurge now, for tomorrow—who knows?

I needed to relax into the glow the liquor had provided and forget the rest.

Forget Noel Ormond.

Forget Glassop and his broken promises.

Forget the Baker & Glassop wasted years and the fact I was now unemployed.

Forget that Hollywood considered my screenplay a pile of dog shit.

Mostly, forget the Wadsworth prognosis and tomorrow's Fortieth. The way all of it messed with my head, had me believing I was already over the hill. Over the hill. Over the hill and far away. Out of sight. Don't disgust us with your liver spots, thinning hair, bat-wing flabby arms, rheumatic joints. Over the hill with you, woman. Be gone! At least become invisible. Greer, in her new book *The Change* declaring post-menopausal women become invisible to the rest of society.

For a moment downstairs I had not been invisible, at least not to the hotel's man. Until something younger passed across his field of vision. How soon before such an insult no longer matters?

The flesh withers around an unchanged spirit. I read it somewhere. Or something akin to it. Passed it off at the time as a whining woman's lament.

I appraised my duty-free extravagance, the sensational Chanel. Wasn't I owed the comforting indulgence of a magnificent piece of art? Of course, I was. And the shiny black leather Chanel bag was a work of art. Classy, the entwined C's and the authentic heavy silver chain. Expensive. So what? It won't matter what's on your arm soon, Cynthia Lorraine. If they are right, the medicos, then before long you'll be stepping out in tracksuits, your hair up in rollers. Schlepping around in sneakers to ease your corns and bunions. Carrying your onions home in a string-bag.

I heard the knock at the door, softly at first, then more insistent.

I ignored it.

Connie, no doubt. Didn't need it. Already have a drink, thanks Con. I'm good. And if it be the Lothario from downstairs, to Hell with him too. I didn't need him, either. Needed no one. Read the sign. Do Not Disturb. Ne pas deranger. Nicht Storen. Fuck off!

I thought about retrieving the envelope, tear it open and for the zillionth time since last week, study the ultra-sound images. Contemplate the weird reality imbedded in those medical images. Go to the dark side. Realize with a shock, how those tiny shadows served to bring my past so viscerally into the present. And how much I missed him, still.

Instead, I laid back on the bed and contemplated the unalloyed joy of pouring another nip. And wondering, briefly, if young Sapphire was having a good time at the library. I loved that child, loved everything about her.

15

CONNIE

There is no more creative force in the world than the menopausal woman with zest.

Margaret Mead

Santa Monica, Los Angeles
Friday 1st May 1992

Connie cursed herself, the New Yorkers and the rushed latte she hadn't needed. Now she was chasing her tail. But at least she'd had a chance to give the New Yorkers a heads up on Cyn's screenplay.

Tightening the baby harness straps, she picked up her pace and hurried towards the Miramar's outliers, the luxury bungalows hidden behind 1930's tropical gardens.

Passing under the shade of a gumtree, she noticed a bicycle with a buckled wheel leaning against the trunk. Someone had come a cropper. It triggered a thought; tomorrow, early, before they all went off to meet up with Nick at Venice Beach, she'd suggest to Sapphire that the pair of them hire bikes and ride around the grounds.

It had been a few years since she'd ridden a bike, but it would be fun. And more importantly, the start of her fitness regime. The gear she bought today was the incentive she needed to start and get back into shape. Mountain bikes. She would buy them mountain bikes. Saturday mornings cycling to the Paragon for tea and scones, Theo and Harry in bike seats, the twins on their own bikes. Foggy breaths. Rosy cheeks and earnest faces peddling against the mountain's winter chill. She could ride hers to work on Thursdays if she were serious about losing weight. BM-FM had a bathroom. She could shower and change but would need to leave home earlier. Drop Theo off to day care. Peddle into Katoomba. Hard, but it was a plan. She pinched the fat bits around her belly and hips, made doughier by the harness straps, and made a commitment; bub off the breast, mum on the bike. And then she could get into the new clothes. David deserved it.

She hurried along the path, wiping sweat from her forehead with the back of her hand, feeling her messy Kate Hepburn hair coming adrift, the pin holding the topknot coming loose and long tendrils escaping.

She undid the knot, shook her head vigorously and let the heavy weight of curls cascade down her back. Unseemly for a woman her age to have such wild hair but how could she find time to get to a salon. And anyway, while Rosemary might give her grief about her unkempt appearance, telling her a woman risked losing her man if she neglected her looks, she knew her man approved of her long hair and ample curves. At least he whispered these sweet bedroom lies often enough to thrill her.

Looking up, she was just in time to side-step a hotel kitchenhand coming towards her pushing a loaded trolley of god-knows-what in his teetering pile of cardboard boxes. The kid hadn't seen Connie, so she forgave him. But while dodging cart-boy, she was almost knocked down by a couple of middle-aged kamikaze bicycle riders. For fucksake. You don't need a riot on the streets, the whole bloody town's full of lunatics.

She checked her breasts. Cannonballs.

According to the Miramar's literature, the bungalows up ahead were being preserved as a reminder of a much grander era, a time when the likes of Greta Garbo and Jean Harlow hid their glamor behind the Miramar's stucco walls and palm gardens, rather than parade for the fans in the main hotel. Too late she had read about them. Had she known of the bungalows when the office did their bookings, she would have requested they book them into a bungalow instead of a regular suite in the old Palisades wing. According to the brochures, the Hollywood-heyday classics had also hosted the likes of Monroe and JFK. Even Eleanor Roosevelt frequented them during the war years. She must remember to tell Sapphie. Eleanor Roosevelt. The child would be bedazzled.

She moved across to the edge of the path to safer ground to let the bike traffic whiz by. Pity Nick couldn't get here tonight. He would be the guy to smarten up Cyn's story. The curfew was a bummer. Cyn was having a rough trot and needed a win.

She thought about her own script and wished she'd had time to do more than a rough treatment, but life was too hectic for quiet contemplation. Never enough hours in a day or days in the week. When she had time after baths, dinner, homework, story times for Harry and Theo she was too dead on her feet to pamper to her own creative urges. Between her two mornings a week at the station and tuck shop duty, music lessons, sporting events, birthday parties to arrange and the school concerts she scripted and directed she could never find time for her own writing.

One day, Constance Labelle. One day, m'dear. But not today.

Had Sapphie and Theo enjoyed their day with their sitter?

It was kind of Rita Goldman to stick her hand up to babysit. She only knew the husband, Maurice and then not all that well. But David had convinced her the kids would be safe with the elderly Rita. He wanted her at the lunch, more because he felt strange in Nick's company.

Weird, the dual father thing. It was still, after all these years, a work in progress, she figured as she dodged another bicyclist just in time to save her shins, this time from a woman of certain years. The tanned-to-leather skinny senior wobbled past and at the last minute shot her an apologetic look and waved a rheumy hand dripping with silver rings and scarlet nail polish.

A 'hip' old girl. She admired the woman's outfit; tight white peddle-pushers teamed with a red and white French matelot sweater and jaunty little gob-cap. A killer-Diller in the Fifties. She imagined the woman in her prime, living it up here among the glamour set. Cocktails at six. Into the cot with Clark Gable by eight. One of Hollywood's leftovers, she decided, throwing a glance over her shoulder. No blue rinses. No floral frocks or thirty-denier stockings or flat heels like Nanna Bray. Another way to age, she reasoned.

She was never going to be a Nanna Bray. Nor a sweet Granma Dolly with her fox furs and Ponds Face Powder dabbed around her decolletage so flamboyantly she would emerge from the blitz looking like an ancient Geisha. She intended to arrive at the pearly gates in black leather on a Harley and say to the Big Guy; Done that. Now what ya got for me?

Menopause. When exactly did it kick in? When do you reach for hormone replacement therapy? She must talk to her mother. Rosemary was a miracle. Looked sensational at Seventy-Three. Tennis twice a week. Yoga. Pilates. And no doubt, lashings of HRT.

Hell, menopause? Bring it on. No more tampons or PMT. Goodbye swollen feet, tummy cramps. And the cherry on the pie; sex without ovulation charts, diaphragms, IUDs, rubbers or the pill. Tonight, darling? You bet. And the next, and the next, and the next after that.

She giggled, recalling Miss Stewart's rallying call. Moon goddesses. Their mighty moon fluxes. What they endured for the sake of mankind.

Bullshit, she whispered to the breeze that swayed the palms

16

SAPPHIRE

She was powerful, not because she wasn't scared
but that she went on so strongly despite the fear.
Atticus

Santa Monica, Los Angeles
Friday 1st May 1992

'See, kiddo,' he said to Sapphire. 'You're gonna go out the gate and then you're gonna hang a left onto Wiltshire.' The hotel's commissionaire handed her the map with her route marked out.

Hang a left. Make a left. Back home it was turn left. And chuck a U-ee when you wanted to do a U-turn. But for Nick, it was 'Let's flip the bitch.' Which was so cool.

The sheer exhilaration, hair flying wild behind her, the ocean wind whipping her face, all the while she was punishing her legs to go faster, harder, aware she was handling Mateo's bike with the athleticism of a champion. A girl on a mission. Like the group of demonstrators, young people chanting, some waving banners, marching towards her.

She pulled up to let them pass, smiled and waved as they turned their banners around for her to see. Stop the Violence, Honk if you think the Trial was UNFAIR! And one which read; Give Justice a Chance. Some protesters were wearing UCLA sweaters. College kids. She'd be there in a few years. She saw them hurry to catch up with another lot, all heading towards the beach. She thought about

Rodney King being beaten by the police officers. Students, black kids and white, were angry. She was stunned to see the heavy army vehicles parked across the road. And soldiers with rifles standing by. And choppers whizzing overhead. It was what Rita Goldberg told her while she sat at her table gobbling down the awful chilli dish; the army would be pouring into Santa Monica to protect them.

Goldberg? Goldman? Whatever.

She had an instant flashback to the old lady coaxing Theo to try the chilli. Big mistake, she'd thought and behind Goldman's back, she had scooped out as much as she could from her baby brother's mouth and dumped it in the sink.

More like scare them, than protect them, all this army stuff, she thought. Armed soldiers and their tanks along a beach, a really dumb idea. She might start her article with how scary it felt being surrounded by military tanks and rifles when you stepped out the door on a sunny Californian day. And then include these young protesters. She wished she could interview a few of the students for the article. How would that go down with Muldoon!

She hoped she hadn't got the nice old lady in trouble by leaving the grounds but she was on a mission. She tried to put Connie out of her mind as she peddled like a daemon down Wiltshire. She should have tied back her hair to stop it flying in her eyes. Her mother would go full mental when she turned up at the bungalows to collect them and only Theo was there. At least she had let Goddy know where she was going, so her arse was kind of covered.

Following instructions, both from the commissionaire and Mateo, she hung a right onto 6th Avenue. Acrid smoke caught at the back of her throat. She saw the glow of an orange sky and rising black fumes up ahead. South Central. It must be awesome. She checked her watch; aware time was her enemy. If only Goddy had been in a fit state to run her around her. Adults.

She halted halfway across the intersection to let a silvery blue Benz pass her. She caught a glimpse of the driver's face as the car crawled by. The woman was scared, leaning forward, gripping the wheel as if an invisible force were trying to prize her fingers off it and peering hard through the smashed windscreen. A small boy sat alongside her. Even in passing, Sapphire understood how frightened they both looked.

Completing the crossing, she took off again along Wiltshire, wondering at the violence which must have caused the damaged windscreen and the terror. An angry rioter with a baseball bat, maybe. Like the image she'd watched with hands to her eyes last night in Goddy's room. Whatever, who could blame them for being scared? Everybody was scared. It was a scary time once you got outside the hotel, she realized. She checked her watch. Doubled her pace. She would soon be turning right—hanging a right—at the intersection of Wiltshire and 6th Ave.

Reaching the corner of 6th Ave, she pulled up and waited for traffic to slow down so she could cross in the pedestrian strip, which she had all to herself, noting not for the first time that no one ever walks anywhere in L.A. The place felt eerily empty as she walked the bike across. She pulled her t-shirt over her nose to draw in heavy doses of fresher air.

Mounting the speedster again on the other side, she took off down 6th, heading for Santa Monica Boulevard and the library, congratulating herself on her efforts. What she needed to get from the newspapers was a crash course in what Bill Clinton's policies were on education. And on youth participation in politics. And anything she could find on Chelsea. Imagine being Chelsea Clinton. Imagine it; Bill and Hillary, your mum and dad!

A red car passed her. A sports convertible. When it slowed down, she sped up.

Sounds of heavy metal blared from the stereo. What she noticed as they cruised alongside her was that the driver was a tall, skinny looking long-haired surfie in a bright Hawaiian shirt. The other two filling the front seat were big, fat or muscle she couldn't tell. The middle one leaned across and pipped the horn, grinning back at her. The three of them waved but she kept going. Did the idiots think she was impressed with their wheels? A bunch of drunken yahoos in daddy's open top. She was from Katoomba. She knew their type.

Already, she had the gist of her article in her head. Even the Blue Mountains Argus would want to run it. But it was Mr Muldoon she was out to impress. He could hardly refuse to let her publish it. Their magazine wasn't exactly the Sydney Morning Herald. A Clinton one-on-one, an exclusive. Connie might even invite her on to Blue Mountains–FM to talk about her amazing experience.

She thought about the Democratic Convention. Nick was one of the Hollywood crowd who attended fund-raising dinners for the Clinton campaign. The Convention first, then she'd come back for the Inauguration. Two more brilliant scoops for an Australian student, great stuff for her resume. She would do her thesis on Clinton, one day. By then he would be an experienced two-term President.

The library was coming up ahead. She dodged another bunch of banner-waving protesters. A man gave her the slow-down sign when she swerved to avoid him. Well, what do you know? An actual live pedestrian! Nick always joked that pedestrians in L.A. were as rare as unicorns. And then she saw them, another group of marching kids on the other side of the road, all of them heading the same way as the ones back at the Miramar.

Something was going on down by the beach.

She took off, peddling fast towards the library. Her aim was to gobble up as many reports of Bill Clinton's campaign speeches as she could in the limited time before they kicked her out. She had a pocketful of dimes. She could photocopy. And she wanted to ask Governor Clinton whether he and Mrs Clinton had figured out how Chelsea would handle living in the White House. And when he was President, would he visit Australia? If she could quote from his speeches, Mr Clinton would take her seriously. Everyone respected good preparation.

She heard them before she saw them, the same loud yobbos in their red convertible, their music pumping even louder. Now they were slowing down again, cruising alongside her just as she was approaching the building. She bet they weren't the reading type.

'We know where there's a party happenin' tonight. Hop in!' the passenger in the middle yelled, waving what she imagined to be a tequila bottle. 'C'mon.'

The one leaning his arm out the door whistled her, then the driver gave a loud yippee, a doofus love-call. They were bouncing to the wild music, swilling the liquor and passing the bottle. She knew their kind. Friday night specials, the city kids who came up the mountain to get drunk and chase girls. The animals, the locals call them. There was a rumour a girl had been raped, a student from Sacred Heart. She peddled harder; the massive building so close she could smell the newsprint. A quick look over her shoulder as she finally peddled into the library, breathless but relieved.

The red car was still in the rear, still hugging the kerb, tailing her.

She noted the Californian number plate. Couldn't help it. From when she was first able to read, to pass time on long trips—and to keep them from getting car-sick she suspected—David would get them to make up phrases to fit the plates of every car they saw; a race to see who came up with the best, funniest, fastest.

One hundred-and-seventy-four stupid doofus idiots; 174 SDI.

One hundred-and-seventy-four stoned drunken imbeciles.

Either way it worked. She peddled up the garden path to the enclosed courtyard behind the building. The bicycle rack, to her surprise, was empty. As was the courtyard. It wasn't until she chained the bike and walked up to the big glass doors at the side of the building that she discovered how things were. The library had closed at 3pm to allow staff to get home safely. The notice pasted inside the door said so. No wonder everything looked so deserted. She cursed her luck.

The curfew. Damn!

She looked up at the sky. The sun was low, the shadows lengthening. She looked around at the empty courtyard.

Instinct told her it was time to leave. Soon the streets of Los Angeles would be totally deserted. She was alone in strange territory with a curfew about to make things even stranger. And she preferred not to tangle with the likes of those tequila idiots packed into their Dad's red convertible. Nor come across any more smashed Mercedes' windscreens. Or police choppers. Angry protesters. Tanks and soldiers with rifles. She unchained Mateo's bike and heaved her leg over the bar.

It was then she saw him; one of the loudmouths coming around the corner of the building and sauntering towards her. The chubby one who'd been squeezed in the middle, the horn-blower, wearing an idiot grin as he approached. Someone should tell him he was carrying too much weight to saunter. Like some loser rapper. She estimated he was ten kilos and a good suntan short of being as cool as he imagined he was.

'What ya doin', sister?' he called to her, both hands in the pockets of a low-slung pair of faded grey cargo pants. He wore a blue baseball cap turned backwards. Of course, it was backwards.

'Going home, if you must know,' she said with a forced smile, trying to be as polite as she could while steadying the bike and waiting for the right moment to ride off.

'Hey, bein' friendly's all, sis. I'm Jazzy, by the way. Where y'from?'

'Australia.'

'Wow! What's your name?'

'Piper. But sorry Jazzy, Piper's gotta fly.'

'You look like someone who knows how to have a good time, Piper. Hey, that's a cool name, sis. The guys and me, we thought you might like to come to this party up the beach. Y'wanna come wiv us? Secret location n'all.'

'You haven't heard? There's a curfew.' She had one foot on the peddle, the other keeping the bike steady. She was impatient to be back out on the street, heading home to their hotel. 'Sorry. Ask someone else.' She found the peddles and edged past him.

He jumped in her path and held her handlebars. 'The guy on MARS-FM's been talkin' about it all day. Kids are comin' from everywhere, man. Everyone's gettin' together at friends' houses and then they tell you where the rave's on. "Psychosis" they're calling it. A secret rave party. Deejays, liquor, dancin'. Say yes.'

'I'm saying No, actually.' He was a pest. Nice but harmless. 'Now, would you please let me past ... Jazzy?'

He shrugged but stood his ground. 'Chain it up,' he said, indicating the bike. 'Come wiv us.'

'Look, have a great time at your rave party, okay? I hope it's awesome. And thanks for asking me but I need to get back. They're expecting me and I'm already running late.' She twisted the wheel and started to move off. 'See ya.'

He came in front of her again, his heavy thighs spread as he planted himself and reached out to grab the handlebars. 'We're all kicking off from the Pier,' he said. 'Come wiv us, c'mon. We'll get ya back here, no worries. Drop y'off, wherever.'

She heard the tooting, loud and insistent coming from 6th and recognized it as the automobile's horn.

Had the other idiots dared him? Were they timing him?

She leveraged his hands off the bars again, finger by finger, and saw him glance over his shoulder. She needed to get out of the situation diplomatically, not antagonize him or do anything to bring the others around to see what was happening. Santa Monica streets were not yet deserted but with a sunset curfew they soon would be. And Rapper Boy was standing too close for comfort. She disliked strangers coming onto her like this. Okay to be friendly, but there was something about him starting to scare her. She wished Mateo were here. Really and truly wished Mateo was here. Or Nick. Or David. Her mother. Goddy. Dick the dustman. Anyone who could distract the fool long enough for her to make her escape.

'Chain it!' he said. It was not a suggestion this time but an order.

'Hey, man, what y'all doin'?' the one in the Hawaiian shirt, the driver, called out as he came around the corner towards them. He shot a look at his friend. 'She gonna come to the rave or what, Jazzy?'

'Uh-uh. Excuse me,' she said. 'Gotta go. Thanks for asking, but no thanks.' Standing to gain traction on the peddles, she put all her weight down and took off, grateful for the way Mateo's brilliant bike responded. She left Jazzy and Surfer Joe standing in her wake as she flew past, feeling for all the world like Jody. She needed to get down the path to where it would be safer, out in the open, out on the road.

Suddenly, she looked up and saw the third one coming at her, the tequila-waving one. Long greasy hair, older and bigger than the other two. Muscles earned from gym fees and lots of sweat and grunting stretching the fabric covering his arms and chest. Shoulders like Mr Universe. He wore black jeans, black t-shirt and boots. A packet of cigarettes tucked in the rolled-up sleeve of the black shirt. She attempted to swerve away from him.

Too late.

He reached out and grabbed the handlebars, jack-knifing the bike. Had she not been quicker to respond, the sudden stop would have hurtled her over the handlebars.

'Nice work,' kid, he said with a smirk.

'Get out of my way, please?' She felt her heart beating an unfamiliar rhythm.

'No hurry, babe.' He held the handlebars, grinning.

She shuddered. He scared her but she knew she had to get away. With eyes drilling into the core of his thick skull and her fingernails digging into his hands, she tried to release his grip, aware he must not know her warrior glare hid a paralysing fear, or that her mouth felt drier than Uluru. Or that her heart was racing like a colt bolting out the gates. It was his size, the muscles, the dark gear intimidating her. His boozy breath. This drunken male meant to overpower her.

'What's your hurry, kangaroo,' she heard the surfie call out from behind her.

She turned. 'Please, you're not being fair. Let me go.' She heard muscle man, still holding the handlebars, laugh and turned back to him. 'Let go!' she ordered furiously.

He let his tongue do the work of intimidating her. She was young but she knew what it was about. As he brought his face into hers, she lashed out, scraping sharp fingernails down his cheek.

'Fuck, bitch!' He let go the bike to cradle his torn face. Her getaway moment. She pushed as hard as she could on the peddles. The bike failed to move.

'Gotcha, kangaroo' said the surfie, gripping the back wheel.

17

CYNTHIA

Enjoy what you can, endure what you must.

Goethe

Santa Monica, Los Angeles
Friday 1st May 1992

I found what I was looking for in the Chanel bag; the weed I'd smuggled into the States yesterday. The old trick. Stashed in hollow tubes of Dior lipsticks laying innocently at the bottom of my highly perfumed cosmetics purse. Who would guess? There, among the fluid make-up. Among the loose tampons and mascara wands. Some hairy Californian hippy, a long time ago, had shown me how you melted your old lipsticks, cleaned out the tubes, then stuffed them with the tightly rolled, plastic-wrapped joints. Cannabis to L.A.? The proverbial coals to Newcastle. I know but in a strange land it's best to come prepared.

And as it had been, back in the cut-loose days when I'd screwed my way around Europe trying to forget what I'd done, I still got off on the heart-thumping risk of gaming Customs guys. The heart-stopping seconds while you sweated it out. The kinky thrill as a strange man's hands molests your personal items Your privacy publicly plundered while the Sword of Damocles hovers inches above your head. While you will yourself not to show fear but not really caring because nothing matters to you all that much, not anymore. Except perhaps a little Victory over Authority. A small tilt at civil disobedience. *Resist much. Obey little!* Walt Whitman.

The hippy and I had pulled our little trick on an officious train inspector in Germany when the clown came goose-stepping into our carriage on a mission to harass the long-haired likes of us, backpackers on Euro passes, deadbeats who would have made the pilgrimage to the Bulldog en route to the Fatherland. The hash under the inspector's nose all the time he was checking out our passports. Breathing easy once the fool had dealt with our documents and moved further down the carriage. Fondling each other under the hippy's flak jacket till I climaxed with a mighty yawp as the train pulled into Hamburg Central.

I held the joint in my palm for a moment, allowing myself a grudging smile as I recalled that long-ago piece of mischief.

But then I returned it and reached for the bottle instead. What else to do when they lock you up like this except try to drown reality, prevent the walls—like those giant metal filing cabinets on rollers—slowly closing in on you, slowly crushing you. And you're such a loser you're romanticizing a flying fuck you had with some random a million years ago. Why?

I knew why; because my sex is shrivelling up. I'm on the fast train to crone-hood. A hag to be sung up the mountain because my fecund days are over. Useless to the tribe. A lonely old wart-nosed, whiskered crone with toenails thick as planks. The abyss. At the edge and looking into it. Early onset menopause, that's why. There is breathing space before it happens, however. So, he said. An interval between acts, according to His Nibs. A lead-in to the Big Dry. It's not like you just suddenly fall off the cliff. Professor Kevin Wadsworth, the Macquarie Street big shot gynaecologist. What kind of man does that for a living?

Heavy bleeding. No bleeding. Periods all over the place. Unheralded mood swings. Wadsworth, after having taken one lot of blood, telling me another sample would be required the following month. Two lots, four weeks apart. Necessary to identify what was going on with my ratty hormone levels. Not certain what would turn up in the pathology results. Blood tests, a prognosis hanging in the wind. Although strongly suspecting P.O.F., he counselled. Spontaneous premature ovarian failure.

But Failure was not a word I tolerated. Premature ovarian failure, doctor? How come? Fingers crossed. Holding my breath. Well, my dear—soft-spoken words from the big man behind the big desk—shaking his head—it might be a little too early to concern ourselves. Ourselves? You and me, or just me? But I'd held my tongue. I needed this patronising medico on my side. We shall see what turns up next month, my dear. Till then ...

Over and over, I repeated the mantra as I left his rooms: No need to panic. No need to panic. It wasn't going to be like Boom! It just happens overnight. Not as if one day you're all sexy and nubile—

—fragrant as fuck—

—and then the next, your oestrogen's done a runner and whoops.

No, said Wadsworth on the second visit, his fist jabbed up inside me as he tried to give it to me easy, the fact I was entering early menopause. But a gradual process. Gradual, he emphasised, as if to put my mind at ease. Calm the demons. Gradual, like the slow decay of a rotting corpse. Like the sun going down. Darkness descending. And no sunrise tomorrow. You lose your way in the dark. In untrodden territory. Where do you go from here? How gradual is it going to be? When do I hit the wall? What will life be like post-menopausal? The Change. The Climacteric. How different a woman will I be? Will I even be a real woman? I left the Macquarie Street surgery and walked across the street to the State Library where the books spelled it out for me; premature death, long-term health risks, cardiovascular disease, osteoporosis, psychosexual dysfunction, neurologic disease and mood disorders. At which point I closed the books and walked out.

Lien was not in the office when I returned from Wadsworth's appointment. My lotus flower had taken an early lunch break.

Happy to think, as I flicked through the pile of messages on my desk, of Lien relaxing down by the harbour, daintily nibbling away at her Spartan lunch. Bean sprouts and cold omelette most likely. Unappealing fare but it worked for Lien who had a glowing complexion and a petite figure. My P.A. regularly took her lunch to the local harbourside park, along with her copy of the latest Economist or Business Review Weekly, addicted as she was to the magazines and constantly boning up on the fortunes, rising or falling, of Sydney, Melbourne and Perth's tycoon class. The daughter of a family who sought refuge here in the Seventies, Lien, like her twin brother, had studied Economics at the University of NSW. I often joked she was light years ahead of me in financial matters. Only it wasn't a joke. It was true and Lien, god bless her, knew it.

In our Vietnamese language, Ms Smart, my name means lotus flower, Lien had informed me in her job interview. That's so sweet, Lien. And call me Cynthia. Cynthia's the other name they gave Artemis, the mythological moon goddess. Welcome to Baker & Glassop. I hope you enjoy the agency experience. You're hired.

In Lien's absence, I had time. Not time to worry about how rapidly my female attributes were deteriorating but to concentrate on how fast things were deteriorating at the agency. I needed a strong black coffee and yes, a cigarette. Lien always glared at me when she copped me smoking, all righteous disapproval in an inscrutable Asian way. It was uncomfortable to be the subject of Lien Nguyen's scrutiny, being challenged to do better, be better, give up cigarettes, not swear, not curse. Lien was brilliant, clever, cluey and headed for a far better career than a personal assistant to a Group Account Director who was ready to bail.

I would not forget Lien when I confronted Haydn this evening. With mentoring, Lien was ready to move up the ladder. I lit up, took a welcome draw and finally attacked my messages.

'Hi,' said Lien poking her head around the door.

I all but swallowed the cigarette, just managing to ditch it, believing I'd fooled the clever one. 'Come in. You're back. I thought you must have taken early lunch.' Seeing the scowl, I shrugged, swallowed a mint and waved away the tell-tale smell of burning nicotine. Lien pantomimed her usual look of disapproval while tipping water from a nearby vase into the trash bin. 'Kudos to Ms Nguyen. Bads to Ms Smart. What's happening? Where have you been?'

'Ray asked me to go across the road and collect the dinner suit he was hiring.' Lien ducked out of the room and returned holding up a plastic covered suit package.

'He what!' A rhetorical flourish. I stepped behind Lien and shut the door. 'Say, again!'

Lien shook her short bob of shiny black hair and pushed her oversized, crimson-rimmed glasses further up the bridge of her nose. 'For some wedding or other, Cynthia. Apparently.'

'How dare he! The hide of the bloody man. Getting you to do his bidding. Ray Robb is so typical of the men in this place, Lien. Next time he tries that one on, you have my permission to tell him to go fuck himself. Okay?'

'Okay. If you say so,' said Lien, grinning. 'Wow!' She removed her glasses and wiped them against her shirt. 'You really mean I can do that? Say that?'

'I really do mean you can say and do exactly that. It's not as if the guy's a genius copywriter. He's lead weight in our saddle bags, truth be known.'

'Did you see the story about Campaign Palace in this week's Ad News?'

'No. What story?'

Lien looked sheepish. 'I don't think you're going to like it, Cynthia. They mention us in the article. You, by name.'

'Show me, Lien. Bring it in here.'

'It's under that lot I dropped on your desk.'

There it was. Front page. Above the fold. Campaign Palace. Glorified as the gurus. The smart with-it agency had just picked up the Go Girl account. 'Shit!' I threw the magazine in the bin.

'That's what I said too when I read it; Shit!'

We shared a laugh. I had never known my serene little lotus flower to swear. Lien was so dainty. So polite. In fact, poor Lien would flinch when the men let fly with a curse. But we both understood what was happening here. 'Take his dammed suit and throw it at him, Lien. With my regards. Let him know ... in no uncertain terms ... he has absolutely no right having you run around after him. Okay?'

'Okay.'

'And let me know if he tries to pull a stunt like that again.' I walked around the desk and took my assistant's small hands. 'Will you, sweetheart? You promise? Otherwise, I'm going down there myself now and I'll rip him a new arsehole. I'm serious, Lien. Just let me know.'

'Sure. Wow, again!' Lien left the office with a wave over her shoulder.

I watched my efficient, funny, engaging beautiful young assistant walk back to her own desk. In the eighteen-months she had been with the agency, Lien's talents had shone like a diamond. Young women like Lien were typical of the cohort the agency needed to go after, a good reason why they deserved a role in creating the campaigns. Whenever it was practical, I took Lien along to client meetings these days. So, it was not okay for Ray Robb, or any of the other chauvinist to treat her as their gopher.

'Can I show you something?' said Lien, returning to stand in the doorway.

'Sure. What y'got?'

Lien drew a green plastic, pocket-sized, photo album from her handbag and handed it across. 'Trang's new baby, Bai.'

The album dropped open on a close-up of a newborn, its fingers clenched around a woman's finger. I studied it for a moment before glancing up at my beaming assistant. 'Cute. In a baby kind of way.' I closed the album and handed it back. 'They all look the same to me, babies.'

Lien's phone rang. 'Hold on to it,' Lien said, pointing to the album. 'Babies don't bite, you know.' She left to answer her phone.

The tiny green plastic album sat on the corner of the desk while I flicked through the phone messages, ignoring the bulk of them, only returning two calls, neither of them long in duration, neither important. With nothing more than a sense of duty towards Lien, obviously chuffed with her newly acquired nephew, I pulled the baby album towards me and opened it. Page after page, as I flicked through the album, showed the new-born laying in his crib or being nursed by his parents. A tiny creature nestled in the woman's womb only days before this photograph was taken. A tiny golden child. A miniature god. What must it feel like to carry a human being inside you for nine months and then to deliver it up to the world; to be a mother?

I studied the perfectly formed miniature hands of Lien's nephew, the transparent nails, the chubby wrinkled palms, delicate little mitts that would one day be a man's hands, doing man-like things. A surgeon, a train driver, a scribe, a builder of bridges? The hands of a lover? But for now, the tiny silky-textured wrinkled hands of a baby boy reaching out for his mother. I shut the album and tossed it aside. I had work to do.

'Congratulate your brother, Lien,' I said when Lien came through the door. 'He's done well. Good on him. Now for the sleepless nights, though, hey? And wall-to-wall shitty nappies.'

'You're not the motherly type are you, Cynthia?'

'Nope. You got a problem with that?'

'No. But do you?' Lien collected the album and left the room.

To Hell with this curfew! I decided to light the joint, did so and took a puff. The stuff was supposed to make you happy. I wasn't happy. Why would I be? Shitty morning. Shitty news from him downstairs.

During lunch, at least, I'd been able to appreciate something good about Los Angeles; the shrimp salad and the dry, crisp honey and guava notes of the Robert Mondavi private bin 1990 Pino Grigio. I was still savouring it. California's finest and on a par with anything Australia could produce, according to everyone around the table. Save for our Grange, of course, Connie had to pipe up from the far end.

Unemployed, rejected and the dinner off. And soon to be invaded by two Latino strangers. And the claustrophobia doing my head in.

The whole catastrophe.

Zorba, the Greek. It's what Zorba said in the movie; I got the wife, I got the kids, I got the goat. I got the whole catastrophe. The lament of that happy Greek. A favourite movie. A classic of its era. The big man sure could dance. The elegance of Anthony Quinn standing on the beach, his arms outstretched, one around the smaller man's shoulder, teaching him how to step gracefully to the measured music of the tinkling mandolins and bouzouki.

Whoever wrote the score for Zorba had known something special about the act of love. The theme coming in softly, slowly. Foreplay; gentle, loving, exquisite. Holding back. Teasing. Erotic. Patiently building to a passionate climax. Quinn, the sensitive male controlling every moment of the dance. Body, heart and mind. Zorba, a virile man full of earthy wisdom, a true philosopher. All that can be enjoyed must be enjoyed here and now, said Zorba. And he said a person had to keep moving. Stagnation is death. On a slope, even a stone comes to life. We should look at life as a child and be astonished by it, be awe struck, be bedazzled. Don't over-think life. Reason can be as debilitating as fear. Dance, make love, live life to the fullest!

Okay for Zorba. A man. Try being a woman facing the abyss. But a Zorba, so wise and sensitive, a poet who danced on beaches would understand me, dance me to a sunnier place. The Greek was a man who took life by the throat and wrung it for all it was worth and then on his death bed, howled at the moon.

I needed a Zorba in my life, someone to lead the way. To dance on a beach with me. To join me in howling at the moon. Zorba.

Nick Cristos? No, I doubted the very sober Mr Cristos was the kind of Greek who danced on beaches, danced anywhere. Thinking of Nick Cristos reminded me of Sapphire, which reminded me I should have smartened up my act, thrown back some strong coffee and agreed to drive the poor kid to the library. Some godmother you are Cynthia Smart.

18

CONNIE

Raising teenagers is like nailing Jell-o to a tree.

Anonymous

Santa Monica, Los Angeles
Friday 1st May 1992

She had promised to collect them by five. The story of her life; always running late. Would she need an excuse for Rita Goldberg? Goldman? She ought not to have left them with the woman so she could go to a lunch that didn't need her and then a shopping rampage that had been a little over the top. Self-indulgence, the whole afternoon, she figured as she approached the gates of the bungalows.

Meanwhile, Sapphire.

She thought about her daughter; how had the sulky teenager got along with poor Mrs Goldman this afternoon? The girl was a worry. Everyone warns you about teenage daughters. The horrible years start around the age of twelve or thirteen, so they say. Sapphire was a late starter, for which she was grateful. A dream run, until the demon hormones kicked in and a thorny teenager declared war on her parents and siblings. The sweetest, most considerate daughter any mother could wish for then overnight, a monster.

A small boy on his trainer wheels came up behind on a tricycle. In his rush to get it right, he knocked the front wheel into the back of her heel. It hurt. Young Evel Knievel's father raised a paternal eyebrow as he passed. Sorry, the look seemed to say, but we must let the young be young. He will be a grown man soon enough and then there will be no place in his life for a father's steadying hand. Great. But do you have a plaster for this heel, mate?

Six months now, of coping with an irritable, obstinate, unpredictable, weirdly dressed, absolute pain-in-the-ass, disobedient contrarian of a daughter. Some days it was hard to feel anything but hostility towards her own flesh and blood; a child standing up to you, throwing out a mouthful of cheek, back-answering, occasionally lapsing into sweetness but mostly being a total sulky smart-arse and making you feel you were beneath her contempt. Nick was in for a treat. Poor Nick. Or maybe the child behaved for Nick. Who knew? Probably did, given the novelty of their visits.

She recalled some of the recent flashpoints, the abuse she'd copped from a fired-up Sapphire. Spiteful stuff. Words spat at her with the sole intention of hurting her. And it did hurt, even though she had strong memories of her own spitefulness when her hormones were in flux. Poor Rosemary, the grief she'd given her own mother. But it hurt, the way Sapphie rejected her when all she did was try to make motherly approaches, let her daughter know she understood these were the turbulent years. It wasn't as if she didn't empathize, didn't understand what physical and emotional changes were happening inside that glorious young body.

She consoled herself with the thought that Sapphie would have matured by the time Francesca hit puberty. Franny was a placid kid but she was on the eve of adolescence. If it hit her early, boy oh boy, she'd be dealing with two surly daughters and that was unimaginable.

It was time she took Sapphie aside and talked to her about the risk of fooling around with boys. It was well past the time. How soon can you put them on the pill? Shouldn't she have been the one to slip a discreet packet of condoms into her daughter's underwear draw? Who gave them to her, anyway? Did she buy them? Or some boy, god forbid. She needed to talk to Nick and David. She was unprepared to accept the idea of a sexualized daughter. All those randy boys at Blue Mountain High. Girls dropping out of school. Desperate parents ringing into BM-FM seeking advice from her medical guests. Loss of innocence versus an unwanted pregnancy. She yearned for the time when she and her little girl had toggled between *H.R. Pufnstuff* and the Wombles.

Putting away the children's folded clothes last week, the morning after Cyn's visit to the mountains, was when she saw them. Normally, she would leave the twins and Sapphie's clothes on their beds for them to put away. But Sapphire had to start thinking about packing for L.A. and because she would be going to Nick's, she had to make sure their daughter didn't turn up looking neglected. Nick paid a generous contribution towards his daughter's welfare.

The girl was daggy. Obsessive about the outer clothes but she paid little attention to what went under the weird op shop bits and pieces. That was okay, a pretty girl like Sapphire donning John Lennon glasses and putting on men's baggy corduroys and paisley shirts, smothering badges all over those old vests was okay. She had been young, herself. She and Cyn flower children one day, all floaty and bohemian, then revolutionary Che Guevara or Pattie Hurst tragics, the next. It had been pure theatre and their outfits an essential consideration.

But two condoms in her fifteen-year-old daughter's underwear draw? The sight of those little foil packages flawed her. Sitting there, in the set of draws David made when she was a toddler, the set the crazy girl had recently painted black and plastered with her weird collection of decals and righteous propaganda. She stopped short of the bungalows. Smiled. My God, I love the girl. Quirky as Hell and often harder to fathom than Pythagoras but a star turn.

And then it hit her: Cyn's visit the day before the appearance of the condoms. Of course. Bloody Cynthia's doing! Her attempt to show what a cool godmother she was.

She remembered now, the two of them with their heads together last week. Okay, she had to have a talk to the godmother, tell the godmother to butt out. But no, on second thoughts, Cyn was right to look out for her goddaughter. Loving Sapphie as she did, naturally she was concerned. Cyn, of all people. Yes, she could give her a pass, poor soul.

She was taken by surprise when a figure in black hoodie, black jeans and dark sunnies suddenly shot out from the bushes, the fool almost knocking her over. Probably curdled her milk. Like the idiot who'd monstered her as he'd pushed past her in the elevators. She was ready to shout abuse at this one, as well but like last time, the brute moved too fast.

She stepped up to the Goldman's bungalow, knocked on the big wooden door and waited, still feeling rattled by the figure in black.

He disturbed her. Something sinister about him. Then again, the dark sunnies, the black gear, the hood, maybe he thought it gave him an air of mystery. Probably a wannabe movie star. A kid from Milwaukee who'd Greyhounded it into L.A. on a dream and a prayer. In character and hoping to trap one of the movie men sitting around in the lobby. Poor kid. She wished him well. It was that kind of place, Hollywood. A company town and everyone desperate for recognition.

It was only then it struck her; it was the kid from the elevator. But with no tennis gear or tennis bag. So, what had he done with that murderous sports bag? Dumped it in those bushes? And if so, why? If he hadn't been rushing off to play tennis back there in the lobby, why the goddam hurry to burst out of the lift, practically crawling over her to get out? And why the frantic hurry just now?

She knocked on the door and waited, still wondering.

19

CYNTHIA

Promises and pie crusts are made to be broken.

Jonathon Swift

Santa Monica, Los Angeles
Friday 1st May 1992

You can check out, but you can never leave. Try escaping the hotel tonight and some wet-behind-the-ears pimply kid in army boots, camouflage gear, an AK-47 and an itchy finger is going to take a pot-shot at you.

The networks were having a field day. It struck me they had suspended their advertising in favour of riding the wave of excitement, wall-to-wall riot images and breathless reporters radioing in the drama they were seeing on the streets. Great for getting eyeballs on screen but would clients want their products associated with violence, looting and death? Or maybe the content was good for promoting sales, frightened citizens anticipating Armageddon. Lay in the loo paper, stack up on baked beans and bottled water.

Not my concern. I'm no longer in the business.

I was about to grab the remote and hit the kill button when I stopped. Flights were being rerouted into the Los Angeles International Airport, causing serious delays or cancellations. They wished to keep the jets high enough over the area of looting to prevent small-arms fire from reaching those airplanes, a federal aviation spokesman said.

Damn! A curfew was one thing, being shot out of the air was another matter. I poured another thimble of the Glenfiddich, sipped it slowly and being in the moment, followed its glorious passage down into the deep cold recesses where I presumed my soul dwelt. I curled into a foetal ball, hugging the crystal glass to my chest, protective of the small joys the universe was allowing me this day.

It was Saturday back home. Brunch on a sunny outdoors table at Zigolini. A stroll through Paddington flea market. Tennis at Rushcutters Bay. Or maybe hit Berkalow's and pick a good book for an afternoon in the hammock. In the evening, perhaps catch Mahler at the Opera House. Maybe I should have offered Mrs C my Sydney Symphony subscription tickets.

Thoughts of my cleaning woman caused me mild alarm. The photographs from Hawaii. I'd pulled them out of mothballs, intending to take them to the meeting and left them sitting on my desk. I should have put them away, hidden them from sight. It was a wonder I hadn't trashed them years ago. I rolled over, killed the sound on the TV and shut my eyes.

Baker Glassop & Smart. A slice of Haydn Glassop and Phil Baker's agency, a voice in the way things were run. Partner. Women given a chance. The promises so often discussed at the time the affair began. The inducement which brought me to the agency and to Glassop's bed. Not immediately, he said, but soon. A promise. He would put it to Baker. Insist on it. You have my word, darling. Discussed so often during expensive dinners at Jonah's, our Whale Beach hideaway. Even whispered in my ear during the heat of our love making. Always the prize he held out but had failed to deliver.

Threatening him with the incriminating evidence—there in the snapshots—was blackmail, a dirty trick, but so be it. I would finally hold his feet to the fire. Enough excuses. Enough backsliding. Enough of blaming Phil Baker. Play my ace card. Slap the proof of his long-running, adulterous affair down on his desk and watch him vaporize. Go into that meeting knowing I had clout, produce the photos and threaten to wave them under the nose of the precious Mrs Glassop, let the woman know what transpired at the Clio Awards in Hawaii four years ago and what had continued for a torrid two and a half years thereafter. I knew I could walk out with the partnership, so petrified was he of what Naomi could do to his financial situation and his dreams of retirement.

The young Hawaiian photographer going around the ballroom, snapping guests, snapping the Baker Glassop Agency's debonair CEO in his smart white dinner jacket, getting the killer shot of him embracing his colleague on his return to the table with his trophy.

Kissing me. More than a professional embrace. A candid shot. And the following days, the same young man photographing us as we lay close together on the beach. Closer, much closer than work colleagues. And taking other shots of the lovers sipping their Mai Tais in the palm lounge of the luxurious Hotel Hawaii on Maui. Snap! Our romantic—and for Haydn—adulterous escapade recorded in full living colour against a backdrop of swaying palms and Hula hussies. Souvenired, because at the early stage of the affair I was crazily in love with Haydn Glassop.

That thought brought me back to the moment. I opened my eyes and stared up at the ceiling. Love. It makes fools of us all, blinds us to the truth. But now I had seen the light, hallelujah. Done forever with Haydn Glassop, his agency and the industry. I had a movie to make. Pity, because as Partner I could have heralded in a new order at B&G. Given a few good women a chance.

As it turned out, my bad-arse blackmailing intentions probably wouldn't have secured me the partnership, anyway. The JWT merger was already in play. At least as reported in the pages of Ad News. And given the accounts I was losing, thanks to an agency mired in the previous century, the JWT boys would never have offered me a position in the new shop. A Group Account Director's desk is where the buck stops. Being saddled with middle-aged white males determined to cling to fading glories are no excuse for lost accounts. What would JWT know or care about how the misogynistic atmosphere at Baker & Glassop, which started at the top and filtered all the way down, kept stymying my best efforts to pitch winning campaigns.

I noticed the room was chilly. Americans love their air con. Too lethargic to get up off the bed and adjust the temperature, I settled for pulling the covers up and challenged the chilly air to do its worst. If it brought on a head cold and stopped me taking off to New York tomorrow, so be it. Who even knew if their planes were flying?

20

CYNTHIA

Peace is not absence of conflict; it's the ability to handle conflict by peaceful means.

Ronald Reagan

North Sydney CBD, Australia
April 1992

No slowing down to admire the expansive view of the harbour—spectacular as it was at this hour of the morning—only the rhythmical clicking of my stilettos on the wide marble staircase to crack the silence.

Monday morning, 6.30am, and I was possibly the only person in the building other than the man waiting for me upstairs. As arranged.

Unusual for me to call him at his home on a Sunday evening but I had spent the weekend stewing about the lost accounts. Stewing about a lot of things and still stewing now as I strode down the corridor headed for the big corner suite and ready to make things happen. Ready to strike. A golden-haired warrior charging into battle for a cause. For the right to plant her flag and declare the territory taken.

I sprung him sitting with his back to the door, feet up on the window ledge, staring out at his uninterrupted view of Sydney Harbour, the jewel in the nation's crown, a privileged view from such a great height. Sydney's skyline—the lush green Botanical Gardens across the Harbour, stately old Government House, the Conservatorium of Music, the Bridge, the Opera House, the high-rises of the Eastern Suburbs, the white sands of Neilson Park, the iconic lighthouse at Watson's Bay and the Heads, North and South Head—Haydn's primary focus these days as he considered the horizon beyond those Heads. The big brassy yacht lay at anchor in Rushcutters Bay. Retirement had become his loadstar. Now more than ever seemed it right to strike. I stood fixed in the doorway, feet apart, arms stretched above my head and clutching the door frame. An aggressive stand befitting my mood. There was fire in my belly.

More importantly, there were photographs in my Gucci. The news that we had just lost another account, one I'd been desperate to win, had done it for me. Now was the moment for the squeeze. I had given nothing away in last night's terse phone call but my strident tone and the way I had abruptly hung up on him after locking in this meeting would have given him something to think about.

'We need to talk, Haydn.'

He muttered something which I missed, so I continued to stand four-square in his doorway staring at the back of his head. He could not ignore my presence forever, even though he would, no doubt, feign zero interest in what I had to say about the partnership. But at least he'd turned up, so he must realize he had a case to answer. If there were one thing Haydn Glassop desired, it was to have a pain-free retirement. No dramas. Lately he had said to the agency he was living for the day he could be quit of Baker & Glassop, quit of the whole advertising industry and sail off into a glorious sunset with Naomi and the boys.

He was an idiot. With Phil Baker preoccupied sorting out a merger to save their sorry arses, the agency was suffering a vacuum at executive level. His dereliction of duty caused a knock-on effect. The agency was mired in the past and going down the tubes. I wasn't going down with it. I had troubles enough if Wadsworth could be believed. But I also had my project. Getting *Surrender Song* made would be my future, not this moribund agency, unless I could ring in the changes, which meant I needed executive influence if I were to guide it into a future more respectful of the female species. Glassop's stubbornness, his disinterest in changing the old-boy ethos, meant that had not happened around these parts so far. Given half a chance to recruit some female creative talent, I could be pulling in serious dime for the agency.

The man continued to ignore me in favour of the view.

'Hey, you over there? Love rat? We need to talk.' I was never sure if the love rat tag had the effect on Haydn I intended. Maybe he revelled in it. He had certainly never apologized.

I watched the expensive polished Ferragamo boots come down off the window ledge and the silver-haired doyen of the Baker & Glassop Agency slowly swivel his chair around to meet my gaze. I saw the quick movement of his hand as he slipped under the blotter the business card he had been nursing. With what I learned yesterday from Lien, who heard it from Marcia at Reception, I guessed he had been thinking unclean thoughts about Miss Japan, Mr Yakima's personal assistant-come-translator.

Glassop leant back in his sprung chair, pushed it away from his ego-sized desk, hoisted the boots up onto the surface and rested his arms behind his tilted head. A man-pose. Okay. What ya got? I'm listening. None too subtle.

It was an attitude of studied arrogance and if it were his first move in this power play it was a pathetic one. If meant to intimidate me it wasn't working, especially not once I glimpsed the bony knees beneath the alpaca trousers. Old man's sharp knees. I hadn't been there for some time and I bet his balls had grown bigger as well, hung looser, and that he clipped his ear and nose hairs twice weekly now days. He grinned, and I saw malice in the detail. That was okay, I was locked and loaded and ready to take him on because what the clown did not know was if he failed to capitulate, I was prepared to blow his comfy little domestic world to smithereens. Goodbye retirement. Hello divorce lawyers.

'Nice chair, hey?' he said, letting the grin linger around the corners of his thinning lips.

'Sure. Nice chair.' The now sixty-two-year-old had boasted to me many times about his black leather Eames Soft Pad desk chair, a 1969 purchase made by his late father. I suspected Haydn valued it simply for its iconic status. The man was too self-centered to entertain any trace of familial emotion.

'I hit a great shot off the sixth at the—'

'I wanted this meeting yesterday, Haydn.'

'They told you I was at The Lakes, babe. Great shot, but did m'bloody back in.'

'You stood me up.'

He sprung forward in the chair and spread his elbows on the desk. 'If this is you coming to me with another one of your gripes, mate, forget it. I'm not in the mood.' He cranked his neck from side to side and winced. 'Fuck the Japs. I should have been out on the water, not chasing a bloody white ball around the dunes, arse-licking our way into the Yakima account. Baker can take them next time.'

I stared across the room at Yesterday's Man and wondered how I had ever considered the fool sexy enough to take to bed.

'I'm suffering here, mate. Be kind,' said Glassop as he rotated his upper body and groaned.

'Okay, you took one for the team yesterday, Haydn. Good on you. You're a hero, no risk.'

I let go of the door frame and stepped into the room. Approaching his desk, I raised an eyebrow and indicated the blotter. 'Wasn't Mr Yakima's pretty little translator-come-buggy-driver-come-whatever any compensation? Ah, the silken charms of Miss Murakami. The way I heard it, she looked at you with her sweet almond eyes and you went to water.' I came closer and leaned in, my hands on his desk taking my weight. 'It was the young lady's card you were drooling over just now when I caught you, wasn't it?' I cocked my head. 'Well, wasn't it?'

My face across the desk was too close for Haydn's comfort. He sat up straight. I took my time to scrutinize him, up and down, my intention being to discomfort him. It was true he could still be considered a handsome man. Aging, but handsome enough. The sailing life had left him lean and tanned, his crop of silver hair adding gravitas. Though, even as his lover, I couldn't have nominated the colour of his eyes with any certainty. Now I could see they were a dull shade of green, the whites yellowing and showing a fine tracery of red at the edges. I straightened up and smiled. 'My god, the ageing Lothario of the advertising industry.' Our break-up had been brutal. I'd stayed on, despite it, and from then on, we had not engaged in any conversation even remotely personal. Now, it seemed, he wanted to get chummy.

'She's a real cutie, the little Asian lass, Cynthie.' He reached for the business card and waved it at me. 'Let me tell you, she was pretty impressed with the performance of yours truly.' He paused, then with an imbecilic grin, added, 'On the course and—'

'Of course.'

'Off the course.'

'Very droll.'

Glassop grabbed his right shoulder with his left hand, rolled his arm and grimaced. 'Twelve on a scale of ten, this fucking pain, mate.'

'Jesus, Haydn, man up!'

'Piss off!'

'Okay. I can see this is useless. It's your back, right?'

'My back, yes. Have pity, woman.'

'You want to do this later? After a couple of aspirin?'

'Yeah. Let's. Thanks, pal. Appreciated, right? I'll owe you.'

'You're not wrong, my friend. Not wrong at all.' For now, I was willing to cut the man some slack, lay down my weapons and just unload my other grievance. Surrender under torture doesn't count, anyway so blackmail was in abeyance. But I couldn't help wondering what he would say tomorrow, or tomorrow, or tomorrow whenever his back healed and I presented the snapshots? Oops? The Miss Japans were no more than balm for his failing manhood, empty boasts for the lads in the locker room. Maybe Naomi looked the other way or these smaller transgressions went unnoticed. If his wife had ever caught him in a serious love affair however—as ours was—it would surely wipe the smirk off his face, have him sitting up straight in his expensive Eames chair.

I would not let him off the hook beyond a day or two. Meanwhile, he needed to know how far I was prepared to go to protect my reputation in the industry. Losing my last two accounts would be the last two I lost. 'Haydn? Remember how I—'

'For Chrissakes, are you still here?' he said, looking up from scratching around in one of his desk's lower draws. 'What?'

'Remember how I pleaded with you to give me a female creative team to work on the Femmtex pitch? And for Go—'

'Yeah, yeah. Go Girl. What's happening with that lot downstairs? I've just heard about Go Girl. Femmtex. And now Go Girl. We lost them both.'

'Great, you're actually catching up on agency business. The word came through on Go Girl Thursday night. I bawled them out Friday morning. They're clots. Dullards. It's part of what I wanted to discuss yesterday.' I sat down. 'But you were otherwise engaged,' I said, indicating Miss Murakami's business card.

'Bet the Hell I was.'

I leaned into him again. 'You better believe it, Haydn; Go Girl was probably the final straw for me—unless something changes around here.'

'That's what all this is about? Same old, same old? Gals in charge? Your own little bunch of ball-breaker hairy-legs downstairs?'

'For now, at any rate. There's a sting in the tail but we'll leave it for when you're feeling better.' I shrugged, tossing my hair away from my eyes and securing it behind one ear. 'You know what?'

'What?'

'We might as well not have bothered showing up for either of those pitches. Femmtex or Go Girl. And yes, I'm sick of the sound of my own voice but you should have given me a female to work on those two accounts. Either an art director or copywriter. Preferably both, of course.'

I studied him; the way he was trying to intimidate me with his off-handedness. Good try but I still hold the ace up my sleeve and his wife would take him to the cleaners if she knew about the affair, no matter how long ago it had happened. It would be enough it had happened. I knew where Naomi Glassop was coming from and knew the mother of their three boys would go in for the kill. Meanwhile, I needed to get the agency sorted out. I was determined to get some female intelligence happening. Cynthia Smart, remember her? A feminist icon. A goddess of the industry. An inspiration to the sorority. Where are you these days, Stewy darling?

I saw him wince as he tried to straighten up. It seemed his pain was genuine. 'Are you going to employ at least one female copywriter, Haydn? A female art director, too ... maybe?'

He did not look up.

'Well? Are you?'

'Piss off. I'm supporting enough of you cunts as it is.' He swivelled back around in his chair to stare out his window again.

I chose to ignore the vulgarity or to take exception to the fact he had just equated my value to the agency with that of the eighteen-year-olds who brought him his mail. I studied the back of the man's head. The picturesque view of the harbour and the Sydney Opera House filled in the background. I had taken Sapphie to a symphony concert there on Friday night.

'They're undermining me, Sapphie,' I said as we stood in the crowded foyer of the Concert Hall during interval, nursing our Perriers and observing a Manly Ferry berthing at Circular Quay.

'Don't cop it, Goddy.'

'Sapph, I'm still fuming.' It had been tough enough learning Phipps Creative had snatched the Femmtex account the previous week but learning we'd also lost Go Girl to Campaign Palace's geniuses was a custard pie in the face. Lien and I had corralled everyone who worked on both the pitches and herded them into the boardroom.

'They're failing the agency, failing me, Sapph. That's what I told them, in no uncertain terms'

'Bet y'did.' The girl was grinning while keeping her eyes fixed on the ferries coming and going. 'Give 'em Hell, Goddy,' she said, turning to clink her Perrier with mine.

'I waved their storyboards at them. Told them they were paid to be brilliant, not ordinary. I scratched the word BRILLIANT on the whiteboard and underlined it. You should have seen them wince. The screech I made as my felt stylus slid across the slippery surface put everyone's teeth on edge.'

'Ouch!'

'Something off the wall, a little crazy. That's what I said I'd wanted from them, Sapph. The Palace keeps coming up with it. Mojo sure keeps it coming. Cheeky stuff. Original stuff. That's what I had a right to expect. And campaigns pitched at women, for women! I needed to have the goods to present to the client. God knows, I threw enough dollars at the research. And I shed blood honing the briefs for them. Any creative worth his bloated pay-packet should have been able to give me winning pitches for those accounts.'

Sapphire put a consoling hand on my arm. 'You are too good for them, Goddy. You told me you were ready to leave that place. You told me you wanted to be a screenwriter, not an advertising executive.'

'You should have been in the room, Sapphie. When I turned from the whiteboard, I caught the condescending look Steve Pearson shot Ray Robb.'

'Yeah?'

'Yes. They're two of my creative guys.'

'Probably put your hissy fit down to PMT.'

'I was fed up with listening for over an hour to their pathetic excuses.'

'Sounds like you were totally, totally pissed off.'

'You should have been there. You'd have laughed. I dismissed the under-performers with a poetic flourish. Stand not upon the order of your going but go at once!'

'Shakespeare?'

'Shakespeare.'

'Good for you. At least you have style, even if they don't.'

'Lady Macbeth, with her clear thinking on pathways to success, Sapphire. Lady Macbeth's my favourite. Like her, I operate in a brutal male environment. One where females who make it even to Account Manager are as rare as virgins aboard a P&O cruise.'

'They're idiots.'

'It's cringe-worthy stuff they keep giving me. Dull, dull drivel.'

'They don't understand women, that's their problem.'

We clinked our Perriers again. The bell began ringing throughout the lobby. It was time to return to our seats.

'My ideas are too edgy for B&G,' I said as we joined the throng taking the wide staircase up to Door 14. 'Ray Robb actually came out and said my Alice Cooper concept was gross. Gross, Sapph. Then Pearson—' I mimed him hitting on the pockets of his flak jacket '—fumbling for his precious Zippo, reckoned it would never get past F.A.C.T.S. anyway.'

'Facts?'

'Federation of Australian Commercial Television Stations. Nup, no way, said the agency's resident genius.' I mimicked my colleague's pseudo-Outback accent, "I mean, give us a break, mate. Even if Warner Music let us have it, the client wouldn't want ... blah, blah, blah." Honestly, Sapph, you'd have to hear that lot to believe what I put up with.'

'You reckon I'm not surrounded with idiots, too? Try our headmaster, Goddy. A total dictator, old Muldoon.'

'I mean, I knew for certain Warner would let the agency have the rights. Alice Cooper's a feminist.' Again, I assumed my colleague's voice. "They'd freak out, over at F.A.C.T.S., mate—go into meltdown, mate. And we woulda had to slap an OA-rating. Couldn't put it to air before 9pm." He's wrong.'

'I know. You get heaps watching TV after nine o'clock.'

'Plenty of female eyeballs on the screen after nine, you're right, Sapph.'

We were in our seats, with the orchestra tuning up when I leant in and whispered, 'You don't think it was gross, my idea for using *Only*

Women Bleed for a sanitary product tvc, do you?'

'Gross?' said Sapphire, eyes rolling. 'How gross is it pretending we bleed blue ink once a month? Like, women give birth to Biros, not babies?'

Trust a savvy femme like Sapphire Cristos-Labelle to nail it. And others like her. Young women like Lien, too, who would flourish in the industry one day.

Miss Stewart had been right; we were a sorority and had to be strong for each other.

Haydn, his binoculars to his eyes, was still lost in his Harbour Master Dreamtime.

'The Fairstar, look at her, Cynthie,' he said as he eventually swung around to offer up the eyeglasses. 'Take a look. The tugs are guiding her out through the Heads. Mighty, isn't she?'

'Haydn, you are a fool if you can't see this agency is sinking. Those guys at Femmtex really wanted to work with me. Check it out. It isn't me losing these accounts. I'm good at what I do. Bloody good! And there are plenty in this industry who know it, don't worry. It's because that lot downstairs is giving me shit to work with. Their stuff's so ... so ... so bloody ordinary! So yesterday. So not with the zeitgeist. I've been begging you for something to counter all this Commonsense Cookery Book, frilly apron, daddy-will-be-home-at-five-so-look-smart-kiddies bullshit this agency goes on with. The Fifties mentality of that lot downstairs, I'm talking about.'

'Being a tad hysterical, aren't we?' speaking through the back of his skull as he continued surveying the harbour through the binoculars.

I ignored the chauvinism. He was old, what did it matter? 'I need people who know the territory. Who live it every day? The female touch is—'

'What I need right now,' he said with a theatrical groan as he spun his chair to greet my scowling face. 'Come 'round here and rub my back Mrs Ormond.'

'We buried that bastard, remember? Your sailing buddy, my worst nightmare?'

'Be nice to me, babe,' he crooned. 'What say we have this weekend on the boat. Just you and me—get reacquainted?'

'What's this? Not you and Miss Japan? Turned you down, did she?'

'C'mon. Don't be like that, Ms Smart. A relaxed couple of days. For old time's sake, mate. What do you say? For old time's sake? For what we were?'

'This is me ignoring you, Haydn.'

'Not sentimental, not just a wee bit? Not curious to see if the old boy can still perform? Remember how you liked—'

'Look, I know Phil is talking to Walter Thompsons. Or if it's not them, then another of the majors. Baker & Glassop will be swallowed up. I understand. But if the agency could just lift its game in the meantime, then we'd all be in a better bargaining position when you sit down at the table. You've had me working with both hands tied behind my back for years. Your golden boys ... downstairs? They don't cut it, don't strike the gongs. Their stuff sucks. All of it. It really sucks, Haydn. They're floundering. They're not cutting through and you don't seem to care. It's such a macho world down there. You have no idea. We have to wade through a fog of male pheromones to get to the photocopiers.'

I hadn't scripted this meeting but knew this would have been the moment to hit him with the ultimatum. The photographs were burning through the leather of my handbag. I leaned in closer and spoke softly. 'I've got more than one shot in my—'

'Is this your movie nonsense?' He was smirking again. I had an urge to slap the smug face. 'Cynthia L. Smart, Down Under's answer to Cecil B. De Mille.'

'Go ahead, old sport. Ridicule me all you like but don't expect to walk the red carpet when it premieres. Yes. I have another life. Does that surprise you?'

'So, what's it about, your movie?'

'Forget it. You'd never understand. Not you. Not in a million years, Haydn.'

I picked up the antique letter opener from his desk and ran my fingers down its golden shaft. Back in my office were designs for the stationery and letterheads I'd played around with. Baker, Glassop & Smart. It had a certain ring about it. The Smart Agency. I saw him arch his back, wince and try to realign his posture. His pain was genuine, if self-inflicted. I wasn't a total harridan. I stood up and made for the door, turning at the last moment. 'It can wait a day or two. Meanwhile, stay off Miss Japan, let you back heal, we'll talk. Okay?'

I left without looking back to catch what would no doubt be another smirk. I had gone in with an ultimatum and a gripe and on both counts came out empty handed. Because of his pain I'd pulled back, gone easy on him. It could wait, because I hadn't finished with Haydn Glassop, not yet. Not by a long shot. To use one of his own nautical terms; I might have altered tack but we were still heading into the storm.

21

CONNIE

To sound the alarm is not to panic.

John F. Kennedy

Santa Monica, Los Angeles
Friday 1st May 1992

Despite being still shaken up by the one in black, Connie was instantly charmed by the vision greeting her as the heavy wooden door swung open.

'Hi,' she announced to the woman standing in the doorway bouncing Theo on her grandmotherly hip. Theo was happily twiddling the lady's fine white hair between his baby fingers, obviously not traumatised by any motherly neglect on her part, she reasoned, holding the smile.

'Sapphire's not back yet I'm afraid, dear,' said the lady, laughing and ducking her head from the next assault on what remained of a once fine head of hair.

The smile froze. 'What do you mean, Mrs Goldman? Not—'

'Goldberg, dear. Goldberg.'

'Not back? Not back from where?'

'He's a hungry little fella, this one, isn't he?' Rita Goldberg said as she extricated the baby's fingers from her hair and tickled him under his chin. 'Call me Rita, dear.'

'Rita. Where's Sapphire? Where did she go? When? Where?'

'It's okay, dear. She just wanted to go bike riding. Ride around the pathways inside the grounds, she said. Although, mind you, there are wonderful riding paths out front. Along the beach. Very pretty views. She told me the hotel lends out the bikes. Over by the gym. It's nothing to worry about, I'm sure. There was a nice young boy with her.'

The bike with the busted wheel. On the path coming here. Sapphire's bike? A boy with her? Stay calm, Constance. Stay calm. 'Okay. But how long ago was this?'

'Oh, quite a while, actually. Let me think; I was just putting the—'

'What? An hour ago? Two?' She could feel fear rising like an incoming tide. She lifted Theo from the woman's arms and secured a now squawking Theo into his Baby Björn.

'Maybe more. She raced in for lunch and then was off again. I fixed her a bowl of chilli, chilli and a big cool glass of iced tea. With lemon and a little mint. She liked it. They probably got talking to other young people. You know how they are at that age. Teenagers. They're curious. And friendly. Always someone new to meet and greet. Won't you come in, dear? Plenty of iced tea. You look a little … well, overheated, if I might say so.'

Not just overheated, outright giddy! The sensation was no longer a mild incoming tide but a tsunami of concern for her eldest, crashing onto the shores of her consciousness. Sapphire not back. Her daughter out there somewhere in that world of mayhem and murder.

She snatched the offered nappy bag from the sitter.

'Thank you. Could you ring us the minute Sapphire comes in, please? I must let her father know. And keep her here, Mrs Goldman. Goldberg. Don't let her leave till one of us comes for her. Promise?'

'Of course, dear.'

'We will come and get her. One of us will collect her,' Connie called over her shoulder as she started down the steps. 'Just make sure she stays with you, okay?' And then she realized she had used this vague woman's kindness. 'And—Rita—thank you so much. It was wonderful of you to babysit for me.'

Running at a trot, trying hard to keep a level head, not wanting to become irrational, all she could think of now was the one in black. They're curious. Always someone new to meet and greet. Irrational, but what if he had run off with her daughter. A boy with her? Every male under retirement age would be a boy to that one back there.

Why hadn't she enquired about the 'boy'? She had no right going out today, gadding about town, leaving her children with a woman like the elderly Rita Goldman, a woman she knew fuck-all about. What was Rita? Sixty-five? Seventy? Rita and Maurice, David's accountant colleague, here for some convention or other. She had said they were too old to baby sit, but David assured her the bungalows were safe. It would be fine.

Well, it wasn't bloody fine. One of her two children she left with a stranger was missing. Fifty percent not fine, David. In a crazy town like this, with the sun going down, a curfew about to kick in and weirdos everywhere and what do you know; the girl up and disappears. If she's been out on a bike all afternoon, probably she doesn't even know about the curfew. Yanking the Baby Björn straps tighter around her waist, she ran for the main building. Hadn't someone in the lobby told her about that radio station? Some nutter calling in and saying unless they started reporting the truth, the whole town would get shot up. Rich people's places, the imbecile had said. Rich people would get shot up. Like people who stayed at the Miramar. People in Santa Monica.

The crazies would be out to get them tonight. It was coming closer. It was Armageddon out beyond those gates. She could feel it. How did she know Sapphire hadn't gone out on the street? She might have heard the library was on fire, the local one. Santa Monica's library, they reckoned. The child might have gone with other kids to check it out. It's what kids did. Or been kidnapped by the one in black.

Don't panic, don't panic, don't panic stupid woman. Just do not panic.

She tugged the Baby Björn straps even tighter, until they dug into the excess tummy fat and with determination to lose it starting tomorrow, doubled her pace. A cyclist flew past, coming near to skittling her. She took the steps onto the pool area two at a time, a hungry Theo bellowing at the top of his lungs, kicking her ribs, not making it easy on her. Smelling her milk.

Past the swimming pool, into the hotel and straight for the elevators where she caught her breath and stabbed at the buttons as if poking out the eyes of an enemy.

Theo was apoplectic. And now she realized he smelled rotten, as well. The child was packing a load. She stuck two fingers in the top of his diaper, pulled the soggy fabric aside and sniffed.

She gagged. Something had died in his gut. His bum would be red raw. How long had that woman left him sitting in his own shit? God forbid, she had fed him chilli or something just as evil? She had packed his Cream of Chicken and his shredded pineapple pieces and a full packet of rusks. Had he been given cows' milk rather than the breast milk she'd left with the woman?

She continued to wait on the lifts, praying for one going up. The sight of the three, all stuck up on higher floors only heightened her agitation. A young kid carrying a fruit and champagne basket stepped into the service lift further down the row and for a moment, she thought of hitching a ride with him. A Latino youth in white hotel kitchen uniform, she noticed how handsome he looked with his olive skin and jet-black curls under his cute cap.

A curfew baring down on them. Where in god's name was her child? Please let my little girl be safe. Jude, the patron of lost things, I'll go to church on Sundays. Do a novena. Just let Sapphie be upstairs in the room when I get there. Please. How could she explain it to Nick if anything happened to their precious girl? Her heart jumped its corral just thinking of the child lying hurt and alone somewhere in this raging town. She moved along the lines of elevators, stabbed the row of buttons again. Nothing was happening except her rising panic and the toxicity of Theo's diaper polluting the air.

She could feel sweat dripping down the back of her legs, could feel milk leaking from her nipples. Having exchanged the ridiculous high heels for her Nikes, it felt as if her feet were swimming in warm piddle. She jigged Theo to quieten him. If the lift didn't get here soon, she would run up seven flights of stairs, baby and all. Women could lift whole cars off their kid's body, she'd read it somewhere and she believed it. She took in three deep breaths. Irrational panic was bad. The adrenalin rush would sour her milk, give Theo colic and then they would be up all night with him. No, he was way too old for colic. And Sapphire might well be sitting upstairs watching TV, anyway. Relax, Connie Labelle. Deep breaths. It would be okay. It will be fine. It will be okay. It will all turn out right in the end. It must.

She cursed the elevators again. The one stuck on Three was finally coming down. Sapphire, if not upstairs, was probably walking up to Rita Goldberg's door. She had probably been trying out some kid's bicycle. God love her, she would have had a wonderful afternoon exploring the grounds. Making friends with kids her own age, by the sound of things.

She needed to keep in mind her child-rearing philosophy, safe freedoms. You plant the seed in sunshine, you nourish it, but you hold back with the pruning shears or it will never reveal its true nature to the universe.

It will be fine. Sapph will be fine. Oh, Jesus and Mary but you pong, little fella, she whispered in Theo's tiny ear.

You put the cake in the oven, you set the timer. No fussing, no opening the oven door. That would not be good for the cake. She ought not begrudge her teenage daughter these discovery years. It was only natural she wanted to spread her wings.

Just not in a city on fire. A city of flying bullets and demented looters. A city under military guard. They shoot teenagers here, the National Guard. She pictured the bloodied bodies of the Kent State students on their campus grounds but quickly dismissed the image, aware she was catastrophizing what would turn out to be simply the result of a vague old woman not being sufficiently across the details of the job with which she had been entrusted.

They would talk about all this, she and Sapphire, have a good laugh at her motherly stupidity, her proclivity to press panic buttons. Then maybe there would be an opportunity to discuss the condom business. An easy segue.

She stepped into the empty elevator and pressed the Seventh-floor button, grateful no other passenger was sharing the ride with her and Theo. The child's backside smelt like a meat packing plant in lockdown. Putrid. Pity anyone who steps in here after us, she thought. It surprised her that even when her tummy was in such a knot, butterflies in free-fall, she could still raise a giggle over the goings-on of her kids. There was no reason to laugh about an errant daughter, however. The sun was fast going down. It was dangerous out there. Men with guns. Lunatics threatening annihilation. Weirdos in black hoods.

Nothing funny at all about her darling daughter gone missing, her Sapphie riding out through those big iron gates into who knew what kind of nightmare. A riot might excite the rebel in her, have her charging in to the thick of things. This Los Angeles today wasn't Katoomba on a sunny Saturday, marching for the environment through the village, one of Sapphie's extra-curricular activities. An old habit, but why not; she crossed herself and prayed silently to Mother Mary for her little girl's safe delivery.

22

CYNTHIA

You cannot swim for new horizons
until you have courage to lose sight of the shore.
William Faulkner

Santa Monica, Los Angeles
Friday 1st May 1992

So warm and comfortable under the covers.

I had dozed off. For how long I had no idea. Didn't much care either. Nowhere to go. No one to see. I sat up and thought about topping up my glass, one more little nip of the glorious Glenfiddich to wipe away the blues; zap the likes of Noel Ormond, Haydn Glassop, Professor Wadsworth, the Hollywood wunderkind Spinak, Arthur Anderson's faint-hearted heroes, lover boy downstairs and yes, the head-up-his-arse Nicholas Cristos, too. I climbed off the bed, grasping the nightstand to steady myself while the B-Double road train passed through my cranium.

The second blood test confirmed it. My future in the advertising industry was a joke. It wasn't any belated moral reckoning that spiked my blackmailing plans last week. Wadsworth's doomsday diagnosis had been a reality check.

I tossed back the dregs and climbed into bed. Of all the likely reasons the gynaecologist had given for a woman my age suffering heavy intermittent bleeding, nothing—not uterine fibroids, not even the possibility of endometrial cancer—had come remotely close to what was depicted so clearly in the ultrasound slides. Sent to him for vaginal bleeding, I left his rooms staring down not only accelerated old age, osteoporosis and heart disease, but something so bizarre I was still trying to process it. Little wonder I hadn't left the envelope behind for Imelda Cartwright to see.

I pulled a pillow over my head. I could easily start blubbering. The world was against me and my life falling apart. I eventually unfurled myself from the foetal position and swung my legs over the side, sitting there with my head in my hands.

Minutes must have passed. I ignored the bottle, my eyes fixed on the view outside the window. There was a new life for me out there, somewhere. If only I could buck up, get out of the fug I'd been in ever since the prognosis.

The professor was an antediluvian. His old brown Chesterfields, his dark panelled walls, the whole brown gloom of his depressing Macquarie Street surgery. It was redolent of a bygone era, that surgery. So was the prim and proper Miss Craig. What I needed was to snag myself a gynie who lived in sunshine, who operated in the present rather than the past, who was plugged in to the science of the female condition. A doc who had some tricks up her sleeve.

From the fridge I took a Coke and gulped it down, wiping the drips from my chin with the back of my hand. Why not? I reached in, grabbed the sinful confectionary and unwrapped it. Sinking my teeth into the squashy caramel chocolate felt orgasmic. Why do we insist on robbing ourselves of these small pleasures? Connie was doing okay carrying all that tubbiness. Time to stop obsessing about being skinny and start giving in to pleasures like these. I finished the bar and tossed the wrapper into the bin then went across to stand and stare out the ocean across the road.

If menopause was a universal condition, then there must be scientists somewhere in the world addressing the issue. It was 1992, for godsakes. I simply needed to find a clued-up medical genius who knew about premature oestrogen failure and could give me hope. The old boy was wary of prescribing hormone replacement for someone so young, he said, warning me of the dangers of long-term usage. To Hell with that. I would speak with Rosemary Bray, ask her for a referral, get a second opinion, a third or fourth ... a fifth, six, seventh. Audition the whole bloody medical universe until I found someone prepared to tell me the end was not nigh.

Whatever the new life awaiting me, it would be up to me to earn it. No one owed me anything. No one was obliged to make it happen for me. And for certain, it was not going to happen while ever I was locked up in this sorry joint. What I needed to do in the short-term was to change into gym gear and go downstairs. That was it. A killer work-out and then the pool. Fifty laps. Clear my head. Thrash things out in the water. Don't let them get you down, love, that was always Paddy's advice. What he always said when things looked blackest and pulling the covers up over my head seemed the only thing to do. Don't let 'em get you down, girly. Well, I'd show them. I would conquer my fears about cronehood.

And yes, along the way, conquer Hollywood, too.

Having surprised myself for adopting this positive pathway to my Forties, I retrieved the bottle, held the crystal glass up to the fading afternoon light and admired the luminosity of the amber liquid as I poured. Amber. Like Wadsworth's waiting room but way more stylish. More comforting.

Uh-huh. No. No more. I poured the liquid back into the bottle, screwed on the lid and went across to where my travel bag sat waiting for me to plunder it for my gym gear.

In the bathroom, I brushed my teeth, splashed cold water on my face and pulled my hair back in a tight ponytail. I checked myself out in the mirror and began removing my jewellery; the diamond studs from my ears, the charm bracelet and the Piaget from my wrists. I unclipped the watchband, carefully laying the expensive two-tone 18 karat white and gold timepiece on the shelf above the basin alongside the earrings. All trappings to impress Myron Spinak this morning.

Lastly, I reached beneath my hair and unclipped the long fine golden chain, always warm because it always lay close against my heart. I let both the chain and the Claddagh ring drip slowly into the palm of my hand, clutching my fingers over it, my eyes closed as I held it to my chest a moment before setting it aside with the other jewellery.

23

CYNTHIA

Only the dead have seen the end of war.

George Santayana

Mosman, New South Wales, Australia
1968-70

He had come looking for a job. A part-time one. He could manage Friday afternoons and Saturday mornings, the eighteen-year-old announced to Meghan Thomas, the young casual who was minding the shop because Moira had left earlier in the afternoon to collect Connie and me from Central Railway after our school excursion to Canberra.

He was a reader, he told Meghan. She was only the casual, she told him. Mrs Smart is not here. He dug the classics, he announced to Meghan, more preoccupied with his athletic physic than his reading list. Catcher in the Rye, James Joyce, Huck Finn, William Burrows, Jack Kerouac, Catch 22. And he also loved poetry, he added for good measure. The Romantics, y'know. Keats and Coleridge. Wordsworth, naturally. William Butler Yeats. Oh, and Heaney, Frost and Allen Ginsberg.

The eclectic reader with the Byronic curls and the eyes to fix the legend was a builder's labourer who worked alongside Paddy on jobs around the district, a builder's labourer who carried a copy of Dharma Bums in the back pocket of his Yakka shorts and read it at smoko. Paddy spoke fondly of his young off-sider. Jesse McKenzie's love of reading impressed Paddy, himself a keen reader. It was Dad who had spotted the opportunity for his wife to lease the vacant shopfront in Dirk Street at a rent that would make running the second-hand bookshop she had always dreamed about a reasonable proposition. Once the lease was signed, he made a commendable effort to bring the neglected old building up to scratch.

Then he suggested Jesse would make a great part-time assistant. The kid's saving up to travel, said Paddy by way of explanation the night we sat around the dinner table talking about the bookshop's happy progress. Wants to take six months off work to see the world before he's off to night school. Landscape architecture. The kid's strong as an ox and sensible. He'd make a go of it. Give him a few hours a week in the shop and you won't be sorry. I promise. He looks the part, believe me.

Not that the proprietor of the surprisingly successful Dirk Street Bookshop had said she was looking for another casual. She had Meghan Thomas for rush hours. But my father reckoned her blossoming enterprise could benefit from a good-looking youth like McKenzie behind the counter. Keen as a whistle, honest as all get out, and knows his onions when it comes to books, said Paddy. After all, he cunningly pointed out the night the subject of hiring Jesse McKenzie came up, females make up the bulk of readers, people most likely to come into the shop and browse. So, what's wrong with giving them a strapping young bloke like McKenzie who knows what he's talking about to advise them on what to read? What to buy? Couldn't hurt, love, he persisted. He's every mother's son. You'll love him. Your customers will too, Moisey, I promise.

Fact was, Paddy had a soft spot for Jesse McKenzie.

Within the first few weeks Jesse had not only boosted Mother's book sales with his applied knowledge and charm, but in an entrepreneurial spirit he had set up a small record bar down the back of the shop. A handy way to introduce kids to book buying. The honey trap, Paddy with a certain pride, called it. Two turntables and earphones, each in small soundproof booths Jesse and Paddy built out of second-hand ply, and which I helped Jesse paint and decorate with album covers and posters.

Friday afternoon and Saturday morning business flourished as the young people poured through the doors to hang with the cool young disc-jockey. The Dirk Street Bookshop became a favourite meeting place the days Jesse's customers put on their headphones and moved their bodies to Born to be Wild, Hey Jude, Mrs Robinson, Harper Valley PTA, Angel of the Morning and the rest of the Top One Hundred. Invariably, they walked out with not only an album or two under their arm, but copies of the popular Rolling Stone magazines and a couple of pre-loved paperbacks. Not that Moira ever gave Paddy credit for the increased sales. Or Jesse.

I was a gawky high school kid when Jesse walked into my life.

It was the sweet curls falling into his eyes, his golden suntan and his lean yet strong physique that heated my sixteen-year-old blood and made me murderously jealous when Meghan Thomas blabbed that he drove her home after work in his white souped-up old MG Sports with the noisy exhaust pipes, the bomb he parked out front on Dirk Street twice a week. It made me jealous enough to try and spike Meghan Thomas, get her fired by hinting that their assistant might be touching the till.

It was the crush that saw the end of the pigtails and a new, long straight crop of blonde hair, at least for after-school appearances. Free-flowing and heavily fringed in the style of Carnaby Street model, Jean Shrimpton. I began haunting the bookshop, my interest in Edna O'Brien and Virginia Woolf hitting stela heights as I thrilled to the sensation of the new boy so close behind me as we studied the rows of shelves, leaning over me to retrieve the book he thought might interest me.

Friday afternoon after school, after taking a fragrant bubble bath and throwing on my mini skirt and boots, I would ride my second-hand Malvern Star up the hill to Dirk Street, hide it in the back lane and sashay into the shop brandishing a bighearted offer to help out during their rush hour.

Sadly, my Saturday mornings were taken up with either training in the pool or tennis coaching, which gave Meghan Thomas free run at hot-shot Jesse Mac. Until, one Saturday morning the girl failed to show up. Peritonitis, her father explained when he radioed in to explain his daughter's absence. While hospitalized, Thomas fell for the young intern who'd rescued her appendix postoperatively and gifted them to her in a screw-top jar of formalin. Farewell, Meghan.

School ended in November. I had months of summer holidays in which to indulge my new-found love of books. Moira offered me two full days a week in the shop. Thursdays and Fridays. Other days, Connie and I waited tables in the outdoor cafe around the corner. By now, anyone could see that Jesse had begun seriously noticing the proprietor's daughter.

And the proprietor began noticing Jesse McKenzie seriously noticing her daughter. Young ladies were supposed to set their marriage sights several levels above a builder's labourer, even a well-spoken and presentable youth with a yen for literature and an intention to go on to study landscape architecture. Meet my mother, the snob. The Ladies College had been her idea, the reason I was made sit for the Commonwealth Scholarship when we were still living in Glen Iris.

But I knew I had Paddy's blessing when Jesse and I started dating. I had turned seventeen, Jesse nineteen. Horse riding, abseiling, surfing and tennis; with movies a way to slow down. The MG was our joy, our sin.

Moira spoke in urgent whispers the night she caught me sneaking back into the house at 2am, my blouse open, bra in hand and my hair a tumbled mess. Poor Mother, standing there in her blue chenille detailing the dangers of uncontrolled youthful passion, her voice thick with broken sleep. Feelings you get down there, Cynthia, she said, pointing to my nether regions. They can very quickly get out of control, young lady and when that happens—well—they can get a girl into serious trouble! Your virginity is like money in the bank. Remember that, child. When a man takes it out, he loses interest.

With my hand protectively at my neck, I had backed into my bedroom and shut the door. The hickie I examined in my dressing table mirror was a sign of love. I truly did love Jesse McKenzie. He meant the world and then some to me. My life revolved around the idea of us as a couple. We spoke of our big plans. Finish our studies and then set out together to explore Asia before we settled down. The money each earned from the bookshop and the café jobs were all in the service of the dream.

It was one sunny morning, a Thursday morning, when the dream took a direct hit.

I was in the shop, attending to an elderly woman enquiring about a Women's Weekly pattern book when I looked up to see Jesse standing in the doorway.

This was out of the ordinary.

He stood there in his work gear; grey Yakka shorts, a navy-blue singlet, chunky socks and his big clumping work boots smudged with clay, or maybe cement. What teenage girl could fail to thrill to the vision presented to her that morning? Not me. I went to water, instantly forgetting about knitting books and valued customers.

From his muscled calves and powerful arms, to the way he wore his dark hair secured by a red bandana. And the gold earring. Jesse McKenzie was a dreamboat. Always when near him, I was struck with a violent urge to rip off my clothes and collapse naked into his arms and let him make love to me. In a constant state of arousal, jabbering to Connie endlessly about Jesse. Jesse is hot. Jesse loves the way I do my hair. Jesse this and Jesse that. Jesse, Jesse, Jesse. I get it, okay? Connie said. He's Mr Wonderful. You're in love. Romeo and Juliet. Gimme a break. Are you doing it, yet? You are, aren't you!

No, but it was only a matter of time, Moira or no Moira. I intended to surrender my virginity on my Eighteenth and that was just around the corner. The heavy petting sessions in the MG constantly had me running inside to hump a pillow between my legs. The physical frustration of being scared to go all the way was killing me and Connie agreed. Go for it, said Con.

He continued to hang in the doorway that morning, apologising for his dirty boots, until I made the move.

'Jesse!' I excused myself from the customer and ran to embrace him. His visit thrilled me. He had found himself in the area and dropped by to say hello. Or so I thought.

'Cyn?' He held me away from his body and searched my eyes.

'What is it?' I could see from the troubled look clouding his face he hadn't dropped by on a social visit. He produced an envelope from his back pocket and handed it to me.

It was eleven o'clock on a pleasant summer's day in February 1970. The sun poured in through the Federation leadlight windows, throwing rainbow patterns across the well-warn timber floors. It was a warm and pleasant day outside in Dirk Street, the sweetness of gentle harbour breezes drifting through the district. Down by the shore young mothers were pushing strollers through the park, stopping frisky toddlers running off on their own. Old men on benches were feeding seagulls. Joggers were jogging. The blue-rinse ladies were shopping for navy blazers and plaid skirts at Simone and consultants in suits were waiting for cabs to take them to lunch in the city.

Everything was normal in Mosman that morning. Except for what was happening to me and Jesse.

There was no need to open the long manila envelope boasting the Australian Commonwealth Government's seal. I knew what it contained, had secretly dreaded it. In that moment, the bottom fell out of my world.

'Open it,' Jesse urged.

The Department of Labour and National Service had sent Jesse McKenzie his call-up papers. He had been drafted. For two years. And because he was one of the fit and healthy recruits, one year of it, at least, would be spent fighting in the jungles of Vietnam.

Vietnam was a galaxy far, far away from our ordinary suburban Mosman. How could it be that what was happening in some distant country—one we knew so little about, jungles and paddy fields that belonged to strangers—was about to crush our perfect world? The possibility of Jesse getting the call-up had been a constant threat since he'd registered. Only as a vague possibility, however. Something I figured I could ignore, given the odds. Connie and I had been cheering the boys who burned their draft cards on TV but I knew Jesse didn't feel the same way we felt about Vietnam. Jesse was ready to answer the call. The McKenzies did their patriotic duty. He came from a family whose relatives fought in WW1, WW11 and Korea. He had a godmother, an ex-Army nurse who'd served in Singapore and who had published a small book about her experiences, one Jesse promoted to any of Moira's customers who so much as hinted at an interest in war histories. No way was he hostile to the Vietnam war. Connie and I never shut up about the obscenity of it.

She and I had even sneaked off in our school uniforms to a meeting in North Sydney to hear Jim Cairns speak against Vietnam. If we argued over the merits or otherwise of Australia's involvement, Jesse found urgent things needing his attention. And he tried to convince me it would be a cheap way for him to see the world before college and before we settled down. His closing argument was the promise of a cheap housing loan for returning troops. The builder in him ate that one up. It would give us a kick start in life, he said. And after all, the time would pass quickly. I had my studies to keep me occupied.

The document said they were ordering him to report the following month to the Marrickville Army Training Centre for his final medical and then to board a bus with the others for distant Kapooka army base and months of training before shipping out. Only the healthiest among them would get to see the real action, take their chances in the jungles of Vietnam. Lucky Jesse McKenzie.

Army boots, not these familiar dopey work boots standing in our peaceful little bookshop, the sun pouring in through the high leadlight windows, throwing rainbows around out feet.

I was losing him. That was the truth. My Jesse belonged to the Army now. The nation's property. Their killing machine. Armed with deadly weapons and sent over there, wherever there was, to kill on behalf of us, Australians who couldn't point to Nui Dat on a map if our lives depended on it.

Dark clouds rolled in. Winter had come early to sunny Mosman.

24

CONNIE

Panic is the sudden realization
that everything around you is alive.
William S. Burroughs

Santa Monica, Los Angeles
Friday 1st May 1992

'Fuck! Those two will be the death of me!' announced Connie as she burst into their suite, releasing Theo from his sling and lowering him onto the bed. The shower was running in the en suite. 'Sapphie's gone and buggered off somewhere, David,' she called out. 'And Cynthia's not answering.'

'Can't hear you, sweetheart,' David, his voice muffled by soap bubbles and shower noises.

She leant over the baby. 'Your naughty Aunty Cynthia's still got that sign out, hasn't she, bubba. Not answering her door, is she?' she cooed to the infant as she took him to the makeshift change table and unbuttoned his sunsuit. 'Or her bloody phone.' She tickled the squawking baby's tummy as she took the two big safety pins from the smelly nappy and shuddered at the putrid stink suddenly filling the room.

While attempting to shush Theo with more tummy tickles, she yelled over her shoulder at the bathroom door. 'David? Did you hear what I said? For godsakes, man. Our daughter's missing. And a curfew's coming!'

She tried to placate Theo's cries with a soother. 'They're a pair, aren't they, my little darling? Your sister and Aunty Cyn? Both missing in action, naughty girls.' She gave Theo his blue bunny, wincing as she gently eased the heavily soiled terry towelling from his chubby bottom, gasping when she saw how red raw his parts were. His tiny testicles looked fried, as did the creases in his buttocks. This, and the rancid smell, touched off mother guilt. She'd had no right to go out today and leave her kids with a stranger, one who was obviously not up to the job.

Using a bunch of wet tissues, she wiped the mess from Theo's buttocks and testicles as carefully as she could, shocked by the state of his baby skin. Tucking his squirming body under one arm, she carried him into the steamy en suite. 'Did you hear me, David? Sapphie's gone,' she said, diving a wet washer into the darkest creases of the small body and continuously rinsing the cloth. 'Gone! The stupid woman let the child go off on her own. She let a fifteen-year-old go off on a bike with some boy, to god knows where. Outside the grounds, she thinks. Said she went bike riding and hasn't come back. David, there's a bloody curfew about to kick in and—'

'What?'

Connie threw away the soiled washer and opened the shower screen door. At the risk of a wet sleeve, she leant in and thrust the naked Theo at David. 'Wash him. Quickly. Soap him up around his bum and balls, rinse him then hop out. You need to go look for Sapphie because that stupid bloody woman, Rita—'

'Rita?'

The baby was done. She cradled him into a fluffy white towel and then turned off the hot shower tap.

'Yikes! That's cold. Why'd you do that?' he said, turning off the cold tap and stepping out, taking the towel she thrust at his chest. 'Whose Rita?'

The bloody sitter! Your mate's wife. Rita Goldman.'

'Goldberg.'

'Goldman, Goldberg. Who gives a fuck? She let Sapphie off the leash!'

At the fridge she grabbed a bottle of spring water. Nursing gave her a mighty thirst. The stink coming from the putrid nappy prompted her to bag it in plastic and tuck it away before settling down to nurse. The more pleasant whiffs of David's Old Spice and citrus shampoos weren't cutting it. He emerged from the steamy bathroom, the towel around his waist and shaking water from what little remained of a once-generous head of hair. 'Pooh, the boy's ripe.'

'There's air-con. Get over it.'

He came up to her and put his arm around her shoulder. 'You're upset.'

'Upset?' she said as she leaned over the change table carefully dabbing soothing baby balm on Theo's red and blistering skin before pinning on his nappy, fluffing a little sweet-smelling baby powder under his chin and pulling a white Bonds singlet down over his belly.

'Upset, you reckon? The woman let her go off on a bike, David—with some strange boy, apparently—and to where? Who knows?'

Theo answered with a fart, followed by a squishy liquid noise and then the smell, again.

'Something's dead in there!' laughed David as he handed her a clean nappy, tissues and a wet cloth.

'She's given him god knows what. Not his baby food, obviously,' she fumed as she wiped mustardy shit from an impatient, bellowing Theo's bum. 'I left his jars with her. What was she doing!'

Her busy hands continued wiping at the putrid toddler mess. 'Oh god, David, look at his poor little chaffed bottom, will you?' The scalding rash was her fault. She washed Theo's bottom again and applied the salve. 'His poor little testicles, Davey, god bless him. Why did I expect a dignified old woman like the one in that bungalow to attend to a baby's shitty backside?'

The job done, she ducked into the bathroom basin, picked up one of the hotel's tiny circular soaps and fumed at how reluctant it was to produce a decent lather. Poor little mite had probably been sitting in his own shit for hours. She wiped her hands and returned to the bedroom, still chastising herself. She had no right dumping Theo in a stranger's lap today. End of story. Rather than curse, she would have flowers and a Thank You card delivered to Mrs Goldman tomorrow. 'Did you hear me? Sapphie's gone. Our daughter has disappeared in the middle of this chaos, David. We have to do something.'

'Missing, you said?'

'Yes! Missing,' she shouted. 'Stop being obtuse. Hurry up, get dressed. Put anything on. Just go!' She eased herself comfortably in the low armchair, unbuttoned her shirt and opened the flap of her nursing bra to release an engorged breast.

'A good look,' said David, grinning.

'Yeah, a big fat nursing bra? A great look,' she said, raising her arms to David for the hungry, but sanitized Theo. She yearned to ditch the ugly bras and get into the sexy Perla's. Cyn had ribbed her about purchasing the expensive lingerie this afternoon but she reckoned she owed it to herself. All the years of flopping her boobs out for babies, they deserved to be well-housed in their retirement.

Before she allowed the baby to suckle, she cast her eyes up at David. 'How do we start and look for a missing fifteen-year-old daughter in a strange city? One that's on fire—and about to go into lock-down?'

'I'm sure she's okay, sweetheart.' He was focused on drying and dressing himself. 'It's still daylight, Con. She's not a child, anyway; she's sixteen in a few days, remember?'

'You're kidding me, aren't you? God, David, get real!' She put Theo to the breast and winced as the first draw-down of her milk caused the familiar contraction of her pelvic muscles. A jab of pain but one she welcomed because apparently it helped get the post-natal body back in shape. It also meant she would shortly be relieved of her hard and lumpy breasts. With a grin, she observed David with his foot up on the side of the bed, leaning in as he wiped between his toes, paying scrupulous attention to each digit and the spaces between.

'Thank god there's only five more to go,' she said, seeing him change feet and begin the same fastidious routine on the other foot.

He rubbed his back and shoulders vigorously, the hotel's fluffy towel whipping saw-like up, down and sideways across his taut body. At forty-three, her husband was still in good shape. It was only the hairy back prevented him from being her ideal Cleo centrefold, she often teased. The fact his hairline had begun receding was something David wasn't coping with, but she figured it gave him a certain dignity. Her husband was a great catch. Even if Cynthia were the one to have had the first go at him. Students. Long ago. Nothing significant.

He was a handsome guy. Thoughtful and intelligent, too, and hot in the cot for a man his age. Just not a man able to meet her sense of urgency in a crisis. 'For godsakes, man. Leave that and get going. Hurry up!'

David was too relaxed about parenthood. The fact he was playing it cool now had nothing to do with Sapphire not being his biological daughter. He adored her and she had him wrapped around her little finger. They were a great father and daughter team. He was far more capable than she was of coping with teenager petulance. It wasn't in his nature to panic, that was his problem. She could do panic enough for both. A Gold Medallist at Panic. The Mother Knot, one journalist had called it.

'She's in a strange city, Davey. That's supposing she rode the bike outside the grounds. And I bet you she has. Why else wouldn't she be back at the Goldmans?'

'Goldbergs.'

'Oh, shut up! When's this bloody sunset they're talking about going to happen, anyway?'

'You've got to give her some wriggle room. About seven o'clock, I think. Thereabouts.'

'What? The whole of Los Angeles?'

'Yeah, the whole city goes into lockdown.'

'And it's cool to let my fifteen-year-old loose in Crazy town? The place is going up in flames, David in case you hadn't noticed. Idiots are firing at each other out there! Madmen with rifles. Cops with orders to shoot. She could get herself arrested. You heard what that guy downstairs said.' She held out her free hand, palm down, to show it was trembling. 'Look at me. I'm a mess.'

'I'll try the room when I go down the hall. She's got a special bond with Cynthia.'

Her eyes shot up from the baby. 'And you don't … have a special bond with Cynthia?' She immediately regretted the snarky comment. It was an ugly suspicion and not worthy of her. Or fair to Cyn. Or David. She reached out for his hand and looked up. 'I've been trying her room, Davey. No answer.'

'I'll check things out downstairs. Sapphie's with her, somewhere.'

'With a godmother like Cyn, probably in one of the bars, sipping dry martinis and checking out the talent,' she laughed.

David reached for his trousers. 'Just stay calm and carry on. You're doing a brilliant job. He thinks so, anyway.' He indicated his guzzling son.

'I'll kill the little bugger. I'll wring her skinny bloody neck when she gets here.'

'Back home, you wouldn't give it a second thought,' said David, stepping into his chinos and zipping his flies. 'Don't worry. She's fine. I'll bring her back in one piece, I promise.' He pulled a white Polo shirt down over his head. '*Virgo in tacta.*'

'David!'

He leant down and kissed his wife's cheek. 'Kidding. I'm onto it. Relax.'

She looked down at Theo then smiled up at her husband. 'Thanks, pardner. I will. I need to.' She reached for his hand again. 'The accountant's tidy mind, that's my guy. The lawyer's silver tongue. I love you, ol' man.'

David patted his son's curly head then placed his warm hand over the top of Connie's breast and let it linger there. 'Love you too, girl,' he said, dropping an affectionate kiss on her forehead and another on the infant's head. 'Lucky you,' he said to his son. 'Make the most of it, boy. It won't always be this easy.'

'Get going, you!'

It pleased her to parade herself in front of her man. Some experts said breast-feeding was the conclusion to the sex act. In some cultures, dark areole and huge nipples were a turn-on. Despite that kind of assurance, however, five kids and she was fed up with the effects of childbirth on her body and longed for a time before stretch marks and nipples the colour of burnt toast. There is a cream, she recalled having read in a women's magazine, cream you can apply to lighten the nipple. Pretty little pink nipples. No stretch marks. Dream on, lady.

'Get going!' She shooed David out the door. He was right, of course; Sapphire was sensible.

Theo, well into his rhythmical sucking, rested his warm hand on her flesh.

'You be okay?' asked David, surprising her when he popped back into the room to grab his wallet from the desk.

'Mother guilt,' she shrugged. 'It's a complicated thing. I should have taken them with me today. Or not gone out. Not stayed out, shopping all afternoon.'

'Ah, the smell of the burning cross. It must get heavy dragging it around.'

She tossed him an eye roll.

'Martyrdom doesn't suit you, old girl,' he said, stuffing the wallet into his back pocket as he headed once more for the door. 'Lighten up. There's nothing to worry about. I'll have our truant daughter back before you know it. Love you.' He blew his wife a parting kiss. 'See ya.'

The room was quiet. Just her and the contented little boy at her breast. She thought about the others back home. She would ring them shortly. Saturday morning. Franny's netball would be over by now. They'd be at Jack's football match. She hoped the children weren't proving too much of a trial for Ted and Rosemary, especially her funny little Harry who was probably missing her by now.

Theo was going at her as if his very existence depended on sucking every drop of milk from her body. Once in a while he took time out to catch his breath. At this stage, she was anxious to ween him.

Nursing had its drawbacks. It was time-consuming. Often boring. As a distraction, she reached down and with her free hand, retrieved a parcel from one of the boutique bags at her feet, her trophies from the day's assault on Rodeo Drive. Even if she were a pound or two overweight, she could still enjoy perving on the lovely garments.

Shaking the silk shirt free of its tissue wrapping, she held it up, admiring its ivory tones. It was a replica of the shirt she had found in their sunroom last week after Cynthia's visit. Why in their sunroom?

25

CYNTHIA

I'll be a park, and thou shalt be my deer;
Feed where thou wilt, on mountain or in dale:
Graze on my lips, and if those hills be dry,
Stray lower, where the pleasant fountains lie.

Venus and Adonis: William Shakespeare

Santa Monica, Los Angeles
Friday 1st May 1992

I opened the French doors and stepped out onto the balcony, trusting the breeze off the ocean to carry away memories too melancholy for a day like today.

I glanced back at the TV but quickly averted my eyes from the image of a male sprawled face down on the sidewalk, blood oozing from beneath the sheet thrown roughly over the body; a youth left to die in the gutter amid the madness. Some mother's son shot down. And for what? A carton of Lucky Strike? A twenty-four-inch grab-n-go tv?

Soldiers and tanks everywhere. Uniforms and guns. Smoke and bullets. A young man left to die. I leaned over the railing and studied the scene down on the corner of Wiltshire and Ocean. A war zone, I'd said down in the lobby this afternoon. War. A hard act to forget.

A hot summer's night. One to remember but not for the demented chorus of cicadas outside our window, nor for the lush melange of perfumes filtering into the room. Jasmine, gardenia and scented roses climbing up the drainpipes and entwining themselves around the window shutters of the Brays' rambling old Mosman Federation home. A memorable night because I was laying naked beside Jesse. Naked. Moira's daughter. Naked beside her man. Not the dry humping or the desperate groping of two awkward teenagers in a cramped MG. Serious sex. Two lovers locked together, no one to shine a torch on them, no sneaking indoors after midnight fearing the dragon's fire. Love, in and on a bed. A full-sized double bed. A well-sprung mattress and crisp clean sheets.

A mandapam fit for their passion. And all the long carefree perfumed night to enjoy one another, discover the age-old mystery of bodies.

The night, a gift from Connie, sweet devious Connie, scheming to make it possible for Jesse and me to share our last night together in her double bed while she took the hard camp stretcher out back in the old tumbledown shed with its skewwhiff door of peeling paint and rampant choko vines. Darling, darling Connie, soul sister, gifting us our first night together as man and woman. A clandestine interlude between sundown and sunrise, when all too soon the noisy currawongs would call time on us, the joggers come out to jog and smart suited Mosmanites disturb the stillness with slamming doors and clattering garbage bin lids as they set out down garden paths for another ordinary day at the office.

For me and Jesse, however, nothing ordinary about it. For us it was extraordinary, our chance to create everlasting memories. To say our goodbyes.

'I'll always be a part of you, promise me?' he whispered. 'Whatever happens Cindy Lou, you and your Jesse?'

'Always, I promise.'

For Jesse, we were making memories to comfort him for when the jungle threw its worst at him. For me, memories to cling to when the longing became an agony too sorrowful for my heart to bear. Young, though I was, I had the love words for him and I whispered them as I ran my hands over his body, explored the beauty of him. Like a blind person reading brail, I was determined to leave nothing out, determined to commit every part of him and this night to memory. His placid penis that paid instant attention to my touch; the soft skin of his ear lobe and the silkiness of it between my fingertips; the curl of his tongue when I slipped my fingers into his mouth, letting him taste me; the teeth that earlier had nibbled the lips between my thighs; the architecture of his body and face. All of it, because as sure as the sun would come up next morning, I was aware these memories of the Jesse I loved would have to sustain me. Until his safe return. Until the Army returned him to me.

We lay above the tangled sheets, our sweaty bodies intertwined, suntanned legs and arms thrown akimbo across one another, skin touching skin and our breath warm and mingling, smelling of sex.

'Are you scared, Jesse?'

He closed his eyes for a moment, in no hurry to answer. I tried imagining what he saw, what he'd been told, what he'd heard about the place they were sending him.

'Scared?' he said, laying back with arms behind his head and addressing the patterned plaster of the Bray's white ceiling. 'Scared?' said with a shrug of his broad shoulders, the tone of his voice disowning any notion of fear.

'I mean, honestly, just a little. No?'

He turned on his side to face me, propping himself up on his elbow. 'Scared, y'reckon?' Then his infectious laugh. Like an electric shock, it had the power to turn my body into a heaving mass of wild particles, protons of crazy desire. Sex as I had not experienced it until this night of skin on skin. 'Me? Jesse Mitchel McKenzie, scared of a few little guys in black pyjamas comin' at me? Who are you kidding!'

I tossed back the sheet and with arms above my head invited him to feast his eyes on me. I might be a novice but I was a fast learner.

His eyes lit up. 'On second thought, should I be scared?'

Before I could answer him, he reached out and cupped my breasts, sucking my nipples until I felt them contract to fleshy pellets. He grinned up at me to show he was chuffed at how magnificently they had reacted to his tongue. We were both on our L plates but the night was still young. We were learning how it was done and the lessons wouldn't be forgotten any time soon. Knowing, once his hands found my moistness, he'd aroused me again, I wasn't surprised to see him look up and grin. 'I'll have this to come home to, won't I?' he said, raising a quizzical eyebrow when I failed to respond. 'Well? I will, won't I, you little vixen, Jezebel ... you fallen woman?'

My studied silence was meant to tease. Unblinking, I continued to suppress the wicked grin threatening to crack my face. I ummed and ahhd, finger to the lips, eyebrows scrunched as I pretended to ponder the question. Then, in a burst of childish exuberance I leapt across his body and straddled him, captured his face between hot hands. 'No,' I pouted from beneath the curtain of hair blinding us both. 'You. Will. Not,' I growled, tossing my head back. 'Bad, bad soldier boy leaving his girl.' Said while brushing a strangled mess of loose hair away from my face, said as I felt his fingers penetrate me.

Glaring at him with evil intent, I took his hand away and licked the two fingers. No longer grinning, I slid them between his lips. With my free hand, I reached behind my back and took hold of his penis, now once more erect, all the while continuing to hold his gaze.

He took my fingers from his lips. 'Me bad? You bad, lady. You very bad!' he said, taking my fingers and placing his and mine in the soft wet parts of my vagina, pinching my labia and pleasuring my clitoris, that biological wonder. Erotic sensations flooded my body. I tossed back my head and moaned, unashamedly relishing every second of the pleasure coursing through my being, causing muscles I didn't recognize to tense in a glorious way.

'Yes, yes, do it!' I demanded before he slammed his hand across my mouth. I shook it away and tossed my head back, undaunted by the fact we were in the Bray's house and it was the midnight hour. 'For as long as the stars stay out tonight,' I announced theatrically, 'I am Artemis, the goddess of wild nature. And you are ... who are you?' I said, leaning forward to plant my lips on his.

'Me? I'm just the poor sap looking for a promise from his girl,' he said, holding my gaze. 'That's who I am. A bloke holding out for a promise.'

I took a deep breath, swiped a hand across my sweaty forehead and raised my body slightly, tilting my pelvis until I felt us coupling. I straightened up and leant back, knowing now that this gave us both the greatest pleasure. My G-spot, according to Connie's mother's textbooks we had been pouring over. 'I do solemnly promise,' I whispered.

'Then how bad can it be over there?' he said, his hands locked on my hips and beginning to move rhythmically inside me.

A SOLDIER'S LETTERS

1797006X5 Pte J.D. McKenzie
8 R.A.R.
Aust Forces Vietnam
Aust F. PO 3
c/- GPO SYDNEY

To my best and only girl,

Well, here I am, darling Cyn, Your soldier boy… right smack in the middle of the action at last. (by the way, my first trip in a chopper!). We flew into Saigon at night on the big Qantas bird with tracer bullets lighting up the sky. We thought they'd put on the fireworks for us! I knew as soon as I stepped of the plane that I'm far from home … just by the smell of Vietnam – open sewers and rubbish on the streets… the incense and diesel from cars, bikes and machinery. It sure ain't Kansas, Toto! It's May over here too of course but nothing like Spring in Oz. Like when we were down at Burning Palms last Spring with Connie and the others, remember, and all of us ran through the bushes and threw ourselves into the water and then we ran up to our picnic rug (starving! Yeah, in lots of ways!) and found the (bloody!) goannas had run off with our snags! And remember how we got burnt to a frazzle when we fell asleep on the beach (North Bondi) that scorcher of a day last November and finished up too sore to … well, you know … kind of get close to each other for a cuddle … one of your specials! (will the Brass read this! Ha ha!) Do you care what the Brass thinks anyway, my darlin one? Hell, I don't! Probably get court marshalled! Who cares????? Gets me home to you quicker! We sure had some wild fun. Some sweet-lovin times, too. Never (ever!) forget our special times, my beautiful girl. Never! No matter what happens. Always remember it was (and is) just us, you and your Jesse. I'll always be a part of you. Promise? Whatever happens? Always a part of you, yeah?

Are you girls still radical little commos? Been marching again, have we? Spending your nights making those banners? Yeah? Well I guess you won't want the medals your man's gonna bring home? Ha ha ha! Now onto the tour guide part. You know all about the three months at Kapooka, of course (see, I told you I'd write every day … well almost every day!) and all the Basic Training jive and Canungra stuff so here's what happened when we arrived in Vung Tau and the next day were taken on to Nui Dat …

1797006X5 Pte J.D. McKenzie
8 R.A.R.
Aust Forces Vietnam
Aust F. PO 3
c/- GPO SYDNEY

My lovely Artemis, my devine moon goddess, my secret sin!

Bet you'd given me up for dead. Well, we got ourselves caught up in a right little skirmish ... a wee battle that went our way thank God! You've probably heard about it by now. Won't go into detail but just to say I had the crap scared out of me and still can't believe I didn't get hit but came out of it in one piece. Soon be over. Soon be you and me on the road to glory, hey girl? Not long now and we'll be together again and doing the exciting thing! about our future. You at uni, me at college and then wedding bells. How good is that, hey? And how long before the patter of little feet? I'll make a great dad and I know what a little ripper you'll be as a mum.

Thanks for keeping in touch with ma and pop they sure think the world of you (me, too, what do you reckon!!) Wish I ~~was~~ (oops, teacher. Yeah, I know!!) wish I were (subjunctive, right???) there to wrap my arms around you and keep you warm. I've received all the goodies you've been sending. Did I say thanks in my last letter? Hope so. Anyway, THANKS THANKS THANKS sweet Cyndie Loo!

Tell Connie I've found a bloke for her. Lives in Newtown. Rides a Harley. A fair-dinkum Leftie and I've put a big wrap on her and he can't wait to call her when he's home. Jerry's his name. Jerry Nagle. A good sport and a good-looker (but not as handsome and virile as your bloke! Mr Adonis McKenzie!!ha ha!!! Virile for sure. Look out Cyndie Loo!!)

Well, it's late here...10.30pm so guess I'll wrap this up but t'morrow I'll sit under a tree like a true poet and write you a beautiful love letter. In verse (I spend a bit of time scribbling poems You'll see 'em one day I guess unless I look at them when I get back and see how dopey they are in the light of an ordinary Ozzie day!) Or would you rather hear about all the action when I sit down to write t'morrow? all the blah blah about what it's been like since we got back here. No? Okay then, a love letter it's gonna be, girly!!

Till I hold you again,

Your loving Jesse

SWAK xxxxxx

PS...give my best to Paddy and Moira and tell them I'm going to sweep their daughter away on a magic carpet any day soon.

PSS...hope the shop's doing a roaring trade. "Eagle Rock" and "My Sweet Lord" must be selling well, hey?

Jesse xxxxxx

26

SAPPHIRE

To conquer fear is the beginning of wisdom.
Bertrand Russell

Santa Monica, Los Angeles
Friday 1st May 1992

'Quit it! Let go!' Sapphire ordered the two standing behind her who had a death grip on the wheel.

She saw the wannabe rapper disappear around the corner. Was he heading back to the car, starting the engine? Did they plan to abduct her or were they just tormenting her, messing with her head?

'Look, I'm sorry. I shouldn't have done that,' she said to the one whose face she had scratched. 'Please? I must get back. My father will already be sending police to look for me. He knows I'm here and I'm late.' If she could get the jerk to let go her wheel, even for a second, then she could take off and make it out to the street, then she could put on speed and there would be no way to catch her, not on Mateo's bike. They were too drunk, too dumb to move fast. She willed herself to stay calm. Not beg. She had read somewhere that's what turns them on. Be firm. 'Just let me go. Find someone else. I don't like parties.'

'Y'know who you remind me of?' This, from Surfer Joe.

'Sure,' she said with a shrug. 'Jody Foster. Ho hum. Everyone tells me that.' She stood patiently astride the bike, her feet planted, her hands on the bars and her eyes drilling into their dumb skulls, trying to calculate the level of danger.

'And if we don't let you go?' said the surfie who still had a grip on the wheel. He leant in and whispered in her ear. 'We might have other plans for you.'

Using the full weight of her upper body, in one swift movement she spun around and caught him across his ear with her forearm. He yelped and let go the wheel. Only for a second but long enough. She had the break. Taking advantage of the moment, she pressed her feet to the peddles and shot off, racing to the corner of the building, turning and putting on more speed as she flew down the side path towards 6th. Her arm stung from the walloping she'd given him, but it was a pain she could tolerate. She shot a quick glance over her shoulder and saw the rainbow colours of the Hawaiian shirt coming after her.

'Bitch!' he yelled.

It didn't matter. She was on wheels and she was getting away. Her heart raced. Blood rushed to her head as she headed down towards the Avenue and safety. Was it coming out her ears and nose, the blood? No, it just felt that way, as if her head would explode. Then she saw it; the red convertible sitting at the curb, with Rapper Boy perched on the bonnet. He jumped off and tumbled up the path as fast as his bulk would let him. When she looked behind, she saw the surfie coming closer.

'Fucking bitch! Fuck you! You're done!' he called out. 'Grab her, Jazzy!'

Jazzy got there first, his massive bulk looming up in front like some giant monolith as she powered towards it.

'Out of my way!' she yelled, swerving to avoid crashing into him but tumbling the bike and landing hard on the grass verge, the bike on top with its wheels spinning.

'Gotcha!' said the bully as he grabbed her under her armpits and with her heels trailing the ground, dragged her back up the path.

She tugged at his hands. In vain. He was under instructions, not letting go, no matter how hard she tried to unlock his fingers or dug her nails into the flesh. She wanted her mother. Connie, coming at him to land a mother blow across his ugly skull with her rolling pin.

'What y'gonna do now?' he said as he dragged her to her feet and pushed her back into the courtyard.

'The fucking bitch! Let me at her,' said the greaseball as he shoved his surfie mate out of his way.

She saw the marks, angry red scratches down the left side of his cheek. She turned her body violently from side to side, tried reaching up to grab his hair. It was useless. She was their captive. This is how it would be, three of them.

'Back off. I've got it,' said the surfie, dropping her down onto the hard surface and propping himself in front of her, pinning her with his boot. He removed his dark shades, sticking them in his shirt pocket and let his eyes roam over her body. 'But she's gonna say 'sorry', aren't you, babe, hey?'

She attempted to get up but the surfie jammed his foot harder on her diaphragm.

'I'm sorry. Now let me go and you can get to your party.' She shook her head. 'This isn't smart. They know where I am. You don't want to …' The words died in her mouth. She couldn't finish the threat. 'Just let me go. C'mon.'

'Where in Australia y'from?'

'Sydney. By the beach.' Even flat on her back with a foot on her chest, she could talk herself out of this. 'You know—Shrimp on the Barbie—Crocodile Dundee and all that. Did you ever see the movie?'

'That ain't a knife,' said grinning Jazzy. 'This is a knife.' He grinned and waved an imaginary knife in her face. Imaginary, but she flinched. The intimidating performance was probably the bravest thing he had done in his life, she surmised. With luck, this might be just a game for these juvenile idiots. It was still broad daylight in a public place, after all.

And then suddenly the dark one put his hands under her arms and the surfie had her by her feet. They lifted her off the ground and carried her like a rag doll further into the deserted courtyard.

She heard the scream inside her head. Had she let it out? Mummy, mummy help me! It was what she thought she screamed out but had she? And even in her terror, it struck her it had been years since she had called Connie, 'Mummy'. The courtyard was so vast and empty she knew her screams would have no effect. She felt a hand go over her mouth. They dumped her beside a large power box.

Jazzy stood over her, his foot on her chest and waving a penknife, this time an unambiguous threat. The surfie brushed Jazzy aside and she saw the idiot stumble backwards, swaying drunkenly. She tried to get up. The dark one wore a menacing grin.

'No!' she begged as she looked from him to the surfie who had reached for his zipper. She struggled, kicked and tried to free herself from the foot he slammed on her chest. It winded her. She bucked and kicked some more but now she felt the dark one behind her, pinning her shoulders hard to the ground. She flayed her legs, tossed from side to side. Screamed. No use. Her screams echoed around the cavernous quadrangle. They laughed at her. She tried to stay calm and think strategically. She would tell them she had AIDS.

'You don't wanna party, darlin'? Really?' whispered the greaseball into her ear, the one with black greasy hair, the dark smelly one. 'A nice girl like you from Down Under? C'mon.'

'A party. Know what I mean?' said the surfie as he jerked his hips to emphasize his meaning. 'Whadda ya say? Y'wanna live a little?' He reached down and yanked up her t-shirt.

Before he could lay a hand on her breast, she raised her head and spat in his eye, saw her spittle drip down his cheek, watched as he wiped it away with the back of his hand.

Suddenly, she shot her foot up into his groin.

'Cunt!' He doubled over and stumbled backwards, moaning.

Before they could grab her, she rolled over, jumped to her feet and took off. The bike! She had to get to the bike!

They cut her off, the greaseball from behind, the surfie in front. Jazzy caught the keys thrown at him and ran for the car.

The surfie seized her by the shoulders, spun her around and slammed her up against the wall, banging her head and smothering her face with a rough hand. He thrust his free hand between her thighs and pushed his body up hard against hers. 'A little spitfire, hey? And all we wanna do is show you a good time. And we're gonna. Okay? We're gonna. Y'comin' with us!' He clutched her breast with one hand, with the other he kept her pinned to the wall.

She came up with her knee. He saw it coming this time, grabbed it and laughed, heard the other one laughing too, chanting obscenities.

The greaseball shoved the surfie aside and pulled her to the ground, threw his legs across her body and fell to his knees, fumbling with his zipper. She twisted and bucked, managing to free one hand to claw at him, pull his hair. He grabbed her hands and pinned them by her side, bringing his face close to hers. She tossed her head to the side, not wanting to give him the pleasure of seeing her fear.

That's when she saw them.

At the side entrance of the building over in the distance, through her terror she picked out two darkened silhouettes behind the glass doors. Saw the door open and a female in a heavy dark uniform step out and stand in the doorway.

'Help!' she screamed before her attacker could muzzle her.

A man came up behind the woman. Tall, skinny and bent, leaning on a stick. The two had their heads together studying a rolled-out document. She tried to scream again but they had her mouth covered. Only she had seen the adults, see the man turn his back and lock the building.

Not knowing where her strength came from but understanding this pair way over the other side of the courtyard were the only thing standing between her and this violence, she managed to free herself long enough to let out a scream to carry across the deserted area. She saw the uniformed woman suddenly shove the document at the man and take off, screaming, 'Police. Don't move!'

'Let's go! Let's go!' yelled the bolting surfie, finally seeing what was happening, shouting over his shoulder to the greaseball who looked up and saw the woman racing towards them. Still with his fly undone, he leapt off, tripping over his feet in his frantic effort to flee.

Stumbling to her feet and straightening her shirt and vest, she ran towards the open arms of the woman, gasping, trying to catch her breath, collapsing in the woman's arms She felt her knees buckle so that her rescuer had to hold her tight to stop her falling to the ground. They stood locked together for seconds, the woman brushing the hair away from her face and murmuring soothing words into her ear. She hugged the lady. The cushiony chest was the mother she needed.

'Mr Olsen!' the woman turned and yelled over her shoulder, beckoning to the frail man hobbling on his walking stick towards them. 'Wait here, pet. You'll be fine, okay? Mr Olsen's going to help you. He's the librarian. I'm going after them.' The uniformed woman was about to speak into the phone strapped to her shoulder.

'No! Please don't!' she said, grabbing the woman's sleeve. 'No. It's okay, it's okay. I'm okay.' The thought of her parents finding out about this was too much. They mustn't, not ever. It would be the end of her freedom. She was safe. She was shocked and ashamed but she was safe and that was all that mattered. There was Mateo's bike to worry about.

'I'll be back!' the woman said as she waved to the man who had finally hobbled towards them. 'Take her inside. Sit her down, Mr Olsen. I'll be back.'

'Please don't?' Sapphire implored her rescuer, still clinging to the woman's arm. 'They were just drunk. My parents must never know. Please?' Her school friends must never know, either. No one must ever know. 'My fault. I was crazy to come here on my own. This time of the day. It was a stupid idea. Please?' She could see now the woman was a fire-fighter, not a policewoman. 'Thank you, I'm okay. They didn't hurt me. Truly. They're just drunks.'

'They might be drunks but they're also criminals, sweetheart. I saw them. Look at you, your tights are torn. You look ... you look ... oh, you poor baby. They attacked you. God knows, if we hadn't ...' The firefighter left off presuming what could have happened to her.

'You're trembling, darling,' she said, hugging her again, so hard that Sapphire could feel the scratchy bits of the firefighter's uniform on her cheek. 'You've had a shock, a terrible shock. Mr Olsen, thank you. Please look after her. Take her inside and find her something to drink. Something warm with plenty of sugar, okay?'

The librarian nodded and took her arm. She resisted but the fire firefighter, ignoring her pleas, took off. She watched as the woman approached the corner, speaking into her shoulder as she ran. She hadn't mentioned the red convertible. She knew they wouldn't have stuck around.

'Miss?' the librarian said, pointing back across to the library doors. 'Come inside with me, dear. You need to tell us who you are and who can collect you, okay? This must be reported. We saw the attack.'

'No!' she said, shaking her head violently. 'No. You can't say anything. You can't report it. It's okay. It's okay. I'm alright. Thank you. Excuse me, please, I've gotta get my bike. I have to go.' She was on her way to the fallen bicycle, determined to leave all this behind. She feared sticking around out of politeness because a police car might be screaming into the courtyard at any moment. Unless, and she hoped it was true, they were all too busy with the riots.

'Girlie!' the librarian called after her as she mounted the bike in time to see the red convertible disappear down 6th, onto Santa Monica Boulevard. The firefighter had missed them. The woman came walking back, shaking her head. She indicated the grey SUV parked over by the library doors. 'Let's talk about it on the way. I'll get you home. What's your name, pet?'

No answer.

'Your bike? I can pop it in the back. No problem.'

What were her options, she wondered? Parents who would come down on you like a tonne of bricks, grounding you and killing any expectations you had of a fun time this week. No chance of going with Nick to Hawaii—against the fear of what could be waiting for you out there on the streets before you could make it back to the Miramar.

She gave an involuntary shudder and eventually dismounted, allowing the woman to wheel Mateo's bike across the courtyard to the grey vehicle.

'One hundred-and-seventy-four stupid doofus idiots,' she said, more to herself than to her rescuer.

'Pardon?' said the woman, spinning her head around to catch the softly spoken words.

'One hundred-and-seventy-four stoned drunken imbeciles.'

'Right,' the firefighter said, looking quizzically to the equally perplexed librarian. 'One-hundred-and-seventy-four … what did you say?

'Stupid doofus idiots.'

'Okay. Got it. I'm Gloria, by the way, pet. Gloria Martinez. Let's get you inside first, I think. Make you a cup of tea. You've had a shock.' She looked to the man. 'Or maybe we have Coke in the fridge, Mr Olsen?'

'We do. That young Declan fellow. He keeps the fridge stocked.'

No use resisting these kind people. She let them lead her into the shelter of the library, Gloria with her arm around her waist as they walked slowly, letting Mr Olsen keep up with them.

She leaned her head on the kind woman's shoulder and let herself give in to the tears she'd been holding back. She'd felt so helpless back there on the ground. Not just scared but helpless, powerless against them. Her excursion to the library to research Governor Clinton's policies had seemed like a good idea. But it had all gone so wrong.

She felt a sudden surge of anger and resentment as she stepped into the library, not in the way she had a right to enter the place—notebook in hand and ready to work—but still shaken and feeling demeaned. Her rights violated. Needing the kindness of two strangers.

27

CYNTHIA

You can't always get what you want
But if you try ...
Keith Richards/Mick Jagger

Santa Monica, Los Angeles
Friday 1st May 1992

I stood on the balcony, clutching the railing, leaning over to view the commotion down at the Pier where red and blue lights flashed above LAPD vehicles and a crowd of noisy demonstrators gathered.

Cable news and the networks must be revelling in the mayhem. Salivating over their ratings. Three fires per minute. Eight thousand police ordered onto the streets. Tanks rolling into town. Gangs stealing firearms from pawn shops and gun dealers. Drama like this is manna for the cables. A windfall. And back home it was the usual dull Saturday. Back in the room I raided the minibar for ice.

Despite the smoke-contaminated air out on the streets, I returned to the patio and sat at one of the comfortable cane chairs, resting the old-fashioned on the small table. In passing, it struck me how dangerous, having this outdoor furniture here on this high balcony.

Opening my fist and holding it high over the glass, I let the ice slop into the whiskey. No slow balletic rise of glorious drops of amber liquid floating skyward in slo-mo to the accompaniment of symphonic strings, the blue Pacific in the background. Only in thirty-second tvc's, such fantasies. Such lies. The ad men. It felt good to be out of the lying game, even if my plans for an alternative future in the movie industry had hit a brick wall today.

Splashes of the golden liquid glistened on the glass tabletop. I stared at them for an eternity before I bent over and licked them up, every drop. Holding the tumbler up to the fading sunlight, I studied the contents and finally decided against ice, fisting the cubes out and tossing them way out towards the ocean. Eventually, the gym but for the moment, the balcony and the comfortable chair seemed as good a place as any to sit and stare at nothing.

It is a truth universally acknowledged that at this moment Cynthia Lorraine Smart you are a woman with fuck-all going for you. No man, no business partnership, no job, even. And as of this morning, no film project.

No baby, either. A womb too tricky to be of any value to the human race.

Would you do it for me, Con? My last chance, my last chance, sister. Time's running out.

Complicated, said Connie.

Too complicated, obviously. The sisterly ties snapped last week up on the mountain, stretched taught and snapped under the strain of an obligation too onerous to be considered. Surrogacy was not on the menu. Delusional to expect so much, even of Connie.

Shall we take our coffees out onto the veranda? It was a balmy night in the majestic Blue Mountains, too cool for al fresco, but the Labelles took the hint, anyway. I had come to ask something of them and required the right setting. Not their cosy kitchen but the grandness of the vistas.

Unlike me to just shoot up to the mountains on a whim. I was still, after all these years, wondering about the Labelles' Westward-Ho migration. Why the Great Leap Forward, moving from a smart, modern Clovelly house overlooking the ocean to a rambling old run-down timber cottage way up in the god-forsaken Blue Mountains. Maybe there was something to be said for raising families in the clean mountain air; long walks in pine forests, beanies and woolly mittens, snowballs hurled, snowmen built, going home to marshmallowy hot chocolates in front of roaring log fires. I couldn't live the life. The Labelles were welcome to their mountain retreat. Did they do the big swap as part of their breeding program? Why else? Six years ago, I questioned the move and still did. No doubt it was safer than the Eastern Suburbs for raising kids and possibly a better class of humanity than the stock market crooks and their Lady Lunchalots.

Sunday morning, early. Calling them, suggesting I pay a visit.

Sweet Connie jumping at the idea. Sure. Come on up, love.

What should I bring, Con? I'll bring wine and ... what else?

David chiming in, requesting one of the lip-slapping delicious French tarts from Lulu's of Paddington. A favourite of his. Done, I said. See you soon.

Stay the night, they insisted. You're not driving back down to Sydney in the dark.

Ready for the convivial visit—if not for the mountain hike the rosy-cheeked mountain folk forced on me—I arrived mid-morning and found the whole family rugged up and ready to yodel. Accepting David's offer of his cashmere coat and woolly scarf, I trudged the nearby forest with the family. Off in search of dry twigs and cones, the children gathering basketfuls for David to add to the roaring log fire he already had going in the living room.

We ate late afternoon hot dogs around the fire, adults and kid, even a couple of random juveniles who seemed to have materialized while Connie was preparing the shoulder of lamb for our dinner—rubbing it lovingly with garlic, olive oil, lemon juice and the all-important dry oregano—and I was busy peeling bucketloads of potatoes. No Bray roast dinner was ever complete without Rosemary's legendary crispy hassle-back potatoes. The usual minted green peas and cauliflower au gratin would complement the roast, said Con, topping up our glasses with David's favourite beverage, the Grange Hermitage we'd sneaked from his cellar.

It had been that way for Connie and me since we were kids. During our Mosman girlhood Rosemary had taught us how to bake the perfect hassle-back spud. Her trick in preparing the potatoes was to ram a metal skewer through the half-way mark of the big Sebagoes or Desirees so that when she sliced down into them to create the regularly spaced cuts, her knife hit metal, stopping at the right point. She would spread sliced onions across the base of the big buttered blue and white Corning-ware dish and nestle the spuds in there before carefully pouring homemade chicken stock around the base. A sprinkle of pepper and salt, a dob or ten of butter and into the furnace. If the Frenchie got off on the smell of madeleines, then hassle-back spuds were our remembrance of things past.

Con could serve up a decent meal, I grant the woman that. Homely cooking but satisfying. Two Tyrrells Hunter Valley Semillons from my Paddington cellar with the mains and one of David's favoured sauternes to wash down the exquisite pear-and-custard tart from Queen Street. Not enough in the tart for the whole tribe of hungry little Labelles, but tough luck. Given Lulu's prices, it was adult food. Had I thought of it, I could have brought up the pile of leftover Easter eggs sitting in my fridge. Connie fed the children first, the youngest ones, that is. As a teenager, it was apparently mandatory that Sapphire be included on the adults' table, which made things awkward and not part of my plan.

How about you start with the dishes, my darling girl?

You want to talk grown-up crap, right? I should just shut up and go to bed, right?

Kind of.

Okay. That's all you had to say, godmother, dearest. I shall vamoose. It is a far, far better thing I do than I have ever done. It is a far, far better rest I go to than I have ever known. *A Sale of Two Titties*. Goodnight, all.

And so, there we were, finally; three adults. Three old friends. Closer than salt and pepper. Under a mountain moon. A favour being asked and all three doing their best to navigate what they knew was about to be one of the most awkward moment of their lives.

The embarrassment was palpable when husband and wife turned down my outrageous, selfish proposition. I witnessed it in all its poignancy, knowing my friends understood the hurt I felt. God, the hangdog looks. I had come begging and they had kicked me to the gutter. Turned their faces from me. Connie's womb not for hire. No gift of a child for the barren friend.

Around midnight, after he came into the kitchen to find me alone with a glass of wine in my hand standing among a sink-full of dirty dishes and wishing I were dead, David switched off the bright kitchen light and came across to me, pulling me away from the sink and putting a consoling arm around my shoulder. He kissed my forehead. As would a brother, had I a brother. Then he hugged me. We love you, Cyn, he whispered. You know that don't you? All of us, we love you. He looked up when Connie came into the kitchen to fill a glass of water. We love her, don't we, Con? he said, releasing me.

Connie at the sink, turning off the tap, looked at both of us and shrugged. Of course. Goodnight.

The terse dismissal weighed heavy in the room. For Connie, I guess it was resentment, having been asked tonight what I'd asked of her. For me, mortification. Absolute abasement.

What do you say we open a bottle, Con, I said, trying to keep her in the kitchen, hoping to ease the tension? Take a walk in the garden. Let's drink. The night's still young. The night might be young for you, Cynthia, said Connie but I've got five kids to get off to school in the morning. Knock yourselves out, you two. I'm off to bed. Acknowledging the rebuff, I watched her disappear down the hall and into the bedroom. Fair enough.

I turned to David and raised my glass. Honestly? Me with a kid? I took a swill and tipped the dregs in the sink. I'm not cut out for motherhood. Too selfish. You did me a favour, you guys. It was a rush of blood to the head. I grabbed the half empty merlot by the neck and with my glass, walked into the sunroom. Night's young. I'm fine. Go to Connie. She needs you. I'm good. I'll go get some more logs for you, Cyn. Back in a flash.

Later, much later, after we had finished off a bottle of the Labelle's finest and smoked a joint of native mountain weed—with David kneeling, adding logs to the fire and his back to me—I did the unforgivable.

When he turned around and stood up, I offered him the glass. And then I offered myself.

The flashing red and blue lights of two NYPD black & whites screaming along Ocean brought me back to the present. The whiskey, hot and fiery as it flowed through me, left in its path a carapace as brittle as lava rock. I continued to stare into the void of a violent sunset. As I'd said to David, I wasn't the stuff mothers are made of. I was no Connie Labelle, that was for certain.

The police were heading north, passing a group of protesters who, on cue, waved their banners and shouted at the cops. Good for them. I imagined Sapphire in a couple of years doing the same. Sapphire, my precious—and these days precocious—goddaughter, growing up too fast. In no time, at university, a young woman of the world. Connie had all the luck. I smiled, recalling the teenager's supercilious but erudite Charles Dickens quip last week.

The sight of two army tanks stationed further along the avenue near the Pier was jarring. Troops in camouflage uniforms and boasting a serious display of weaponry standing ready for action. The tanks, the soldiers, the protesters, the police cars and the billowing flames underlined the life-and-death gravity of what was Los Angeles tonight. CNN had its live coverage of the fires raging on Normandie and 79th Street. Now a shot of a lone pedestrian, a Korean man trying to put out the fire devouring his property, armed with nothing more than a garden hose. The Korean didn't deserve the grief.

I returned my gaze to the unnatural sight of a militarized beachfront outside my window. And in other parts of L.A., burning cars, burning buildings, ugly black clouds of smoke blanketing the city. Livelihoods being destroyed as I stood looking down on it all. Lives shattered. The stench must be putrid for those in the thick of it.

What time was it? And what did it matter anyway, I was a prisoner of the Miramar. Step a foot out of line down where those tanks were rolling into position, where six thousand locked-and-loaded National Guard were now, according to the bulletins, patrolling the wider city radius, and if the bozos didn't gun you down first, they'd for sure arrest you. Los Angeles tonight.

I wondered how Connie would handle the curfew. Locked up with two kids in a small space and her drinks soiree to organize. But Con had an endless capacity for handling mayhem. God knows, I'd got a close-up of the family variety, a la Katoomba, last week.

28

CYNTHIA

A quarrel between friends, when made up,
adds a new tie to friendship.
Saint Francis de Sales

Katoomba, New South Wales, Australia
April 1992

Bedlam has many faces and Chez Labelle could rightly lay claim to one: Its name is Chaos.

Beyond the bathroom walls, Monday morning madness reigned at the home of the Katoomba Labelles. I shivered as I stepped from the tub, reaching for David's emerald green terry towelling bathrobe hooked on the back of the door. Even in summer it was cold on the mountains and god knows, despite my Nordic Celtic heritage, I loathed the cold. Bending double, I shook out my wet hair and flipped it back over my shoulders, spraying water against the tiles. The mirror was too steamy to check it out but before I stepped into the bath, I'd noticed the regrowth. Due for highlights. Claude could do them. Or maybe wait till L.A. Find a chic salon. Westwood or Bel Air. A place where the stars hang out, where I might find myself sitting next to a Susan Sarandon or a Meryl Streep. A girl can dream. I was trying to think of anything other than think about last night.

I leant my aching head against the wall and tried to tune out the cacophony down the hall long enough to picture myself sitting in a gold and white boutique beauty parlour. A place with gilded chairs and mirrors, huge vases of elaborate floral arrangements, black and white marble floors and beautiful people fussing with busy scissors and combs. I pictured myself sitting there reading my screenplay when Meryl, noticing the script, raises a curious eyebrow. By the time we're foiled up and waiting for the goo to do its work, Meryl mentions some young up-and-comer she'd like to have read the screenplay.

A blood-curdling scream shattered the pretty picture. Siblings going crazy somewhere in the vast old house. Tearing each other apart, by the sound of it. Poor Connie. This, every day? Kill me now.

I left the sanctuary of the steamy bathroom with its pink and black décor, its huge square art deco basin, its corroding copper gargoyle taps, and stood for a moment outside the door, clutching the bathrobe tight around my body. Far off down the hall, in the nether regions of their playroom area I could hear the shrill screams of the sparring Labelles competing with a blaring TV. As if that weren't enough, over the top of their battle cries and the nerve-shattering voices of moronic cartoon characters, I heard baby Theo bellowing his lungs out. Presumably for Connie's boobs. The child was only ever happy when he was sucking, piglet-like, on his mother's teats.

They were doing my head in, the children, but sooner or later I had to make it out to the kitchen and face the madness. And face Connie. One of these days we might laugh about what happened last night. But not today. Today, feelings were raw and stepping out to meet Connie in the harsh light of this Monday morning madness was a challenge.

I found the domestic goddess standing at her kitchen bench slathering sloppy greasy butter across an endless row of bread slices. Connie was wrapped in a faded purple kimono, which I remembered from a decade ago when the two of us went on a girls' week to Byron Bay. It has a hand-painted fiery dragon climbing up the back of it. A beautiful garment I'd made her purchase and surprised it still survived. I took a deep breath, marshalled my thoughts, and walked bravely into the kitchen and put a hand on her arm. 'Morning, my lovely one.'

Silence. Connie went to the fridge, returning to take up the buttering with a renewed vengeance.

'Feeling okay?'

'Why wouldn't I be?' Connie, not looking up from her labours. This was the cold shoulder. The message clear. Back off. Okay, I was being punished and deserved to be. It was an outrageous thing to ask of another woman, even your best mate, your soul sister. If only I could take back last night. The whole disastrous night.

'Con, I—'

'Hey, turn it down, you lot!' screamed Connie. 'And get a move on! It's past eight.' She ceased her buttering and holding her knife in the air asked, 'How do you feel, lady?'

It was a loaded question. But how loaded? 'Hung over, I guess. You?'

'I'm a feeding mother, remember? Early to bed, early to rise, makes a woman—'

'Healthy, wealthy and wise.'

Connie gave a shrug and went back to buttering. Resentment fouled the air.

'You're a good mum, Con. They love you and it's no wonder.' I rested my hand on Connie's shoulder for an instant. 'Everyone loves Connie Bray.' I planted a kiss on the side of her cheek before heading for the picture window across the other side of the cavernous family room, making sure, in my bare feet, to step gingerly around wooden train lines and Lego blocks scattered like votive offerings on the thread-bare Persian rug.

'Apologies for the mess,' said Connie. 'Try getting them to pick it up.'

'Tried a wooden spoon?' I said as I looked out through windows still clouded with early morning mountain frost. 'Never hurt us, did it?' With the sleeve of the bathrobe, I wiped the glass to make a viewing space. It was a magnificent sight. Across the gorge, way off in the distance were the iconic Three Sisters. When I leant in and breathed heavily onto the glass it fogged up again. No matter.

I stayed, staring at the distorted view. 'Our mums used them, the spoons. A whack across the back of the legs. Remember? Didn't hurt us one bit. Kids need to know who's boss, Con.'

'The coffee pot's there,' Connie, with a nod and no pretence at pouring for her guest. 'Orange juice in the fridge. Sorry, I'm running behind on these lunches.' She looked up for a moment to direct her voice to the back of the house. 'Turn that dammed thing down, you, guys. Or turn it off, better still!'

'You're yelling into the void, Con. No one's listening, hon. Mind if I turn this up, though?' I indicated the small radio sitting on the sideboard near the family's fruit bowl. 'Keating's up in Kokoda.' I looked at Connie. She had stopped spreading and slicing. Her hand was at her forehead, eyes closed. 'You, okay?'

Connie put her hand up. 'Sure, sure I'm okay. Didn't drink last night, but I've still got this punishing—'

'I've got Panadol in my bag. Hasn't cut through my pain but yours might be of a lower order. I'll go get it.'

'Idiot. I'm breast-feeding.'

'Which means?'

'Which means, what the Hell do you think it means?'

'Well, someone's dragging her Cross around this morning. Are you sure the Almanac of Perfect Mothering forbids Panadol for lactating women?' Martyrdom was wearying.

'He won't give me Barbie,' sobbed Francesca, the nine-year-old Labelle as she came tearing into the kitchen. 'He's ripping her clothes off.'

'Stop tormenting your twin, Jack! Grow a brain, why don't you?' yelled Connie as I watched how adroitly she slapped cheese and tomato down on two of the buttered slices then topped them. 'It's too late to be playing with Barbie, anyways. Put her away.'

Connie reached for the bread knife and the metal sandwich slicing aid. She held it up for show. 'A little knick-knack I picked up at Vinnie's. Lends the job a sense of professionalism, don't you reckon? Labelle's Delicatessen.' She used it to slice neatly through the two sandwiches.

I copped the facetiousness. Con was driving home a point: Don't expect détente this side of an apology. But for all the lack of sensitivity last night, it was still me and not her who'd copped the lousy prognosis. Connie's hormones were thriving, her life overflowing with joy. I turned back to the vast mountain vistas and the valleys beyond the window.

Harry, the four-year-old—or had he turned five—came bursting out of nowhere and stood at his mother's side, his big blue cow-like eyes fixed on her. 'He's got your eyes, Con. Big baby-blues and those long dark lashes. A handsome little tyke. How'd you manage it?' I said, gazing on the mother and son tableau.

Connie shrugged. 'It happens.'

Well, I'd tried. I returned to tuning the radio knobs to the ABC's A.M. program. 'I wonder if the Prime Minister's actually going to walk the Kokoda Track or if it's just a photo op? I can't see it, really; Keating traipsing through the mud up those mountains in his Zegna suit and Ferragamo boots.'

Silence.

'I'd love to do the Kokoda Track someday. We should do it, just you and me, Con?'

'As if.'

'Yeah, I reckon we should when you've—you know—weened Theo. Us, doing the famous Kokoda Track together.' I wasn't giving up.

'Trail,' came the voice at my back. 'It's Kokoda Trail, not track, I believe.'

'Well, is it now, miss?' I spun around and caught my goddaughter entering the room. This could be an icebreaker.

Sapphire came and stood beside me at the window. I put my arm out to welcome the teenager and left it resting on the girl's shoulder, loving the warmth of human contact. 'And what would you know, young Sapphire Cristos-Labelle? And by the way, how about starting with "Good morning darling godmother."?' I looked across at Connie, still at the kitchen bench, and whispered. 'We're just a little short on pleasantries this morning, Sapphie.'

The teenager grinned. 'Morning Mummy,' said Sapphire, throwing her mother a bundle of air kisses from across the room.

'I love this goddaughter of mine, Con.' I rubbed cheeks with Sapphire. 'She's a special girl,' I added, slapping Sapphire's backside. 'Whacky as all-get-out. I got high hopes for her. I think she's going to rock the world, someday.'

'Our little ray of sunshine,' muttered Connie from her bench.

'Ray of sunshine, hey? I know this much; she won't stop growing. She's going to be taller than both of us. What are you feeding her?'

'She's not feeding me,' whined Sapphire. 'They keep me locked up in a dungeon, feet chained to the floor. Bread and water once a week. Save me, godmother, please? Save me. Take me away from all this!'

'Funny girl. Really, how tall are you now?' I looked across to Connie. 'What do you reckon Mother of Many over there? How tall is your darling daughter?'

'Play lunch and lunch, little lunch and big lunch. Okay?' said Connie, as she beamed love down at Harry. 'What we call these lunchbox things depends on which teacher is in charge on the day, doesn't it little man?' She looked up from Harry and across to her eldest child. 'Who do you reckon she looks like these days, me, Nick or David?'

A slight thawing. 'Your chin and mouth, your dimples. But she's got eyes like a cat.'

'Amber. Cat's eyes. Nick's.' She turned back to her son. The small boy looked pained, impatiently waiting for his mother to return her attention to him and finish making his sandwiches. 'Okay, young 'Arry, I'm on it.' She ruffled the little boy's head. 'He's started demanding I cut his sangers in squares not triangles, Aunty Cyn. Triangles are for sissies, apparently. A chauvinist is our young 'Arry.' Connie was smiling down at the upturned face hanging at her side. 'Two even halves. Crusts off, thank you. Harry's sandwiches are big business around here. Done the wrong way and it can bring on a tantrum that lasts all the way to the kindy gate. Isn't that right, Sir Harry?'

'Indonesia's economy is growing at seven per cent a year these days, would you believe?' I had just caught the tail-end of the bulletin above Connie's prattle.

'Cheese and Vegemite, okay?' Connie held up the serrated-edged knife. 'And cut in triangles, right? Four triangles?'

'Christ!' I swear the child's screams rattled the walls of the old timber house. It felt like a piece of four by two to the back of the skull. I put my ear in closer to the radio, tried to ignore the tantrum.

'Mummy's only kidding, Harry. We make little squares, okay.'

'We're learning in Australian History about the war up there,' said Sapphire. 'Two thousand Australian soldiers died in New—'

'Sixteen hundred, sweetheart. Rounded out. Still set on journalism?'

'Sure am, Goddy. Foreign correspondent.'

'Well, all that back and forth to the States since you were old enough to stand up. You've done plenty of travel for a kid your age, I suppose.'

'A kid?'

'Sorry.'

'Just peanut butter thanks, Mummy,' Sapphire called out to Connie. 'With all the rest that is, of course, my dearest, darling, sweetest one—and could you squeeze some lemon on it, please—please?' She turned back to me. 'The lemon juice stops the apple going brown, right?'

'I wouldn't have a clue. Ask your mother. She's the Queen of the Kitchen.'

Connie looked up from her work and shot her guest a look to kill.

'Sorry.' Irony was not on today's menu. We were back on dangerous ground. My fault.

'You must honour our individuality, darling mother. What we choose to have on our sandwich reflects our personality. It helps to define us.'

'What personality? It's kinda disappeared down the drain these days.'

'Mother! Please?'

'Just saying. I miss she who once was.'

'Yeah, I'm a sour sister. Right, Goddy?'

'You're a nut case, I know that much,' said Connie.

'Don't forget; two kiwi fruits and a spoon, okay?' Sapphire crossed the room to her mother, put an arm around her and kissed her cheek. With a smug look indicating she knew she had placated her mother for the time being, she grabbed her school panama from where it had previously been frisbeed onto the sofa and jammed it over her heavy plaits. 'And my pot of yoghurt, please mummy dearest.'

'She remind you of anyone, Con?' Seeing her goddaughter with plaits and panama I was back with thirteen-year-old Connie Bray, my newest best friend. My God, we had come a long way to get to this uncomfortable morning.

'All the girls in her class are into this kiwi and yoghurt crap,' said Connie with benevolent cynicism.

I noticed her put a hand up to her breasts. The kimono had fallen open, displaying the fullness, rivers of blue veins and tiny stretch marks across the creamy white skin. Milky circles shading the mauve satin where her nipples pushed at the fabric. Con still had last night's mascara under her eyes. Unbrushed curls fell around her face and over her shoulders. For a mother of five kids, I had to admit that Constance Labelle, nee Bray, still had it in spades, what it took to stir a man's blood. A stressed-out mum she might be, but she still looked sensational. As Rubenesque as ever. Even under pressure. That's what healthy hormones do for a woman, I thought and with a shiver, tightened David's bath robe around my skinny body. At the stove, I poured coffee into two hand-painted stoneware mugs, offering one to Connie. The offer was ignored. Down at the end of the hall, the baby's bellowing started up again.

'Should Sapphie get him up and bring him out here, Con? He sounds unhappy.' I wanted nothing more than for the noise to cease.

'I'm too busy, here,' said Connie from her bread buttering bench.

'Will he cop a bottle?'

'Hates the bottle.'

'He tosses his head and scratches her ... y'know... her boobs,' said Sapphire. Throws raspberries at her.'

'He thinks these are his birthright,' said Connie, checking her breasts and grimacing at the stickiness staining her kimono. 'I'm trying to starve him, make him wait for a feed so he'll take the bottle.'

'Like a big fat jersey cow,' said Sapphire, doing her best to show she thought the whole process repulsive.

'Watch your mouth, kiddo,' said Connie.

'On both sangers, thanks,' Sapphire whispered into her mother's ear as she came up behind and pinched her backside.

'That's it, right? That's your lunch order today, is it Miss?' Connie spun around and yanked her daughter's school hat down over her eyes.

'Hey, stop it, you!'

'So, for the sangers it's a peanut butter base with grated carrot, apple and sultanas, plus sliced celery? Oh, and the lemon juice, of course. How could I forget the lemon juice! That do you, Miss? Have I got it?'

'You got it, Mother of Mine.' Sapphire shot a wink at me before turning back to Connie. 'Scrumptious. Ta. Love you, mummy.'

'Where is all this coming from?' said Connie. 'Last week it was sprouts, tahini and grated carrot with dates.' She cast her eyes up to the big wall clock. 'The ABC theme's kicking in soon, you lot,' she shouted to her brood at the back of the house. 'That means it's 8.30, so you better get a wriggle on.' She laid down the knife and stuck her head into the hallway. 'Did you hear me, you guys down there?' she screeched 'Get a move on!'

'Jesus, Con.'

Immediately, I regretted letting fly with the exclamation but like a shard of glass, the screeching had stabbed the base of my aching skull. 'The gorgon knots,' I said with an attempt at humour as I held my head and twisted it side to side. 'Self-imposed. Pity me, not.' Carrying my coffee mug across to the booth in the corner of the large messy family room, I slid my backside in, opposite Sapphire. The massive eight-seater café booth with its high backs and red mock leather cushions dominated this part of the open-style room, serving as the Labelle's main and only dinner table—the original dining room having been converted to Connie's sewing and ironing domain.

The booth, I knew, was David's handiwork. The backyard carpenter showing off his skills. Making a practical assault on seating his large brood. How did it happen, all this fecundity? As kids, Connie used to talk about the pair of us quitting Australia and making our mark in exotic places. To ignore the yelling and screaming coming from the back of the house, I began flicking through the pages of the Sydney Morning Herald, stopping at the world weather report. It would be mild in Los Angeles next week. Well, obviously. It always is. Never rains in southern California. 'You excited about L.A.?' I said, looking across the table to Sapphire.

With a finger to her mouth, the teenager indicated her mother. 'Ssh. Don't let the old girl hear you. She's snarky about the whole thing. Dad, too. They don't reckon I'm due for a visitation. Not till August. But Nick's got two weeks in Hawaii. Doing a reckie for his new movie and it's my school hols coming up and my birthday and you're all going there, so?' Breathless. 'So why not? It'll be awesome. Absolutely awesome, Goddy.'

'By the way, where's this Goddy thing coming from? It's new.'

'About to turn sixteen, okay? Too grown up to keep calling you Aunty Cyn, for crying out loud. I like it. You're special to me.'

'Back at you.'

'Sapphire, please go tell that lot down there they better get a move on—or else,' said Connie as she held up the empty cling wrap roll to demonstrate how cleverly she had managed to eke out the last few wrinkled remains of the wrap for the lunches. 'Made it!'

More sarcasm, I wondered. 'Good for you. And so, to Ms Connie Labelle goes this year's Good Housekeeping Seal of Approval.'

'It's something, at least,' Connie shot back at me as she left her workstation and disappeared into the walk-in pantry.

My God, what had I done to the silly woman's psyche? Con had obviously slept on the perceived insult all night. Well, to Hell with her. It wasn't her facing the void, was it? Out the side of my mouth, in a hushed voice, to my goddaughter, 'Did you get the little package I left in your draw?'

'Ta. Mum would die,' she whispered. 'You won't tell her, will you?'

'Mum doesn't need to know. Not right now, at any rate. She's got enough problems with the little ones. Don't ever feel you can't talk to me, darling. You hear? Whenever. Or your mum, for that matter. She might seem a bit old fashioned, Sapph but she loves you and wants you to be safe.' I held the teenager's hands across the table and looked deep into her eyes. 'Sapphie?'

'Yes?'

'There's no rush, sweetie. You know, don't you? No one's handing out prizes. No deadlines. It needs to mean something special when it happens. You understand what I'm saying? Something a bit special. It doesn't mean it has to be the love of your life but there needs to be mutual respect. Never feel obliged. And never, ever do anything that makes you feel uncomfortable. Never. You hear me? You promise?' I moved around to the other side of the booth, pulled Sapphie into my chest and hugged her. 'It's weird. You're entering this whole crazy business just as I'm leaving it.'

'What are you saying?'

'It's a mystery. It defies understanding, the female condition.'

'What's going on over there?' said Connie, coming out from her pantry and returning to her bench. 'What are you two whispering about?' She looked displeased with the pow-wow.

'Telling your daughter her godmother is getting old.' I looked down at the backs of my hands. 'See these? Look at yours.' I pinched the back of Sapphire's plump white hand and watched as the youthful elastic skin bounced back. 'Now pinch mine. See what happens.'

Quizzically, Sapphire accepted the challenge. The tissue showed almost the same degree of elasticity. 'What's your problem? Seems fine to me.'

'Not too bad now but soon the skin on the backs of these hands is not only going to be covered in brown liver spots and ugly veins, it's going to be as thin as tissue paper. The fat disappears from underneath. The collagen. It's all about collagen, Sapphie. The lack of it, that is.'

'Ask her if she's packed her homework, will you? Please?' Connie, now yelling orders across the hall from the bathroom.

Sapphire rolled her eyes. 'You'll still be you, Goddy—so?'

'So, gather ye rosebuds while ye may. *Carpe diem*.'

'*Dead Poets Society*.'

'Robert Herrick. Look him up.'

'Sapphire?' Connie snapped as she came back into the room. 'Your lunch, miss. Pack it! And go tell those kids down there to get themselves out here. At once!'

The teenager shrugged. 'It's cool. I'm locked and loaded, for godsakes.'

Connie spun around, fury darkening her face. 'Enough with the cheek, young lady. I heard that. Now get moving. Go, do as I say.'

'I'll get going too, Con.' I walked over and dropped my coffee mug into the cluttered sink. I put an arm around Connie's waist. An attempt to patch things up before I headed down the mountain. 'You should have tipped me out, Con. Should have let me drive home last night after dinner. I was fine.'

'Bullshit you were fine.'

Connie moved away, industrious to the last as she stuffed packets of raisins into various plastic lunchboxes 'Give me a break, Cynthia. You were tanked. Hey! Not so quick, young man.' She snagged Harry by his shirt collar as the four-year-old tried to rush past his mother on his way out the door. 'Turn around. Let me smell your breath.'

Connie knelt at Harry's level and had him huff his baby breath at her. 'Oh boy, you little tinker, Harry Michael Labelle.'

'Was David okay this morning, Con? What time did he leave?'

Connie busied herself tying off Harry's shoelaces. 'When you get your big teeth little fella,' she said, squeezing her son's cheek, '—

they'll have to last forever. So, you might think about keeping these ones brushed. Just for practice.' From where she squatted, Connie looked up at me. 'Why do you want to know?'

'Just asking.'

'Same as every morning. Otherwise, he runs into the traffic at Leura.'

Connie stood and faced her son towards the bathroom, spanked his bottom and gave him a gentle push. 'Go on Harry L. Get in there and do what you should have done half an hour ago. I put the paste on your Mickie Mouse brush, now go do it!' She headed to the doorway, leaned in and yelled down the hallway. 'Jack? Francesca? You pair ever coming out?' She turned to face me. 'About last—'

'I'll be gone when you get back from dropping Harry off, Con.'

'Don't let's rush you or anything, Jacko,' Connie, still yelling orders down to the far reaches of the house. 'Just so long as you know old sport, miss the bus and you'll be hoofing it. You, too, Franny. Do you hear me? Get your A into G, both of you.' She turned back. 'Unless they get a move on, I'll be running the lot of them to school.' She closed her eyes and shook her head. 'This madness must seem a long way from Paddington. A million miles from your North Sydney office. About last night. I—'

'You have something special going here, Con. Your children. Sure, they're a noisy bloody bunch, they do a person's head in but they're a credit to you.' I was attempting to make peace in my own way but still it sounded condescending. 'And your old man? He adores you.'

'Does he, though?'

'He's a keeper.' Two old friends, almost sisters, we held each other's gaze, ignoring the hubbub around us as children flew in and out of the family room yelling at each other. 'He's a better husband to you than I am a friend.'

'Why do you say that?'

I took a long pause before I nodded. 'Because it's true. Believe me.'

Connie looked at me for seconds then smiled and patted my arm. 'Hang on, I'm going to throw on my jeans and get Theo up.

You'll want to give him a hug before you go.'

'Sure, she will.' Sapphire's despairing teenage groan. 'Pity poor me,' said Sapphire. 'This is my world, Goddy. A world where your mother comes out with pathetic comments like that.'

Connie doubled back and grabbed her daughter and despite Sapphire's giggly attempts to pull away, held her in a playful bear-hug. 'Get to school, wench!' she said, letting go and tugging a plait before taking off again and disappearing down the hall to retrieve her crying child.

Peace reigned for a moment. Sapphie and I exchanged knowing looks. 'Can't wait for L.A.,' sighed the teenager.

Suddenly the peace was shattered when Connie returned with the squawking Theo on her hip. 'Hungry as Hell.'

Jack came running down the hall, flying out the door ahead of his twin. Francesca, in his wake, left the flyscreen banging on its hinges.

'This goes on every fucking morning,' said Connie. 'Oops. Bad language. Bad mother.' She pretended to slap her own face. 'Sorry Sapph. But it's true, isn't it? Both, in the fight of their lives for the front seat. Every expletive-deleted day. It's torment.'

So is the child's wailing. I wanted nothing more than to be on the road heading home. Maybe a little Bach.

'I love you, gorgeous god-mum,' Sapphire whispered. 'Can I go with you? Can you get me out of here? Everyone's crazy but me.'

Harry came out of the bathroom at full speed, almost knocking me sideways. Connie reached out and stopped him in his tracks. The little boy spun around and opened his mouth wide for his mother, displaying two rows of freshly brushed baby teeth. Connie kissed him and took his hand. 'Nice. Now here's your pack. Off you go. Out to the car. But you're in your car seat, young man. It's the law. No argument.' She looked up. 'It would be great if you could just hang around a few minutes Cyn while I run them around to the bus stop. Then it only takes me ten to drop Harry off. I'll be back in under twenty. Is that okay? I'll pop him in his playpen,' she said, jigging the boy. 'He's started crawling, y'know? Every bloody where. Under my feet all day. Save me having to get him in and out of car seats, alright?'

Theo's crying had intensified. It drilled through my brain. 'You're amazing, Con. You really don't hear it, do you? The noise. The jangle. It just goes straight over your head.'

'Here you go, take him.'

I tried not to flinch when Connie thrust the decidedly unhappy and smelly infant at me, along with the nappy bag Connie took everywhere. I stood holding the child as far away from my body as possible without dropping him.

'He was fed an hour ago so he can wait for these until I get back,' said Connie, indicating her breasts. She swiped her car keys from the sideboard and turned to smile at me. 'Unless you want to try him on yours, sister?'

It was an insensitive thing to say to a childless woman, even if meant in jest. And insensitive to say it to someone who had prostrated herself at your feet only the night before. Tactless, even for Connie. Maybe not tactless. Maybe a shot across the bow; look at me, I'm a mother and you're not. Theo was ravenous.

'Just walk around with him over your shoulder. Pat his back and sing to him. Shove this in his mouth.' She retrieved a soother from her shirt pocket. 'There's expressed milk in the fridge. Just warm it in hot water.

'Ah, no thanks. I'll stick with this.' I swung the blue dummy by its chain.

'Stick him in his playpen with his toys. It won't kill him to yell for a while. Whatever suits you. But remember, he crawls!'

It would be admitting to infanticide if I said what it would suit me to do with the child. 'Twenty minutes, okay?'

'Twenty, no more.' I watched Connie leave the house.

The phone rang. 'What fool would call a busy mother at this time of day?' said Connie, doubling back.

'Ignore it, Con. Whoever it is, their timing's lousy.'

Intuitively, I knew it would be David. Thinking Connie had let the house by now, he would be ringing to see how I felt this morning, touching base to make sure we were back on track after last night's indiscretion. Mine, not his. Back to being David, Connie and pal Cynthia. The immutable order of things which, in my despairing mood and inebriated state I'd tried to skewer. And had David Labelle been other than the decent, loyal husband, I would have succeeded.

'Yeah, why not? Dam 'em. They can call back at a civilized hour.'

'Con?' I held the unhappy baby out to its mother. 'Actually, I'll have to pass on the babysitting. I really do need to get dressed and get on the road.'

'Piker.'

'Is that okay?'

'Sure.' Connie relieved me of Theo and headed for the door with Harry's forgotten backpack and the baby balanced on her hip.

'Con?' I called after her.

Connie pulled up and turned to face me. 'Yep?'

'We're good?'

A moment's hesitation. Then a smile. 'Whadda y'reckon?'

'See you at the airport, then?'

'See you at the airport, sister. Bye.'

'Bye.'

29

CYNTHIA

My guiding principle is this: Guilt is never to be doubted.

Franz Kafka

Santa Monica, Los Angeles
Friday 1st May 1992

In the loo I did a long pee, hot and fierce. Shot it out like a horse for no better reason than I was still capable of ordering my bladder around. But how long before incontinence kicked in? The dribble that spelled death to a social life. To sex. How long before my fun palace dried up and I lost the urge?

I stood at the Miramar's bathroom basin interrogating the stranger's visage, leaning in to angle my face to the light. Being Nordic, I wasn't troubled like so many of my sisters by untamed, rampant body hair. My legs and underarms were shaved only in extremis, only during the warmer months when blonde fuzz sprouted. My eyebrows were well-shaped, fine and just enough to be useful in framing my eyes. No sign of whiskers yet but I should get Connie to check it out. The climacteric approaches and she who is caught with a chin whisker—well—I must remember not to let the sun backlight me. Never leave home without tweezers. For the moment, my reflection gave me a pass. But how much longer I had as a holistic female with all the attractive bits and pieces intact was anyone's guess.

Young Rudi had seemed interested enough in me as a woman. I dried my hands and checked my reflection again, this time from a different angle. At least there had been a spark of interest there, I reflected.

I reached for the phone and dialled 9, already feeling the primal joy.

It was not until Reception answered that I realized I had no idea of the man's name. And anyway, the young thing at the bar with the cute tush would have her claws into him by now. Game over. I hung up, grabbed the bottle from the bedside table and flopped back on the bed, closing my eyes, deciding the world could spin without me for the duration, the curfew last forever for all I cared. The Katoomba weekend, ugly as it was, had been useful in convincing me I was born to fly solo, a conviction that had followed me all the way home.

The Great Western Highway in morning peak hour; painfully slow getting down off the mountain. And the Bridge, a nightmare. One car had done a Liberace, as Paddy would say. Two more, with lesser impact, had concertinaed into them. I drove past the daisy chain of jammed cars wondering how, in God's name, the bozos couldn't manage to concentrate long enough to know when the guy in front slams on his brakes. I wasn't feeling charitable towards my fellow man this morning. It had been rough up on the mountain, a weekend I wished, on several levels, I could erase. Reset the dial.

I had copped the cold shoulder from Con, but at least we'd avoided mention of the previous evening's core business. It had been no more than a few minutes conversation, anyway. A truncated account of the diagnosis over the first glass of chilled dry white—early onset menopause—and then after David had poured each of us a second glass and carefully replacing the bottle in the bucket; could you, would you, Con? Husband and wife looking at each other and ever so imperceptibly shuddering before slowly shaking their heads. For all three, the moment had been mortifying.

And it still felt that way as I cruised into North Sydney's CBD, drove in under the building and parked the Mercedes in one of the spots reserved for the Baker & Glassop executives. No doubt Connie was also pissed-off with me for keeping David up so late.

Grabbing my bags, I stepped out of the car and slammed the door, savouring as ever, the sexy sound of a luxury door closing. A solid sound, one that spoke of fine German engineering. Click. The remote lock. A decisive sound. And significantly, one that banished all thoughts of a Fisher Price baby seat sitting prettily on the back seat. That fantasy had perished in the mist.

Strolling across to the elevators and contemplating the years served at B&G, and that they were about to be in my rear mirror, I figured my time for enjoying the luxury of a Mercedes Benz was coming to an end. No Partnership. No Mercedes. Would I really have forced the partnership ultimatum on Haydn, carried out my threat to expose the adulterous husband?

For all that it reignited the screaming headache just thinking about the mob back up on the mountain, the weekend's heavy dose of family life had done me a favour, focussed me. I would go quietly. Hasta la vista, baby. Aloha. Goodbye. Farewell and fuck you Haydn Glassop. I just couldn't do it to another woman. A weekend of the Labelles and their closeness had shamed me out of becoming a homewrecker. Seeing a loving, if weirdly chaotic, family in action and understanding the sacrifices Connie must make daily just to herd that impossible lot of screamers safely through a day—let alone through their lives—and how much her husband loved her for it was sobering. A family unit is a precious thing and who was I to mess with the model.

It wasn't Naomi Glassop's fault, or her children's, that the husband and father was a philandering creep. A man who broke promises. I would have liked to stick around long enough to improve the agency's recruitment policies, stack the place with clever creative females but not at the risk of making a selfish bitch of myself. The Glassop family's happiness wasn't a thing to mess with.

That was the problem with love-rats, I reasoned as I waited impatiently for the lift to come down to the basement. They know we are morally superior to them, being over supplied, as we are, with empathy and decency. They count on it.

When the elevator doors slid open, I moved aside to allow a quartet of giggling schoolgirls to tumble out. I stood aside and let the elevator rise without me. I wasn't ready. I needed to stretch my legs after the long drive and time to pull myself together. After all, this would be an ending and endings required management. Fresh air and a cigarette, for starters.

Stepping out into the light of day, I paused for a moment to revel in the sunshine before moving around the corner to the shadier side of the building where I could take in the harbour views—the saving grace of the North Sydney CBD, the narrow glimpses of the harbour between the skyscraper canyons.

Ignoring passing pedestrians, I leant back against the building that housed the agency and closed my eyes.

The scene I made in the Labelles' sunroom had been pathetic. Worse; it was perfidious. Treacherous. I had tried to rekindle the spark from long ago with my best friend's husband. Thank god David had been a gentleman, because I had been no lady, no friend to either of the Labelles. He understood, he said, as he'd unclasped my hands from around his neck and gently eased my body away from his. Cyn, let's not do this, hey, he said as he bent and picked up the silk shirt I'd let fall at his feet. Let me help you upstairs, he whispered.

I was still leaning in, clutching the basin and staring at my image in the Miramar's mirror. They say stare at your image in a mirror for ten uninterrupted minutes, not taking your eyes off your reflection is a way to the soul. But what I needed more than soulful introspection was to get my sorry arse down to the gym and do a workout. But an industrial-strength caffeine before I attempted public spaces. The Glenfiddich required a little watering down.

I left the bathroom, switched on the jug and shook two envelopes of coffee powder and one of sugar into a white mug. Apart from anything else awry in my life, going to bed tonight and waking up with two strangers in my room was going to feel very bloody weird but I better get used to the idea, I reasoned as I dropped onto my hands and knees, lay my head sideways and looked from a low angle along the floor.

The envelope? I needed the envelope!

What would these women be like?

Where was it? I thought it had landed under the chair. I must find the envelope before they did. How do you say "Shit! What's that?" in Spanish?

I crawled further along the floor, my cheek resting on the rug. Tempted to just stay on the floor, close my eyes. A long, rough day. Jet lag. Where was it? I had to find it before the women arrived. But okay; if I can't find it, nor will they. And I ought to be taking a shower. Wake myself up. Sober up ... before they lob. The whiskey was finally catching up with me. I closed my eyes.

Just a nap, ten minutes of shut eye.

30

CONNIE

I call myself a domestic goddess.

Roseanne Barr

Santa Monica, Los Angeles
Friday 1st May 1992

She let the silk shirt drip from her hand, watching as the lovely garment nestled again on its bed of crinkly tissue paper in the boutique bag at her feet. She looked down at Theo, guzzling his way to a full belly and smiled. The eternal cameo, Leonardo's Madonna and Child. Later she would try on her Rodeo Drive booty. Tonight. For David.

She eased Theo off her right breast, locked him onto her left and drifted into a dozy otherworld.

She found the shirt under the Bali cushions, spotting it while vacuuming the sunroom, Monday morning. Odd that it should turn up over on the other side of the house, she said when she phoned Cyn at her office to let her know she'd found it. Not really, Cyn replied. Although they'd made up a bed for her in the spare room, she hadn't been capable of climbing the stairs at that hour of the night, she laughed. The morning, actually. You saw the evidence, Con, she said. You saw how much booze I put away after you went off to bed.

She pictured it; their visitor wandering about in the night, pissed and then finding her way around to the sunroom and just passing out on the big cane sofa. She understood the gynaecologist's diagnosis had jolted Cynthia. It was bad timing; to finally be hit with the yearning for a child just as your body is letting you know it's too late. Cyn's biological clock had played a lousy trick on her, no risk. But self-medication on alcohol wasn't the answer. Probably hormone replacement was a better way forward.

It would have been great therapy had the screenplay been given the nod today. The work required to polish the script would have given Cyn something to think about other than her retreating hormones. Pity she was leaving tomorrow. Nick was the answer. Nick, with his writing skills and his great connections. She eased a drowsy Theo from her breast and playfully squirted a jab of warm sticky milk in his face to wake him up. He giggled before greedily latching back onto her to suckle with renewed vigour.

She knew she'd disappointed Cynthia by not agreeing to the surrogacy business. It irked her, though, the notion of surrogacy. Even IVF troubled her. She hated to hear people refer to harvesting their eggs. Dorothy entering the henhouse in a gingham apron and a basket over her arm. It was a woman's ovum for godsakes. Not a chook egg. Do we make omelettes from ova?

A cosy setting last week for that awkward conversation. Theo and Harry tucked in and fast asleep, the twins in their room giggling in the dark about god knows what. And Sapphie in her bed, reading. Just the three adults alone, out on the veranda, sitting in muted candlelight, gazing up at the stars. She pictured it; the proposition having been put, hers and David's refusal reluctantly delivered, and then Cyn standing abruptly, grabbing the wine bottle by its neck and taking the veranda steps two at a time, disappearing down to the bottom of the garden.

Cold mountain air. Standing there, staring into the darkness. What had the poor soul been thinking.

She had the distinct impression there'd been more to the gynaecologist's diagnosis than Cyn let on. She seemed to be holding something back. After stacking the dishes and turning in for the night, she'd lain awake wondering and hating herself for not being able to give her sister-in-spirit what she'd asked of her. But it was a mighty imposition on any woman to carry a child for another, give birth and then surrender it. Is that all I am? A womb for hire. Good old Con, the breeder? By the time David finally climbed into bed alongside her, she'd worked herself up into a tizz. Just a housewife with nothing to do but whelp. The Stepford wife stuck up in the Blue Mountains with five kids, her Wednesday and Thursday morning on 2BM-FM the limit of her corporate life—if being an unpaid community radio host was corporate anything.

She pulled out a red t-shirt of Harry's from the laundry basket and folded it. Cyn had her North Sydney office, her smart business suits and a P.A. to dance attendance on her. So what? This precious family she had created. Nothing topped that.

She rifled through the basket looking for socks to pair up. It was tough that as this stage she couldn't accept the fulltime breakfast position they were offering. Theo's stubborn resistance to weaning was a curb on any ambition. Presently, she was able to take him along with her but that was ending now that he crawled and was resistant to his playpen. She couldn't expect the girls in Reception to put up with a demanding toddler running all over the place. Sure, she could take the TV job and employ domestic help. Plenty of women on the mountain had finished rearing their own kids and would be grateful for the work. But did she really want another woman mothering hers? Shouldn't she be the one with the responsibility for their journey towards responsible, caring adulthood?

No paid housekeeper was going to design Book Week costumes for Harry. Or sit with Jack and help him research his project on Australia's wild river systems. Or make dioramas of Uluru for Franny. Or help with tuck-shops at two different schools. Or edit Sapphire's essays before she submitted them. Being a featured host would mean being high-profile in the community, attending promotional events and opening village fetes. A nanny was okay if getting a job outside the home arose from necessity.

She lifted a pair of David's jeans from the basket and folded them. He was still slim-hipped, god love him. She knew women who worked full-time. They were doing it tough, poor buggers with no option but to put on heels and get out into the workforce. For her, it would be a matter of vanity, the Morning Show. It would mean leaving the house practically at dawn, which meant another woman coming in and packing her kids off to school.

Francesca and Jack's bottle green school jumpers. She rubbed the soft wool against her cheeks. Fresh green apples. She hand-washed their woollens in shampoo and conditioner to keep the fabric soft. Note to self; shop for perfume next week in L.A. Her signature fragrance these days—poop and baby spew—needed to make way for Van Cleef and Arpel's *First.* Her Van Cleef used to be a big turn on for David. Before Children. B.C. Back when they had their bed to themselves and her man could take pleasure in slowly disrobing her, caressing her body, each enjoying the carnal pleasures of luxuriating in unhurried, erotic foreplay until the excitement built and he thrust into her and they made it all the way to heaven. Labelle, le sensuel.

She slid her hand into her jeans and touched herself, not surprised to find she was wet. She giggled. Who but you, Constance Labelle, could get horny folding laundry! She needed to get Theo up, give him a quick feed then collect Harry from kindy. Stay a craven horny slut. Tonight, she would feed the kids early. Homework, baths, bedtime stories and lights out. She'd open a bottle of wine over a candlelit dinner—the chilled Frascati sitting at the back of the fridge. Later, take a couple of warm cognacs out onto the veranda and catch the moon over the mountains—wearing no knickers and panting for her man.

She grinned at her wickedness. It had been a long time since they'd made love outdoors. She plucked out David's favourite black—but now faded—tee and folded it, the two sleeves doubled into the centre to keep the Ramones logo whole so that he could pick it out in his draw.

She thought again about Cynthia and hated herself for harbouring resentment towards the person closer to her than her own siblings. In fairness, she had glimpsed the other side of the successful career woman last night, saw the vulnerability. It was sad to decide you wanted a child and then be told it wasn't possible. Then again, the woman had made her life choices. And had gone on making them all these years. The trendy terrace in Paddington, the antiques, classy furniture, Business Class travel, luxury holidays, expensive outfits, Mercedes cars. No one to have to look after but herself. Not a care in the world. Just get up and take off whenever the urge took you. She was onto the whites now.

How many items of clothing had she plucked from washing baskets over the years? School uniforms, dresses, shirts, pants. How many had she washed, ironed, folded and put away? David's shirts and shorts, her own clothes. Their undies. The sheets, pillow slips, tea towels.

Just the nappies alone, for fucksake. Dealing with the shitty ones, shaking the baby turds into the toilet bowl, hosing the stubborn ones down the laundry sink, pushing the resistant stuff through the plughole with the end of a wooden spoon kept on the sink for the purpose. Scrubbing, rinsing, boiling all those hundreds and hundreds of terry-towelling squares in the copper over the years. Never disposables. She would never put her babies in those toxic atrocities. Hanging out the squares. Bringing them in. Folding. Stacking. Putting away. And then doing it all over again the following day. Christ, any wonder women like Cynthia Smart expected women like Connie Labelle to bear their children for them. A welcome interruption in the poor bitch's boring life.

She reached for the mug of coffee, now colder than August.

Coffee. Sometimes it lets you down. She waited while the java warmed in the microwave. The taste rarely lives up to the tantalizing aromas, the waft of Eastern spices filling the car on the way home from the supermarket, tantalizing the taste buds, carrying you off to romantic places. Oscar Wilde reckoned Niagara Falls was a bride's second disappointment. For her, it's all too often her coffee beans that disappoint. She had never witnessed the spectacle of the Niagara Falls so didn't know if she would be disappointed by them. What she did know, however, was that she had certainly not been disappointed in David Labelle's honeymoon technique. She put down the coffee mug and dragged a pair of Jack's football shorts from the pile. Bugger, a three-cornered rip. One more for her bottomless sewing bag.

Rosemary had to have a talk to Cyn about hormone replacement therapy. She would call her mother tonight. Rosemary had been on HRT for years and swore by it. No one was more glamorous, or together as a female than Dr Rosemary Bray, still with her busy Mosman practice, still playing championship tennis every week and still collecting husbands. With her eye on the clock, she went on folding. She had to think about collecting Harry.

Finally, a beautiful thing; an empty washing basket. She tossed it in the laundry and came back into the kitchen to brew herself a fresh mug of coffee. She would take it out onto the sun deck and contemplate the Three Sisters across the gorge. Sweet moments to herself to be savoured before the after-school madness kicked in.

She took Theo off her breast, put him over her shoulder and rubbed his back, aware at ten-months, he was well beyond the need to be burped but old habits die hard. This little man would be her last. Where was David? And where the Hell was her delinquent daughter?

Theo's eyes were milk heavy, the grateful smile, lopsided. She cradled him in her arms ... as she had done when he was brand new and hummed to him while soft music played somewhere off in the background and she thought of home, picturing Jack and Franny in their sporting gear and Harry down for an afternoon nap. No wonder another woman wanted a go at her ova. She did produce miracles. The phone rang. She lunged for it.

31

CYNTHIA

Don't wait for the right opportunity: create it.

George Bernard Shaw

Santa Monica, Los Angeles
Friday 1st May 1992

Shrill, the ringing sound coming from the far reaches of another universe.

I circled up out of the fog. My first thought: how long had I been asleep? My second: the woman doesn't give up so easily, you can't hide forever. I wiped the warm dribble from the corners of my mouth, dragged my body across the room, pulled myself up off the carpet and squatted on the edge of the bed. Reaching over for the phone, I attempted to quash an exasperated sigh. 'Yeah, Con. I'm still thinking about it. Drinks at six, right?'

'Oh, you're there. Ms Smart?'

'Uh.' My head was playing host to a thumping great hammer-and-anvil show. Sitting upright made the pounding worse. 'Guess I am.' I reached for my cigarettes but remembered I was quitting. Coffee. I needed it strong and I needed it now. Remembered I'd been waiting for the jug to boil.

'This is Reception, Ms Smart. Our porters are outside your door. They have the beds and would like permission to come in and set them up. If that's possible?'

'Sure. Why not? I'll let them in.' The phone's message light was flashing. Obviously, they had been trying to reach me. And Connie as well, no doubt. 'Have they been out there knocking for long?'

'Yes. We apologise but—'

'It's fine. I'm sorry. I know everyone must be flat out. Strange times, right?'

'Yes, Ms Smart. Strange times. Thank you.'

'The women? Are they here, as well?'

'No. We'll let you know.'

'What time is it, please?'

'Four minutes past six o'clock, Ms Smart.'

'Fuck!'

'Ms Smart? Is everything okay?'

'Oh, sorry. Ah—yes. Everything's fine, thanks. Jet lag, that's all. Look, would you tell the women to come. Whenever. Now. Straight away if they wish. Please let them know this is their room, too. I'm going to the gym anyway. For a long walk,'

'That is very kind of you, Ms Smart. Thank you. And you have messages.'

'I'm sure I do. I'll call them back.'

After hanging up, I grabbed the hotel bathrobe and wrapped myself tight before opening the door on the two men standing before me; both Latino, one I put somewhere north of fifty. Powerful shoulders, stubby legs and a smile sitting affably beneath a canopy of black eyebrows. His moustache was noble. The name on his green work shirt pocket announced him as Arturo. I looked over the top of Arturo's pepper-and-salt mop of slicked-back hair to the other porter. This one was a different story. He looked like trouble; not to me, but to the young femmes of Los Angeles. Not long out of his teens, I presumed, and sufficiently tall and good-looking enough to be a self-assured Alpha male. Macho Man's tag told me he was Juan. Don Juan, what else? Young Juan stepped around Arturo into the room, his back against the door, holding it ajar with both arms for his colleague while unabashedly sizing me up and down with eyes destined forever to break female hearts.

Oh, to be young. And then I comforted myself; I'd just been mentally undressed and fucked by this kid half my age.

A quick reconnaissance of the room. I straightened the bed and dashed into the bathroom to hide the Glenfiddich, rinsing the glass and catching my reflection in the mirror. I bent over and shook my hair out, which increased the throbbing but was a necessary adjustment. Upright again, I ran a comb through the length of my locks to straighten out the kinks. The left side of my face was red where I'd been lying on the floor. I pinched my cheek to erase the rug imprint. Only after splashing cold water on my face and drying off, after wiping away mascara smudges beneath my eyes and painting gloss across my lips did I feel respectable enough to welcome Arturo and Juan.

'I'm Cynthia, by the way.'

'Signoria.' Arturo nodded politely.

'I'm sorry. You've been knocking and I didn't hear you.' I made a point of killing the sound on the TV, as if it were to blame.

'We came back two times,' said a grinning Don Juan, two fingers held up to make his point. I knew he knew I'd been caught out. I raised an eyebrow at cheeky lover boy while no-nonsense Arturo stepped past us with his load of bed linen, beckoning his young offsider to look lively and wheel in the heavy stuff.

While the two workmen set up the beds, I returned to the bathroom and applied moisture cream and makeup then, dashing back out to gather up a fresh white linen shirt, a pair of dark navy cotton slacks and my new Jody Boffa espadrilles, I returned to the bathroom and fussed with my image. The three pain killers I gulped down with Evian would slow the hammering. A proper industrial-strength espresso downstairs would clear the fog and then, maybe, a brisk walk around the grounds. All depending on how I felt when the elevator hit the lobby and I had to step out into the mass of humanity I'd been avoiding all afternoon.

First, the phone's blinking light. While I craved permission to crawl into bed and go back to sleep, I had to steel myself to chase the messages. Connie. I would need a convincing excuse for giving her soiree a pass. Apart from not feeling sociable, I had jumped the gun on the drinks business. More alcohol and I'd fall flat on my face.

'Oh, Hi. This is Cynthia Smart, Room 708. My messages, please.'

There was a bank of calls for Ms Smart; two from Mrs Labelle, two from Ms Gloria Martinez and an international call from Mr Richie Yang.

'I'll take the Sydney number, Mr Richie Yang, please.' I scribbled down the number, adding a question mark. Connie's could wait, and Martinez would be one of the maids organizing their check-in. Because the porters were here, that call could also wait. 'Thank you,' I said and hung up.

The Sydney number piqued my curiosity. Richie Yang? I had no idea. From the prefix, it was somewhere around the Paddington area. Saturday afternoon back home. I pressed the button for an outside line, then dialled and waited for my connection to the mysterious Mr Yang. This better be good. Long-distance calls dialled from the Miramar cost an arm and a leg.

A knock came at the door as I waited. It would be the women, the maids. I nodded to Arturo to let them in.

Connie, with Theo on her hip and toting the ubiquitous nappy bag burst into the room. 'Cyn, thank god you're here, love,' she gasped, no concession to the fact she was interrupting a phone call. 'You have to mind him for me.'

'Shush,' I signalled Connie, using the handpiece as a pointer to indicate she should introduce herself to the porters.

Connie turned from Arturo who was cooing over Theo. 'Cyn, sorry. I have to rush!'

'Con, just a minute. Please.' I heard the familiar clicking sound along the wires.

'Hi, Cynthia.' It was a familiar voice on the other end of the line.

'Lien! What are you ...? I was given ... oh, of course, your boyfriend. Richie ... from Ernst & Young, right? God, I'm a dope. I should have remembered.'

'Cyn,' said Connie, determined to interrupt.

I felt Con's tap on my shoulder and turned sharply to look up at her. 'What, what is it, Con? I'm—'

'Niall's had a heart attack! He's in North Shore intensive care. I have to find David.'

'Lien, I'll have to call you back. Don't go away, okay?' I replaced the receiver and stood up, relieving Connie of the baby. 'Niall Brennan? A heart attack. Oh my god, Con!'

'And Sapphire's not back, either.'

'So?' As though Sapphie being late home was on a par with a man's heart attack.

'Went bike riding and hasn't returned. Not unless David's found her. Or she's back at the Goldmans' place. God knows where she is. What a day! I cancelled drinks, I'm sorry.'

How should I handle this? 'She's sixteen next week, Con. She'll be fine. There are kids shooting around everywhere on those hotel bikes, cruising the beach paths, exploring things. She's fine. You go look after David. I'll look after Sapphie. And this little guy.' Obviously Sapphire hadn't informed her parents she was cycling to the local library and I wasn't about to dob the kid in.

'Gotta pack a bag for him then find the bugger and get him on a plane. If it's a possibility. If you see that child before I do, tell her I'm going to kill her. Literally kill her!' She pointed to Theo, now settled on the bed. 'He's had boob. He'll go to sleep for you. Here's his dummy. Stick those pillows around him to stop him falling off but don't let him smother. Sorry, gotta rush! I'll check in.'

'Niall, Con?' I grabbed Connie's arm. 'He's only—what, forty-two?'

'Forty-three,' said Connie, pausing in the doorway. 'David's going to want to fly back tonight, for sure. He and Niall—'

'I know. David thinks the world of him. More like as a brother than his legal partner. God, he'll be devastated, Con,' I said, going back to the bed to put the dummy in the whimpering boy's mouth. 'Forty-three's young. Let's hope he's okay.'

'We'll see,' said Connie. 'A heart attack's a heart attack. Fingers crossed. Gotta find the boyo.' She took a last look at her contented infant, nodded to Arturo, ignored Juan and let the door slam in her wake.

'Oh, boy, your dopey mummy,' I said as I leant over to arrange the pillows around Theo. 'She's a force of nature.' The wide blue Connie-eyes had me pinned as if daring me to look away. I smoothed his blonde curls. 'A bummer of a day, little fella.' He spat the dummy and shot me an old man grin. He understood, said the creases in the tiny brow. He had seen it all before. I couldn't help but smile. An old soul. 'Yep, a real bummer, young Theo Labelle.'

Arturo and Juan, for reasons beyond my understanding—perhaps they'd forgotten a piece of the bed business, or maybe they needed a coffee break—indicated they would be back. I made my international call, going straight to the point when Lien picked up. 'Hi, Lien. Tell me; why's your man's looking for me? He's a lawyer. Am I in trouble?'

'Cynthia, this is exciting. Well, we think it's exciting.'

'Out with it, my little lotus flower. The suspense is killing me.'

'It's all about the World Wide Web and how things are going crazy over there in the States about new media. The internet.'

'What's the World Wide Web got to do with me?' The call was costing me a fortune. 'Can you give me a hint, a clue?'

'Richie's firm handles areas of Saatchi & Saatchi's business. They'll be one of the early adopters and'—'

'Saatchi? Or Richie's firm?'

'Saatchi, of course. You're heading across to New York tomorrow and he wants you to meet with them. Richie told them how talented you are and how frustrated you've been at B&G. He did a big sell on you. Honestly, Cynthia, your ears must have been burning. Anyway, they're dead keen to talk to you, maybe have you come aboard, help them get a foothold in the Asia Pacific region. It's all about integrated marketing, building niche units. Some of the biggest players over there in the States are starting to set up boutique agencies, spin-offs from the parent group. I've been reading about it. McCann, Young &

Rubicam. Saatchi. All the majors. You'll be in New York next week. Listen, I know this call is costing you plenty. I'm talking fast, okay? I'll get Richie to radio in when he gets in from squash. He can explain.'

It was possibly the longest string of words I had ever heard from my former P.A. 'Apart from all that, is everything okay, Lien? It's crazy as hell, here. As you've no doubt seen.' Or maybe it wasn't such big news back home. My parents were yet to call.

'I know you say you're over the whole advertising business but wait till he calls you. Honestly, this is different. It's big. I promise. There's a whole new world of advertising and marketing coming, according to Richie. And you could kick something off over here, Cynthia. Head up something big. Just think about it. New media.'

'Leave your man to enjoy his weekend, Lien. Give him a big smooch from me and let him know I'll call from New York on Monday. Radio in.' God, the jargon. They've got me doing it, now.

'Cool. I'll—'

'That's Tuesday …for him. We can talk about it then.' I had no intention of being rushed into anything. It could wait a day or two.

32

SAPPHIRE

The only weapon that we have in our hands this evening
is the weapon of protest. That's all.
Martin Luther King Jr.

Santa Monica, Los Angeles
Friday 1st May 1992

'Come on, Piper, away from this lot,' shouted Niesha, the tall black girl with the wild curls who had hold of her by the arm, yanking her away from where two skinny white students in red bandana masks stood taunting the cops. 'Sit, babe. Y'hear me? Sit and don't move.'

'Sorry.'

This afternoon, as they'd stopped to cheer on the straggling group of chanting, banner-waving UCLA students coming towards them down 6th Avenue, it was Niesha who stepped out and took her by the arm, assuring a worried Gloria they were heading down to the Pier to take part in a strictly non-violent sit-in. Gloria had been anxious to return her to her parents.

Just a half hour, she pleaded with her rescuer when Niesha promised it would be a peaceful sit-in. To get material for her article, she begged. It was on her way home. Just up the road to the Miramar, and finally she had worn her saviour down. Since arriving, their group of peaceniks had been joined by a larger band of demonstrators, rumoured to have marched all the way from Montana and San Vicente Avenues. They were peaceful.

But further down on Ocean, tear gas had been thrown at rioters. Niesha heard from a student running through the crowd that a Molotov cocktail had been hurled at the courthouse and a police car set alight. Local buildings were being graffitied. These were clearly different kinds of protesters on their way here and it was probably why more police and National Guard were turning up.

She was sitting cross-legged, chanting along with the crowd, listening to the speakers—convincing herself that her parents would approve of her taking part in this historical protest—when she caught sight of Gloria through the crowd.

It was clear from her worried look the firefighter thought she had lost her, Gloria who looked super powerful standing up there, towering above the sea of straggly students, searching the gathering. She could see Gena Davis playing Gloria Martinez. She'd tell Nick about it. The dark firefighter's uniform with all the belts and badges and jangly bits. The fluoro stripes. And the two-way radio stuck on the shoulder. She shivered to think where she would be now if Gloria Martinez hadn't been there for her this afternoon. Today, she was gathering friends; Gloria, Niesha and Mateo. Many of these other students, too, had welcomed her into their midst. The word had got out that she was Crocodile Dundee's niece. How, she didn't know but probably Niesha's prank. That was cool; she could talk crocodiles for hours. Knives, not so much.

'Here! We're over here, Gloria. Hey? Over here!' she called out, jumping up and waving her arms She was about to take off when she felt Niesha restraining her.

'Uh, uh, baby. Sit down. It's good. She's seen you.'

'Over here!' she continued to yell to the firefighter, now speaking on her cell phone, until Gloria flipped and pocketed it and began stepping around bodies and dodging banners on her way through to them.

'Thank God! I thought I'd lost you,' said Gloria, hugging her. 'Listen, sweetie it's time to pack up and move on. There's trouble on the way. I can't stay, I'm afraid. It's a nightmare in this town. It's all hands, on deck. I've been called away.' She looked around. 'I finally got through to your godmother.'

'Yeah? And?'

'Told her you were marching for justice,' she said with a grin.

'Wow.'

'Yeah, wow.'

Gloria looked hard at her for a long moment. She knew what her rescuer was thinking and she was thankful.

'Nothing else, though,' said Gloria, patting her arm. 'Just that you'd left the library to join a student protest at the Pier. "Pull her out of there! Drag her by the hair if you must!" was the reaction, I got. She wants me to bring you back straight away. I can't. I've just been ordered in the other direction.'

A loud noise; a bang close by. The three crouched. Defensive. Hands to their ears. She looked from one friend to the other. What could she say? She wasn't leaving. This was her story. Protesters were running in all directions now, several landing where she was sheltering with Gloria and Niesha. She ran out and picked up a girl who had tripped. 'Come over here. Stay with us,' she shouted above the clamour, pulling the girl back to the wall.

'Could I have that number?' Niesha said to Gloria Martinez. 'The godmother's number.'

She watched as the firefighter gave Niesha the Miramar's phone number and Goddy's room. She frowned at her new friend. Niesha must know she'd have her own godmother's contact number. The hotel's number. And Goddy's extension, as well. She wasn't a baby.

Niesha caught the look. 'It's just in case we kinda get bothered—get separated,' she said, throwing her arms out to indicate the mayhem. 'In case anything happens.'

'Like?'

'Like ... well, like they try to arrest you. Listen, I think you're a great little urban terrorist, Piper but let's face it, you're new to this kinda thing and kinda young, honey. If y'all know what I mean.'

'I'm sixteen! Almost. And old enough to know what they did to Rodney King.'

'So, looks like you're not about to quit,' said Gloria. 'Can't say as how I blame you.'

'She's with me, I'll see she gets back to her hotel. It's just up the road.'

'I tried,' said the firefighter with a grin and a resigned shrug. 'You have my card, Sapphire, right?'

She patted her bra. 'Yes, I do, thanks.' She let Gloria take both her hands, bring them up to her lips and kiss them. Gloria held her face and looked hard into her eyes. They were sharing a moment before Niesha's time, the deserted library courtyard.

'Think about it, sweetie. Promise? And remember I'm here for you, your witness if—or when—you change your mind. And Mr Olsen. He saw it, too, don't forget.'

She walked a short way, arm-in-arm with Gloria. 'I do remember.' She hugged the firefighter who had been so kind to her. 'Thank you for everything. Thank you so, so much.'

'Stay strong young Sapphire Labelle. Piper. And keep your head down, okay? I'll drop your bike off in the morning.' A final hug and the firefighter waved goodbye, her head bent over and speaking into the two-way as she disappeared into the crowd. For several moments, she stood watching her disappearing friend, lost in thought, oblivious to the commotion building up around her.

'Six minutes to curfew,' yelled the voice from the LAPD bull horn, shocking her out of her revery. 'Get on your feet. Leave at once!'

She looked around and saw Niesha jump up and cup her hands to her mouth.

'Freedom of speech,' yelled Niesha. 'Our First Amendment right.' She was yelling over the heads of the mostly still-squatting protesters. 'The First Amendment. "—the right of the people peaceably to assemble." So, we hang in, guys. We stay down. And we stay cool.' She squatted again amid loud cheering and banner waving.

'The magnificent Niesha!' said the black student sitting in front of them. He turned around and saluted. 'A patriot who knows her American Constitution.'

'She should. What y'reckon? She's studying law.' This from a white girl who leant across others to flash Niesha a high five.

'Yeah, she knows we're within our rights to stay put,' yelled another protester. Latino, this one.

'I'm in awe of you, sister,' the black student said as he grabbed the megaphone of the kid sitting alongside him and passed it along to Niesha, who eagerly took it and gave the two boys a victory sign.

'Remember your First Amendment rights. We are doing nothing wrong. Stay here and stay strong,' Niesha shouted through the megaphone.

Niesha was something else. Dreamily, she fantasized about living here in L.A. fulltime so she could hang out with the older girl. And others like her.

'Justice! What do we want? Justice!' And the crowd answered Niesha's call. 'When do we want it?'

'Now,' they yelled, keeping the call going until the interruption.

'Leave now or get arrested,' the voice of an LAPD officer beaming out the order on his bull horn.

Niesha was on her feet again, the megaphone to her mouth and her fist raised in the air. 'No justice. No peace. No justice, no peace,' she yelled through the megaphone, grinning when the chant was taken up by the multitude.

The LAPD cop again. 'Leave at once or be arrested.'

The protesters, at least most, stayed seated. This was awesome. But she wondered how she could ever fit it all in to one article. The kids will never believe me. Remembering how her class had fisted the air over a sighting of Chrissy Amphlett at the Hydro Majestic, she could hardly blame them. Chrissy Amphlett. As if. A random Goth, more like it. She put her hands to her mouth and joined in the crowd's loud booing.

'We got rights, pig,' yelled the student sitting to her left, brandishing his banner.

Her heart was racing. She was aware the mood had turned ugly. The LAPD was not on its own. Around the grounds, along the boardwalk, she saw the National Guard moving in and heard sirens. And now, a chopper overhead. Media people with cameras were everywhere. This would be on the news. The blue and red lights of police cars coming towards them added to the sense of danger. Her mouth felt drier than December grass. She felt tingly all over. Palms sweating. She knew she shouldn't be here.

'Two minutes to curfew. Leave now.' It was loud. No one could say they hadn't heard the order. She threw a glance at Niesha.

'Piper?' said Niesha as they rose to their feet. 'I don't reckon you should stay, babe. Our state laws restrict minors—anyone under eighteen—being outdoors or in public places during certain hours, let alone a curfew like this.'

'No! It's my right.'

Niesha shrugged. 'If they arrest us, at least they'll make sure they get you home, I suppose.'

'I'll get myself home.'

'No. They will see you home, rest assured.' She shrugged again. 'And hit your parents up for the administration and transport costs. Under California state law.'

The chanting was so loud and aggressive now it was making her pulse race so fast it felt like wild horses racing across her chest. It was only adrenalin. She knew all about adrenalin. They talked about it in Biology. Fight or flight. The platypus totally lacked an adrenal gland, the reason it was so shy. Students done with chanting were shouting, running at the blue line. She stood to get a better view of what was happening.

'Here!' yelled one of the youths, football-flinging a full bottle of water to her which, surprising herself, she managed to catch on the full.

'Get 'em!' he yelled, beckoning her to follow him into the reinforced line of police now ranged against them, shields held up and batons at the ready.

She was looking around for Niesha, being pushed and shoved in the melee when suddenly, a thudding pain shot up her leg and she screamed as she landed spread-eagled across the boards, having copped a billy club across the back of her calf. Her busted knee! Mateo's plaster was hanging off. She bent among flying feet and examined her injury, spitting on the open wound to ease the pain. She noticed a splinter had jammed in the cushion of her palm. With the tip of her fingers, she extracted part of it.

'Babe,' said Niesha, kneeling beside her and taking the splintered hand. 'Poor baby.'

'I'm good. It's okay. We've got needles and tweezers back at the hotel,' she said, brushing her friend off and getting to her feet while sucking her hand, trying to pull the remaining wood out with her teeth. She saw the youth who had thrown her the bottle bravely barrelling into the thick of the mob as he and others were being pepper sprayed and copping batons on their heads, backs and legs, anywhere the cops could land a blow. For a moment she hesitated, amazed she still held the bottle. She had gone down with it and survived. Why be here if it's just for singing and chanting. She felt her leg stinging from the walloping. They shouldn't have done that.

When the student looked back—impatiently signalling her to throw—she ran in and flung her missile as hard as she could. Always the joke of the team at school for her lousy sportsmanship, she was amazed to see it had connected, if only with a shield. But a connection. She was in her stride. No stopping her. She looked around for the youth and saw him go down, felled by one of their rubber bullets. It was then that a tear gas gun exploded with a bang nearby and she was enveloped in a suffocating cloud of putrid stinging, stinking air. She turned and ran.

'Quick!' Niesha grabbed her.

With her eyes shut tight against the enveloping smoke, she took hold of Niesha's hand and blindly followed her through the crowd, across the boardwalk to a clearing alongside an ice-cream shop. No way she could open her eyes to see where she was going without the painful stinging sensation forcing them closed again. It was a toss-up as to which felt worse; her busted knee, her calf muscle, her splintered hand or her burning eyes. She slid down the wall, onto the warm boards, cursing the LAPD bullies.

'Here, rinse.'

Gratefully she took the bottle Niesha thrust at her and bending her head all the way back, splashed the cool water into her eyes. After wiping her face dry with the hem of her t-shirt, she looked around at her fellow protesters. Some were running from the tear gas, tumbling over each other in their haste to escape while others, too stunned to move, stood gasping and choking. Through the smoke she saw kids dodging another onslaught from baton-wielding cops. From inside her shirt, where she was attempting to gasp unpolluted air, she let out a mumbled hallelujah!

'I got one, Niesha! I got one!'

'Good for you, babe.'

She took another go at rinsing the toxic gas from her eyes with the next bottle Niesha produced from her canvas bag. She couldn't believe how quickly their peaceful protest had turned violent. It had felt awesome before; people honking their horns in solidarity as they'd marched down to the Pier with banners, and then as she sat on the boardwalk singing and chanting along with the crowd. Awesome, until the police started surrounding them, yelling at them about curfews and ordering them off the street. Bludgeoning everyone with the kind of sticks they'd used on Rodney King. She had seen the video. Over and over and over; their boots and batons going at him.

'Monsters!' said Niesha as she squatted alongside her and leant her head back to rinse her own eyes with the rest of the water. 'Look at them. Pigs. Cowards, all of them.'

'Cowards, you're right.'

Involuntarily, her hand went to her cheek where she knew a bruise would be working its way to the surface. The backhander he gave her, jerking her head so hard she thought it would spin 360 degrees. Anger was the colour of red. Their stupid convertible was the colour of red. Her bruise would be the colour of red before it turned purple, yellow, green and every other colour of the rainbow.

She felt the terror of their groping hands all over her body. Leering. Their vile grins while she struggled to free herself. Their filthy hands grabbing her breast. The powerless feeling and the indignity of being held down, smothered. Their drunken breath in her face. The fat one's knife threatening her. Their jeering, laughing, scary circus clown-mouths mocking her. She shut her eyes tight and shuddered. She would never forget or ever forgive them. She looked around at her fellow protesters; the non-violent and the violently angry, all on the right side of justice.

'Let's go, come on, honey.' Niesha urging her to her feet.

She stayed leaning against the warm timber for a moment longer. 'Cowards should pay,' she whispered; the words so softly spoken only the angels would hear and know her intent. 'One hundred-and-seventy-four stoned drunken imbeciles.'

'What's that, honey? Never mind. Let's go. It's time we beat it.'

'You know what? I'm not leaving.' She indicated her splinter. And the violent red mark on the back of her calf. Her busted knee. Her red and watering eyes. But not the other, not the cheek. 'I've had enough of bullying for one day.' She jumped up and ran forward, her hands to her mouth and her lungs opened, shouting with the crowd. 'No justice! No peace!' 'No justice! No peace!' Over and over. Breathless, she turned back to where Niesha was talking to a youth with a bloodied forehead who was sitting further along the wall. He hugged a bunched-up canvas banner. Niesha took one end of the long pennant and unfurled it. The student attempted to struggle to his feet with the other end but fell back. He looked pale, as if the hit to his head causing the blood flow had flawed him.

'This is Kane, Piper.'

'Hi, Kane.'

'They attacked him with billy clubs, beating him around his head and across his back and his legs. Right, Kane?' The sorry student with the long blond hair bloodied by the blows nodded and tried again to stand.

'Stay put,' said Niesha, bending over him and settling him. 'By the looks of you, you need to rest. Are you okay? Do you need water?'

'Only to hurl at the cunts,' spat the injured student.

Niesha shot her a look, embarrassed by the word being said in her presence, she supposed. She watched as Kane tried to struggle to his feet, holding his end of the banner.

'Here, I can take it,' she said.

'Piper? Really, babe?' Niesha was pulling on the banner to straighten it out. 'You're okay to go in there again?'

No Justice, No Peace! was painted on Kane's banner in thick black lettering.

'Let's do it.'

33

CYNTHIA

When you're a teenager, 'No' is a complete sentence.

Anonymous

Santa Monica, Los Angeles
Friday 1st May 1992

I rejected the idea of alcohol. I had a baby to look after. In the calm after the Connie whirlwind and the job offer coming out of the blue, I laid down alongside Theo's warm little body and thought about Niall Brennan.

I recalled the man's kindness to me in my student days. Warm hugs without strings, aware I still nursed a broken heart. A complex man. Niall could smash it on the tennis court, surf the biggest waves and then go home and bake a cake. It was Niall, in our uni days who taught me how to mix lemon juice, olive oil, mustard and honey and shake the jar, dressing for the salad that accompanied his beef stroganoff and brown rice specialty. All I'd ever known of salad dressing prior to Niall Brennan was Moira's Condensed-milk, Keens Mustard and brown vinegar horror.

Strange how such silly things came to mind when the poor guy was lying in ICU. Strange how Niall and David, both law students—but miles apart in other ways—had cemented a solid friendship. Strange, too, how their student friendship had affected hers and Connie's lives. With Seventies left-wing politics as important to us as our pass marks, we became habitués at the Newcastle on George Street,

The Rocks pub being the lair of the Sydney Push. Intoxicating for Connie and me to mix with the arty crowd—most of them older than us—who congregated around the big, polished bar most afternoons nursing their beers and heady opinions.

Connie, a student at the next-door Julian Ashton School and me up the road at Sydney Uni, eventually fell into company with the two third-year law student pals, Niall Brennan and David Labelle. Connie had been making goo-goo eyes at Niall Brennan for weeks with no luck. It was David who eventually made the moves on us. I smiled at the memory; Connie pairing off with Niall while David and I enjoyed a brief fling. It was in Niall's company, however, where I found comfort. He had lost an older brother in Vietnam.

Naive as we were, Connie constantly bemoaned the fact Niall showed zero interest in getting her into the cot. Until the penny dropped and we realized sweet, clever Niall was gay. No such problem with the fledgling lawyer Labelle. David and I had wasted little time in finding our way to an available bedroom.

The chubby form lying next to me, warm and talcum-powdery snug, let out a babble of baby sounds before nestling further into my side and falling back to sleep. A tapping on the door. Connie had forgotten something.

Juan and Arturo, returning with pillows, let her in.

'Here's the key, Cyn. Oh, he's asleep. God bless him.' Connie lowered her voice. 'He'll need his solids when he wakes up and I've gone and left them on the bloody bench. And I left a note for Sapphie to come to your room when she gets back. I'll keep ringing.'

'When's he going to wake up? When will you be back?'

'I've packed David's bag. Now I need to find him. I'm sure he's found our idiot daughter by now. We'll have to check on flights. Book his ticket and get him a rental. No idea, Cyn.'

'Okay. It's fine.'

'Okay? You sure?'

'Sure, I'm sure. Get going. I'll be here when madam gets back. She can't have gone far. I'll keep her here.'

Connie grabbed me in a bear-hug. 'Thanks, babe. I owe you. Bye.'

'Bye.' I closed the door and stood for a moment, wondering if Connie had smelt the booze on my breath. Obviously not. No way would she have left Theo with me.

Coffee. I needed coffee. If not the good stuff from downstairs, then at least the powdered kind. I glanced across at the precious bundle left in my charge. I was done with alcohol. I put on the jug and, waiting for it to boil, thought about the two strangers sharing my room. The phone rang as if by telepathy. The maids, this will be them.

'Cynthia Smart?' said the woman on the other end of the line. 'Ms Smart?'

'Yes.' I caught the Latino accent.

'Oh, thank goodness I've caught you. I hope she's not in too much trouble.'

'Sorry?'

'She joined up with a group of uni students, kids from UCLA protesting about Wednesday's verdict. She wanted to let you know she'd be back within the hour.' There was a pause on the other end of the line before the woman spoke again. 'Only that was a while ago, I'm afraid. I couldn't get through to you.'

'I was in the gym,' I lied. 'Who wants what? Look, I'm sorry—you've caught me out on this one.' If I hadn't given up the cigarettes, I'd be lighting up.

'Your goddaughter, Piper. We're at the Pier. There's a crowd here now. Peaceful—well, kind of,' the voice trailed off into ambiguous territory.

'The Pier, you said? And you mean Sapphire, not Piper, right? Sapphire?'

'Piper. That's what she told me.'

It caught me off guard, until I recalled Sapphie recently floating the ridiculous name. Her reporter's bi line. 'She uses Piper sometimes. It's Sapphire,' I said with a sigh. 'And I thought she was going to the library? She's on a bike, right?'

'Yes, I have it in the back of my Pajero. She wanted me to let you know she was okay and—'

'Why me? Why not her mother? Her father? She specifically asked you to call me?'

'Ms Smart, I kinda got the impression Piper—Sapphire—figured you'd be a bit cooler with the message.' There was a pause, long enough that I thought the woman's phone had gone dead. 'There was a bit of a problem at the library,' said the caller. 'I wanted to bring her back to the hotel straight away. She was ... she said—'

'Yes?' Something had happened. 'Please, what did she say? What kind of problem? She's okay, right?' I whispered, not wishing to be heard by the porters fussing about with bed linen. There was another pause. Martinez was holding back on me. This was killing me. Where were the parents? Any of them. Why me? 'Sorry. You were saying, Ms Martinez?'

'Well ... what happened at the library was—'

'What is it?' I whispered. 'What's happened to Sapphie?'

'I just think she might need some motherly advice. A little TLC as well.'

'Someone's hurt her!'

There was an even lengthier pause. 'I guess she'll tell you, herself,' said Gloria Martinez. 'She missed the library. It closed earlier this afternoon. I was there doing an inspection. There'd been a fire.'

'Oh, Jesus! Sapphie, is she—'

'No. The fire was put out. She was ... look, I'm sorry I couldn't get her message to you earlier.'

'I can see you've been trying. Thank you. I'm sorry. An hour ago, you said?'

'A little less, maybe. She's fine. I'm not letting her out of my sight. I'm with the L.A. Fire Department. Gloria Martinez. Badge number 5301. She was really set on joining these young protesters. Apparently, she's a budding reporter. The students invited her to join them. One of them gave her a banner to carry. She seems in her element, I must say. I said I'd try and stick with her, drop her and her bike back when she's ready.'

'When she's ready? No way. She's ready now! Tell her there's a curfew coming!'

'I'll give you this number. Although my phone's playing up—sorry, it's crazy here—yes, as I was saying, my phone—but keep trying. You should get through.'

I saw Juan, with hand signals, asking where they should position the made-up beds. I nodded at the window area. He pointed, needing confirmation.

God Almighty. 'Yes, please,' I said, not bothering to hide my frustration. I wasn't a parent. I didn't need any parental problems I grabbed the hotel notepad and returned to the woman on the other end of the line. 'Sorry, I've got two porters here putting folding beds together—long story.' I took down the woman's information. 'Where, exactly did you say all this was happening?'

'We're down at the Pier. She seems like a sensible kid. She thought you'd be worried, knowing she was going to the library and it closes at five or thereabouts.'

'And she's not wrong! Drag her away by her hair if you must. Boot her in the arse and send her back'

'Wait a moment. There's—there's some activity—something's happening. More are coming. Hundreds marching! The cops are moving in!'

'What? What's happening? Ms Martinez?'

'Wait till I go grab her. Hang on.'

This was extreme parenting. Not the warm cuddly stuff laying over there on the bed. I had a sudden feeling of helplessness in the face of danger. I reviewed the possibilities. Frightening things could be happening to Sapphire. The TV images were fresh in my mind. Big men with big guns. Police, National Guard and Bush's military goons. Kent State University. Four kids lying dead on the ground. Blood oozing from their wounds. Any one of the men out there on those streets tonight are going to be capable of shooting first and asking questions later if serious trouble breaks out.

I fretted for the woman to come back on the line, to put Sapphie on and hear the girl's voice promising she was on her way home.

The phone would not reach the French doors, otherwise I'd be out on the patio, seeing what was going on down at the Pier. Panic was more effective than strong coffee. My synapses were in overdrive. Pins and needles. Sweaty hands. Where the Hell were the child's parents? God knows, she has an abundance of them. Even assuming Martinez was for real and not a kidnapper about to drop a ransom demand on them—how the Hell was I going to relay the intelligence to the parents who were, at this moment, downstairs looking for their truant daughter? How, without cruelling the girl's pitch?

They're going to ground her, for sure. Not let her go to Hawaii with Nick Cristos. I would too, were I Connie. But to be fair, I could understand the teenager wanting to be a part of this momentous political event ... like Connie and me, sneaking away to march in moratorium marches. Pro-abortion rallies. Sit-downs to protest pollution of the Parramatta River. Habitués at the Newcastle pub in our student years. The Balmain cops in '75.

'Sorry. My station was beeping me,' said the firefighter, introducing a note of uncertainty. 'Problems everywhere, tonight. We're busy as ...' The caller was silent again. 'They're trying to move the kids on. It's getting—'

'Pull her out! Drag her by the hair!'

'They're ignoring the beach closure and the curfew.'

'I'm grateful to you, Ms Martinez but just tell Sapphire if she knows what's good for her, she'll get back here, pronto. Would you tell her to call the moment she lands? I'll come down to the lobby and collect her. And again, Ms Martinez, thank—'

'I'm sorry. I must go. It's really heating up. I've got to get in there and grab her. Goodbye, Ms Smart.'

The line went dead. I hurried to the patio. Thick black smoke spiralled skyward from the South-Central area. More alarming was the white explosions of tear-gas. I could see the red and blue flashing lights of police cars on the boardwalk. I returned to the room and noticed Juan waiting at the door for Arturo who had stopped to stare at the screen.

'Oh, my god!' I exclaimed. The two men looked at me. I was transfixed by what I was seeing. There it was, on the screen. Sapphire! The shitty day had just turned a whole lot shittier. Connie was going to kill me!

I would recognize the child anywhere; the yellow mini, the purple tights and the hair. My darling goddaughter in close-up being arrested by burly cops, thrown up against a police car and cuffed. I saw the defiant look Sapphie shot over her shoulder at her aggressor as the plastic strips were locked on and she was directed to line up against the wall with an army of others who had also been arrested. No LAPD force was going to bully that girl.

I turned from the TV and grabbed the notepad, dialled the woman's number but received no answer. Tried again. Still no answer. Should I run downstairs, try to find Connie? No, bad idea. The Labelles had other stuff to deal with. I could sprint down to the Pier and rescue her. I could; but I couldn't leave the baby and could hardly take him into a riot zone. Cristos had a mobile phone. His cell phone, he said when he offered his business card this afternoon. I went to the closet for the blazer worn at lunch. The man answered on the second ring. Even in my panic, the passing thought was that he had a seductive voice, deep voice-over kind of vocals.

'Nick? Nick Cristos?' Uncomfortable about how familiar to be with a man I had only met this afternoon and with whom I'd had zero rapport.

'Sure is. And you're Cynthia. I recognize the voice. How're you doing, Cynthia? I was just thinking of—'

'Look, sorry, it's about your daughter. About Sapphire. I can't get onto Connie or David but Sapphie's at a protest rally along the beach—here in Santa Monica—students—at the Pier and they've just—.'

'What? She's what?'

'Yeah, she's at a protest rally. Don't ask—but I've just seen her being arrested. On CNN, right now. With dozens of other kids. It's

Hell down there. The Pier. Tear gas and loud bangs going off. I can hear it from here. The place is crawling with cops—flashing lights. It seems like a serious riot. I can see from my balcony.'

'The Pier's a symbol. The protesters would be targeting it. Y'certain it's Sapph they're arresting?'

'Positive. She was here earlier. I know what she's wearing; purple tights, kind of a yellow mini and a paisley vest. It's her, alright. I just saw them putting the ties on her wrist. Saw the look she gave them, too.'

'That's my gal.'

'They're throwing the kids up against the police cars. Hands behind their backs while they cuff them. Making them stand in rows against the wall once they're cuffed. That's where she is now, standing against a wall, handcuffed.'

'I'm out the door. They'll herd them into the Pier substation to ticket them. And take their time doing it.'

'Is she in trouble?'

'A citation, maybe. I could be up for a grand, I guess. But she's a minor, so we'll see. Might need David's intervention.'

'He's about to step on a plane. We hope. His business partner ... his best friend actually... has had a heart attack and Connie's putting him on a plane, home. I've got the little one or I'd run down there.' I was looking outside. 'God, the street's full of uniforms—tanks—idiots with guns—smoke everywhere!'

'The Pier, right?'

'Yes, the Pier. The beach is closed but the protesters are refusing to leave, they said on TV. So, the cops started teargassing and arresting them. The media trucks are all over it. CNN showed a woman in a Press jacket getting pushed and shoved. Photographer, poor guy, lost his equipment. It's ugly down there.'

'Foot to the floor. I'm down at Redondo, a good forty minutes away, depending. But I'll get there. I'll fix it, don't worry. She's a minor. And I'm her dad.'

'The curfew?'

'Fuck their curfew!' He cut the call.

With the porters gone and nothing more I could do about helping Sapphie, I lay back on the bed and tucked an arm under the head of the drowsy little boy. When he whimpered in his sleep, I dragged up a lullaby from my subconscious. As I sang softly to him, the words of no consequence, I kept my head turned sideways, the remote in my free hand and my eyes glued to the screen. I caught the ABC replay; images of the police bust at the iconic Santa Monica Pier. It appeared, said the breathy young network reporter, the protesters had just been pepper-sprayed. Police were seen rushing in, wielding batons. A tear gas canister was hurled into the crowd by a burly uniformed LAPD officer, sending bodies—including the glamorous media woman—scattering and tumbling over each other in their haste to dodge the violence.

Now I saw the replay of cops grabbing students and pushing them against parked police cars, cuffing them with ties. My Sapphie among them. And with that impudent look! Carefully, I slipped my arm out from under the sleeping infant and tried Martinez's number again, cursing when there was still no pick-up.

From the balcony I could see to the Pier. The LAPD's flashing lights. The bursts of white smoke. National Guard troops among the rioters. Another thrown canister. More smoke. If only I could scoop the sleeping boy up in my arms and run down there, find Sapphie and drag the girl home. Instead, there was nothing to do but let the drama play out.

Stay calm, Sapph. Stay calm and don't make waves, sweetheart. Your daddy is on his way. Said as a mantra as I came back inside and once again tried to reach the only person on this planet presently standing between my precious goddaughter and the might of those LAPD and National Guard murderous morons.

Eventually I gave up trying to reach the firefighter and checked on Theo, restless now and making aggressive slurping attacks on his dummy as he stirred intermittently and whimpered. I bent over and patted him, tried the lullaby again and felt a strange vindication when my 'mothering' eased him back into his baby dreams I wondered what coloured the dreams of one who had not yet spent a year on this crazy planet. The TV had devolved into talking heads. I opened two sachets of instant coffee and shook them into a mug, poured on boiling water, added sweetener and blew on the hot brew, all the while picturing Sapphie sitting in a cell with a bunch of radical uni students.

I cracked a smile; Sapphire Cristos-Labelle having the time of her young, adventure-hungry life. Today has probably topped even a Clinton scoop. The teenager would remember this day forever. Part of her history, her story; the time in '92 in LA when she was arrested for protesting police violence against a black man called Rodney King. Sapphie would be telling it to her grandkids one day. The tear gas, the cudgels, the pepper spray. The girl was strong, she would come through the better for the experience. I contemplated mine and Connie's radical student days; being chased by cops, thrown into paddy wagons. Never pepper-sprayed, however, or belted with batons. Australia wasn't the USA.

I sat cradling my coffee mug out on the balcony, craning my neck to catch the action down at the Pier when I heard the tapping at the door. The Mexican women.

'Oh,' was all I could manage to blurt out when I cracked the door and saw him standing there.

'Ms Smart,' said a smiling Mr Valentino, cradling a silver ice bucket of Moet wrapped in a white linen cloth. 'Compliments of the Miramar. For your generous forbearance,' he said with a smile, looking past me for direction as to where to deposit the peace offering.

Bemused, I ushered him in and indicated the coffee table. When he turned to look at me, I felt the charged atmosphere in the room. The hotel's man looked from me to the champagne and back to me, again. I knew what mischief was implied but wasn't about to make it easy. Somewhere in the Almanac of Good Behaviour his organization would frown upon, if not downright prohibit, these types of guest relations. A senior member of hotel management, not a junior who would normally be sent on such an errand. I smiled with carnal glee as he deposited the ice bucket and made no move to leave.

'Glasses,' I said, my voice a register lower than it should have been, had I not just been taken by such a pleasant surprise. He was reading my thoughts. Was lust betraying me? I indicated the champagne, noting the tiny droplets clearing paths down the side of the icy silver bucket.

'Let me do the honours,' I said in a voice reserved for sex. When his smile released me, I turned to the bar fridge. Kneeling in front of the small fridge, I was about to retrieve two iced champagne glasses I'd noticed there the night before when an ungenerous thought grabbed me; so much for the sweet young thing from the bar stool downstairs. Here he was ... here with me and not her.

I felt his hands go around my waist then navigate the curve of my hips as he raised me to my feet and turned me towards him. His touch felt electrifying. His body now hard up against mine. The old familiar slow burn that made me moist and ready for the act. His kiss was brutal. Today, I wanted it that way, teeth grinding teeth, tongues greedily exploring each other's interior as he forced my knickers down, allowing me to step politely out of them.

A part of my fevered brain reminded me I had to keep him away from the bed. I pushed him down onto the makeshift one instead.

This was the attention I needed. To Erica Jong fans, known as the flying fuck. Swift, pleasurable and totally meaningless. We climaxed together, silent and savage.

Breathing heavily, but as suave as ever, he straightened up and without a hint of post-coital affection, reached for the champagne bottle on the coffee table while I straightened up, surreptitiously flipped my underwear under the camp bed and ran fingers through my tumbled hair.

'Welcome to the Miramar, Ms Smart,' he said, grinning, holding my gaze as he released the wire cage from the cork. Not Valentino. He was Bogey. Cool. Distant in a supercilious way. The cork popped. Loudly.

And with that explosion, the romance was over. The sudden noise had alarmed the warm and talcum-powdered one hidden among the pillows across the room, till now asleep on the king-size bed. Terrified by the rude intrusion upon his dreams, baby Theo had woken up, startled and now bellowing. Nothing for it but to go across and gather the hysterical infant up in my arms and attempt to sooth him.

'There, there little one. Ssh. There, there.' Explanations would have been pathetic. I did not even try.

The Miramar's Lothario replaced the champagne in the ice bucket and cocked an elegant eyebrow, adopting a smirk so transparently patronizing I could have used the close-up in a before-and-after deodorant campaign. 'Enjoy,' he said, pushing the cork into my hand. Still smirking, he held up two elegant champagne flutes that had been buried in the ice bucket all along. I shrugged.

'Ms Smart,' he said politely, nodding the same formal customer relations nod he shopped to guests. On his way out the door he tumbled the baby's curls.

Nothing for it but to laugh as I stared at the closing door. 'Can you believe what just happened, Theo?' Only on such an extraordinary evening as this, would two horny adults—one the hotel's employee, the other the hotel's guest—dare such a brief and forbidden encounter. I hugged Theo closer to my chest, grateful the child was still a baby, one who couldn't judge me. I paced the room, patting Theo's back and trying out my lullaby routine again until, eventually, his baby-sobs subsided and I became aware of his gentle, rhythmical breathing.

With the sleeping child cradled in my arms, the warmth and weight of him snuggled into my bosom, I lowered myself into the cushiony armchair and rocking him gently, began to think that perhaps it wasn't the worst feeling in the world to be this important to another human being. I was settling the sleeping boy back on the bed when the phone rang. I reached for it before the second ring. 'Yes?' I whispered.

'It's me, Cyn. 'I found David. Theo's asleep, right?'

'He's asleep, yes. For now.'

'Heard from her, yet?'

I thought for a moment. I had a choice: tell Connie her truant daughter had been arrested or tell her everything was fine. After juggling the alternatives and the consequences I decided it wasn't a choice at all. 'Sapphie's on her way back. She's with Nick. Long story. Tell you later, okay. It's all good, though. I'll keep her with me when they get here. They'll be a while, so relax Con. Go find your New Yorkers. Get in line for your buffet.

'Y'sure?'

'Sure, I'm sure.'

'Thanks hon. The boyo will be winging his way home tonight. The kids at Reception pulled a miracle, got him on a last flight out. "Heart attack", that was the password for the Qantas blokes. They must have shafted someone to make room for Davie.'

'Great. Now go eat! Grab me some fruit.'

The champagne sat there with the cork already popped. But I'd had my quota of booze. And I had a responsibility to the small trusting bundle of humanity now fast asleep again on my bed. I took a teaspoon and stuck the cold metal end in the neck of the bottle. An old wife's tale but one I always found effective in preserving the bubbles. From the small fridge, I grabbed a handful of ice cubes and clinked them into the silver bucket. Maybe my roommates would appreciate a nightcap. I fancied the idea of a couple of hard-working, under-paid domestic gals enjoying their employer's complimentary Moet.

I remembered the knickers and retrieved them.

34

CYNTHIA

Dread of night. Dread of not-night.

Franz Kafka

Santa Monica, Los Angeles
Friday 1st May 1992

My tiny bedmate stirred.

I saw a pair of unblinking eyes staring up at me. Theo Jacob Labelle, junior interrogator. For how long had he been laying there, pinning me with those Connie-blue-eyes? And what had he concluded about naughty Aunty Cyn? I planted a kiss on the curly head resting on my arm and was rewarded with an undeserved smile. I smiled back at the little man-child wearing the quizzical expression, welcoming the infant's scrutiny. It was only right others should judge me; I was weary of handling the interrogations alone.

The phone rang. I leant across the bed to pick up the receiver. 'Hello?'

'Richard's given me the details for your meeting in New York, Cynthia.' The excitable voice of Lien. 'It might be a good idea to call ahead. Lock it in. How is it over there, by the way? We're getting all these horror stories about—'

'Sweetheart, I can't talk,' I whispered. 'I've got my friend Connie's little fella asleep on my arm.'

'I don't believe it Cynthia Smart! You? Letting yourself get that close to a baby? What happened? I know; they've kidnapped and tortured you?'

'Torture, yes, but this curfew's been therapeutic, believe me. Talk later. Gotta go.'

God, that girl's funny. I fell back against the pillows. Funny without meaning to be. I stared at the ceiling, wondering how I was going to break the news to the poor soul without damaging our relationship. Lien was obviously excited on my behalf. Then I put thoughts of Lien and her finer feelings aside and thought about Sapphie down at the cop shop. When would her father arrive? Had the firefighter woman found her? Theo grumbled and threw a chubby arm across my chest. I kissed a bunch of his fingers and wiped dribble from his lips. How long before Nick got there? How much trouble was Sapphie in? Theo might wake up again, any moment. I patted his arm and hummed to him, amazed at my ability to concentrate on two kids at one time.

Having chased Connie into the arms of the New Yorkers for the next couple of hours, I realized young Theo would demand to be fed once he was fully awake. It was the child's default position. God forbid, I had Con's expressed milk in the fridge to warm up. But the perpetually hungry infant would also need his solids or he'd go ballistic. His jars, as Connie referred to the mash.

I slid off the bed and arranged his bottle in a mug of warm water.

I checked him out; one fat little arm tucked under his head, the other, heavily dimpled at the elbow, lay above the sheets. His mop of curls clung to a head out of proportion to the small body but all babies' heads were whoppers. They had to grow into them. I'd observed that much about kids if nothing else. I smiled at the way the eyelids fluttered. He was dreaming, god bless him. David and Connie had produced a beauty. A Hallmark commercial, a campaign poster child to move hearts, minds and wallets.

I rested the back of my hand against his rosy cheek. He was both warm and breathing; two sure signs my mothering hadn't snuffed out the tiny life. He was off in Babyland. Best if I could keep him asleep a while longer. I had a sudden urge to go through the script. Not to give it Hollywood oomph but, in re-reading it, improve it. Despite its prospects tanking today at Century City, it was a story I had to tell;

my characters Miki and Jude, victims in their teens who, as adults, find the courage to fight back. The story would not go down well with the church, the military or the establishment, all of which take a hiding. So be it. History was with me. For unmarried mothers, black and white, forced to surrender their babies, times had been cruel. Maybe, just maybe—if my film found a popular release—some in government might be shamed into facing the truth and apologise to those who'd been persecuted by a nation's hypocrisy.

I dug the script from the briefcase I'd schlepped to Goldwyn this morning and with red and green pencils in hand—and banishing all thoughts of the condescending Myron Spinak—sat at the desk and began to read through the draft.

More than once in the reading I paused to wonder how certain scenes would fly with the great Nick Cristos should he ever get around to reading it. In the process, I found myself adopting a more objective eye for the story. Less politics, more drama and even a little humour. Entertain, not educate. Well, maybe a little of both. Connie was right though; my girls were asked to carry too much baggage. I needed to lighten things up while keeping the story's integrity. Meaning I had work to do—serious redrafting—if I were to aim for a commercial release, rather than a grudge film for the converted.

After some time had passed and I'd edited dozens of scenes, I heard pathetic whimpers coming from across the room. Hunger stirrings. I ignored the disturbance for the time it took me to race through a few more pages and then, satisfied, I stacked the sheets to one side. The script was now a work in progress rather than a final draft.

I poured myself a coffee and, in the light of the rudimentary script revisions, assessed the progress I was making towards accepting my on-rushing Fortieth. I'd quit Baker & Glassop, so Item One of my great plan could be ticked off. I blew on the hot liquid and with a sigh, conceded I was probably going to flunk Item Two. No man in sight. If I worked hard at it, however, I was still on track to bring in Item Three, a successful career as a filmmaker.

The achievement of Item Number One and Item Number Three

would mean kissing off the Paddington terrace. And the Mercedes would have to go, as well. Leasing that beautiful beast was money better spent creating the materials and travel expenses I'd need to promote the project. The costs associated with getting over to Cannes next May with some effective brochures and a reel would set me back a pretty penny. It wouldn't be a deck chair in the Bahamas, trying to get *Surrender* green lighted but I was ready to push forward.

I recalled a well-meaning writer/director with a history of getting his work produced. The man had attempted to console me last year after I'd had a rough week knocking on doors for funding. If it was easy, love, they'd let girls do it, the venerable one had commiserated. He was right, there'd be plenty of Myron Spinaks along the way to gainsay me. Many are called, few are chosen, the cynical mantra in the movie business. Well, I'd show them. I was starting to feel more than a little fired up, determined to be among the chosen. My birthday gift to myself: Determination to succeed.

I would not be contacting the bright young things at Saatchi New York next week. A brilliant opportunity, no doubt and so kind of Lien's boyfriend to put my name forward but if all the bells and whistles of the New Media zeitgeist were ringing loud and clear, let others cash in on it. The life was not for me. Lien would be miffed but Lien was young, her whole life ahead of her. In fact, Lien should dive into the integrated marketing—building niche units—World Wide Web area of new exciting advertising. I would have no time or headspace for any of it. I had a movie to make. If it were done when 'tis done, then 'twere well it be done quickly.

If the increasingly noisy complaints from Junior meant anything, it was well I followed that advice and scooted around to the Labelle suite to collect the jars. I wondered if I should let the little guy hold his bottle, suck on it while I was gone. No, he might choke. Instead, I pushed the dummy into his mouth and double-checked the pillows were well away from his face before leaving the room.

Hurrying down the corridor and rounding the corner, I pulled up suddenly when I saw two strangers standing at Connie's door, a solidly built man in a black suit and a female in navy jacket and cream trousers. Oh, my God. Something's happened to Sapphire. I put on pace.

'Can I help you?' I called, still doors away.

'Mrs Labelle?' said the young woman as I came closer.

'What's happened? Mrs Labelle's downstairs. At dinner. I'm Cynthia Smart. I'm minding her baby.' I pointed over my shoulder. 'Back in my room. Please?' I stepped around the pair to insert Connie's key card. 'What's happened?' My imagination was galloping across the badlands of possibilities.

'Nothing's wrong, Ms Smart,' said the woman, smiling as she extended her hand. 'I'm Sarah Nowak, Governor Clinton's regional campaign director. And this is Agent Mooney, the—'

'M'am,' said the man in black, offering me a curt nod.

'The Governor's secret service detail,' the woman completed.

'Oh?' Was I dreaming? Bill Clinton's people?

'We received Sapphire's note,' said Sarah Nowak. 'And Mr Clinton's happy to give—I'm sorry, is Sapphire your niece or—?'

'My goddaughter. But she's not here, right now.' I held the door open. Noticed Agent Mooney's eyes scanning the room. I invited them further into the suite.

'The candidate was touched by your goddaughter's note,' said the campaign director with a kindly laugh. 'She sounds like an incredibly self-confident young teenager. He'd welcome her interview. Apart from anything else, he has fans in Australia who get to vote.'

'Of course. Expats.' I ducked behind the kitchen and knelt at the fridge, wondering as I buried my head in it, how many American expats read the Katoomba High School broadsheet and where this thing was going.

'Umm, no baby food.' I stood up.

'Are those what you're looking for, ma'am?' The agent pointed to the bench top.

I examined the baby food Connie had forgotten to pack; a chicken and veg, a beef noodle and a pear and rice. I scraped up all three.

'Thank you,' I said to Ms Nowak who handed me an empty boutique bag and, after holding a Thomas the Tank Engine bib up for Agent Maloney to admire, dropped it in the bag as well. 'Thanks.' I took a deep breath. 'Governor Clinton? Really? Wow, someone's going to be dark on herself if she misses this opportunity.'

'It would be a pity,' said Sarah Nowak.

'It sure would. You say you got a note from her?' This intelligence amazed me.

'Yes, a sweet note. Delivered by one of the hotel's young kitchen staff ... with yet another basket of fresh fruit thrown in,' laughed Sarah Nowak.

I noticed the agent crack a grin.

'When do you expect Sapphire will be back, Ms Smart?' she said, beating me to the fluffy teddy I was heading for and offering it up.

'Thanks. When? Ah, mmm, probably not too long.' I dropped the teddy in with the bib and jars. How could I tell these government officials that the person they were after is presently in handcuffs, an urban terrorist? 'She's being picked up by her father ... soon, I hope. Look, I'm sorry about this ... it sounds rude of me but you'll have to excuse me. I'm in a frantic hurry. I've left the baby on the bed and that's not a good idea because I've just remembered his mother said he's started crawling. Can I get Sapphie to call you? She'll be desperate to call you. My god, you can't imagine how she idolizes your candidate, Ms Nowak.'

'Sarah. Certainly. We've got the governor addressing a campaign meeting this evening but if we drop by here on our way out… say, in the next thirty minutes or so. … might she have returned, do you think?' Sarah Nowak held out a fluffy bunny, this time.

I declined it. 'You mean … you mean candidate Clinton would actually come down here ... come to Sapphire?'

'Sure. That's why we were sent ahead. Tell Ms Smart,' she said to Agent Maloney. 'The Gov's like that, isn't he, Mick?'

'He likes to get amongst the people, ma'am,' said Mooney in a tone dripping with dread. But the smile that followed was probably because the idea of a fifteen-year-old girl from Australia grilling his guy was a novelty, a welcome reprise from having to deal with the nutters.

'And we … the Gov … thought it more appropriate to conduct the interview in the presence of her parents,' said Sarah Nowak. 'After all, she is a little younger than his usual interrogators.' Said with a throaty laugh.

'How long did you say she had? Stretching it, maybe?'

Nowak checked her watch; 'If she gets in within, say, even the next forty minutes, possibly …' She looked to her companion who nodded. '… we could still spare enough time for her to grill him,' she said with a smile.

I could only imagine what Sapphie had written in her note to the man who was possibly—almost certainly—about to become the next president of the United States of America. But it had obviously tickled the fancy of the next Leader of the free world.

Grilled by a budding young reporter who had just been arrested for breaking the law. Not sure the Gov or his people—particular the slick secret service guy—would feel comfortable with the intel. Maloney had never stopped checking out the suite with eyes I guessed missed nothing, not even the array of Connie's shopping bags littering the room.

'This is really going to break her heart if she misses him.' I looked to the campaign director. 'I don't suppose it's possible to reschedule. Tomorrow?' I was standing at the open door.

'I'm sorry. The governor's going to be tied up all weekend with the riots and campaigning. And a fund-raiser on Sunday before he flies back to DC. We've really got him on a tight schedule, I'm afraid.'

'Sure, sure. I understand. Of course.' How persistent could I be in attempting to negotiate on Sapphire's behalf. 'Just that if there was the slightest op—'

Whoop, whoop, whoop … whoop, whoop, whoop …

A Maserati take-off. The agent, speaking into his cuff, shot a look at Nowak and raced past me, out of the suite and halfway down the corridor. Ready to take a bullet for his man, no doubt.

'It's just a fire drill, right?' I said to Sarah Nowak. 'The city's on fire and I guess they want us up to speed.'

Whoop, whoop, whoop... whoop, whoop, whoop...

Nowak flung her business card in my hand. 'Sorry, Ms Smart. My card. We had drill yesterday. This is for real!'

'I'll let you know when—'

The door slammed.

'—she gets in.' I was standing in an empty suite, Nowak's card in my hand.

Whoop, whoop, whoop... I took a final check for anything that might be vital to the happiness of a demanding little boy and fled.

Attention. Attention. Attention. An emergency has been reported. All occupants walk to the nearest stairway and walk down to your assigned entry floor or main lobby. Do not use the elevators. Walk to the nearest stairway and you will be directed to your building's designated evacuation assembly area. Attention. Attention. Attention. An emergency—a continuous disembodied imperative. The voice over the public address system pursuing me like a banshee's scream down the Labelle's corridor as I dodged panicky guests bursting out of their rooms; men, women and children rushing in the opposite direction, all heading like spooked wildebeests for the fire escape.

Attention. Attention. Attention. An emergency has been reported. All occupants walk to the nearest stairway and walk down to your assigned entry floor or main lobby. Do not use the elevators ...

A popping cork frightened him. He'll be apoplectic over this raucous carry-on, the poor little mite. *Repeat; do not use the elevators. Walk to the nearest stairway. Attention. Attention. Attention. An emergency has been ...*I rounded the corner and came upon a corridor equally jammed with guests racing for the exits ... *whoop, whoop, whoop...* some caught half dressed, some calling into their rooms for tardy ones.

Whoop, whoop, whoop... The elevators spewed alarmed passengers out into the corridor, among warning bells and the screeching of loudspeakers.

Do not use the elevators. Repeat; do not use the elevators. Walk to the nearest stairway. Attention. Attention. Attention. An emergency has been ... People were crashing into each other without apology. It was Black Fridays and Boxing Day madness. Pushing, shoving, mayhem. Guests, charging like animals across the savannah. As I ran, I pictured the cinematic scene; urgent music underscoring the stampede. I kept running towards my room, dodging those coming at me.

Why did I leave him in there? Christ, what was I thinking!

Attention. Attention. Attention. An emergency has been reported. All occupants walk to the nearest stairway and walk down to your assigned entry floor ... 'Ooops! Sorry!' I apologised on the run, then skidded to a stop and backtracked to steady the woman and child I'd crashed into as I'd flown past the pair leaving their room. 'So sorry.' I fell to my knees and gathered up the little girl's Lego box and the spilled pieces, thrusting the box at the woman before taking off again.

Whoop, whoop, whoop... Theo, baby, I'm coming. The wailing of the sirens landed somewhere mid solar plexus. I kept going, pushing my way through the on-coming crowd in a frantic effort to reach Room 708 at the end of the hall. And Theo. Alone. With this cacophony filling the air.

Whoop, whoop, whoop... Connie must never know! Con would've taken him with her. Only an idiot would leave a ten-month-old child alone in a hotel room. I pictured Theo, warm and cuddly, waking in fright. A terrified little boy sitting up in the big bed bellowing, not knowing what was happening in his baby world. Wailing for his mummy. At least it was my fervent hope; that I'd rush in there and finding him sitting up in the bed, still surrounded by the cushions. Any other scenario was too frightening to imagine.

Attention. Attention. Attention. An emergency has been reported. All occupants walk to the nearest stairway and walk down to your...

My hands were shaking as I attempted to push in the card, only to be met with the red light of failure. *Whoop, whoop, whoop...* Come on, come on! For fucksake. Another try.

Attention. Attention. Attention. An emergency has been reported. All occupants walk to the nearest stairway and walk down to your assigned entry floor or main lobby. Do not use the elevators. Repeat; do not use the elevators. Walk to the nearest stairway. Attention. Attention. Attention. An emergency has been ... A few seconds of impatient breathing, until finally, the green light. Open sesame!

I burst into the room, my arms ready to scoop up the poor terrified little sod and join the exodus down the fire escape. *Whoop, whoop, whoop...*

An empty bed! No Theo! *Whoop, whoop, whoop... Whoop, whoop, whoop... Whoop...*

I tossed the pillows to the floor, ran to the other side of the bed. No baby! 'No, no, no,' I whimpered, cradling my head and spinning around until I collapsed on the floor. This can't be happening. I reached up and felt the part of the bed where his little body had lain. It still felt warm. His soother was still there.

*Attention. Attention. Attention. An emergency has...*The bathroom! He's climbed out of bed and crawled in there, looking for his mother. In blind panic, I ran to the bathroom.

No Theo! And then it hit me. I froze.

With a white-knuckle grip on the basin, I stared in horror at my reflection in the mirror as the wailing sirens rang out. This was the worst Stephen King or Alfred Hitchcock moment in my life. A dead baby! *Attention. Attention. Attention. An emergency has been reported. All occupants walk to the nearest stairway and walk down to your assigned entry floor or main lobby.*

He climbs, they said last week. Pulls himself up and climbs onto tables. Climbs onto anything. They laughed about it as David poured the last dregs of the Tyrells Semillon into his glass. Up on chairs. Up on the table. He climbs. *Whoop, whoop, whoop...*

The French doors to the balcony.

I had left them open!

35

CONNIE

A restaurant is a kind of living fantasy in which diners are the most important members of the cast.

Warner LeRoy

Santa Monica, Los Angeles
Friday 1st May 1992

A young busboy approached their table carrying a water pitcher, a white napkin draped formerly across his arm. Tight curls—black corkscrews—pulled back in a bunch from a handsome face. Looking dapper in crisp white jacket, black ribbon at his neck and black trousers. Latino. She had seen dozens of Miramar's staff looking like extras from the set of Huston's *Treasure of the Sierra Madre*.

'Please,' said Connie with a dimpled smile when the boy—with a raised eyebrow and a dimpled smile of his own—indicated her empty water glass. She studied him as he poured. He was young but exuded a mature charm. Deference and charm. 'Thank you—your name is?'

'Mateo,' he said after some hesitation.

'Mateo?'

'Si.'

'I like it. Thank you, Mateo.'

She signaled for him to pour for the other two at her table and as he did, admired the youth's professional manner; ramrod straight back and intense concentration as he dispensed the iced water to the two New Yorkers, wiping the lip of his pitcher to avoid drips and turning to flash her another smile. She wondered what the prospects were for a good-looking and attentive teenager like this. Would he make it as a chef one day? Maybe hotel management? Maybe a career in movies, even? Mentally, she cast him for the role of Ketut. Her script—if she could ever find the time to work on it—was set in Bali. Put good-looking kids like this in *The Sixth Kris* and it could work. For some odd reason, she hoped the young man would succeed in life. Figured he would. 'Thank you, Mateo,' she said as he nodded politely and moved off to a nearby table.

She looked across to Clement Horowitz—a man she learned tonight was a pal of the Village Roadshow boys, having invested in *Turtle Beach*, which had opened in Australia last month to passable reviews. 'Pity my daughter isn't here with us. She'd have tried to distract that handsome young man from his labours. She's a trick. Fifteen-going-on-twenty,' she laughed.

'They kit them out well, I have to say.' Horowitz, now topping up her wine. 'They pay 'em peanuts, y'know, these immigrant kids. Expect them to work their asses off.'

'Shame on them.' She held the basket of bread out to Horowitz. 'These are the wholemeal ones,' she pointed out as she claimed one for herself. 'The unions should demand better conditions.'

'Unions. Blah.' Horowitz, dismissive of both a bun and organized labour, sniffed his wine and eyed the buffet across the room as if preparing to dive in for seconds.

'Hermione? A roll for you, dear? No?'

'Uh-huh,' said the red-haired Hermione in the skimpy-as-hell black Givenchy, Horowitz's colleague and whatever else, whose only contribution to the evening so far had been to carp about the food and the fact she'd been made to line up for it. That, and the confident opinion elegantly expressed that historical movies like Connie's were way too passé to be able to attract funding or a studio's interest. They just did not work, right, Clem? Connie should forget toiling on a story as naff as ancient Balinese majesty up against Dutch colonial cruelty, am I right? A Raj's funeral, his virgins and favourite white stallion thrown into the pit with him? Who cares?

'No?' she enquired again of the redhead, holding the basket of horrors firmly under the nose of her critic. 'Can't tempt you?' It had become a challenge. 'These ones here are sour doughs. No?'

'No.'

She had not only been navigating her way carefully, painfully across the landscape of recent movies, hoping to find common ground so she could segue into Cyn's project but also tippy toeing across America's political landscape. All through drinks and dinner she'd put up with this pair of movie dilettantes and, as it turned out, Bush admirers. She was fed up with their company. She'd cry breast-feeding, swollen boobs and make a dash for it as soon as she'd eaten the fish.

Whoop, whoop, whoop... Whoop, whoop, whoop...

'Fuck!' She spun from Hermione, her elbow knocking over the wine glass, which bounced off the table onto her lap.

'Bugger!' The superb Napa Valley Merlot she'd been raving about only moments ago, now leaching into the white fabric, spreading like a wound across her lap. Ignoring the alarm and cursing, she grabbed the dish of Israeli sea salt and upended it. Mateo's water. She reached for that, too, and drenched her skirt. Radical but necessary if she were to arrest the stain. *Whoop, whoop, whoop... Whoop, whoop, whoop...*

She was about to jump up and run, as were many in the room. Horowitz raised a supercilious eyebrow, shook his head and slowly pushed his soda water across the table to her. Of course, soda water. Who didn't know that? All good. She was a pro with stains. And on any account, if the dress was ruined, she could always run up a quirky little vest or mini for her zany girl. *Whoop, whoop, whoop...* While she continued to pour and dab Horowitz kept eating.

No knickers; she'd worn no knickers beneath the Max Mara tighter-than-tight little Rodeo Drive number. No visible panty-line. No more hefty bloomers for the new Constance. Meanwhile, iced water dripping through to warm fanny was thrilling. Wait till she tells Cyn about it—and Davey boyo. *Whoop, whoop, whoop... Whoop, whoop, whoop... Whoop, whoop, whoop...*

'For Chrissakes, top me up,' said Hermione-in-black, her glass held out to Horowitz to receive the Bordeaux she had been swilling all evening. 'Crazy time to bring it on, their stupid fire drill.'

Whoop, whoop, whoop... These guys knew the lay of the land better than she did, she supposed. She folded her soiled napkin and returned to the distribution of the bread rolls, trying with a studied elan to ignore the sodden Max Mara, as well as the emergency alarm. They were on the ground floor. How urgent could it be.

Whoop, whoop, whoop.... She watched Horowitz upend the empty Sauvignon Blanc bottle into the silver pail by his side and take up his knife and fork. *Whoop, whoop, whoop...*

The alarm, even if only a false one, had her pulse racing and her tummy doing backflips. Indigestion was never far from a reality with breastfeeding and she had left her Quick Ease upstairs. Maybe she could ask that young Mateo kid for carb soda.

Attention. Attention. Attention. An emergency has been reported. All occupants walk to the nearest stairway and walk down to your assigned entry floor or main lobby. Do not use the elevators. Repeat; do not use the elevators. Walk to the nearest stairway. Attention. Attention. Attention. An emergency has been ...

'Oh fuck, it *is* for real!' She was on her feet and throwing down her napkin, not caring how uncool she looked to this pair of sophisticates from the Big Apple.

Even Horowitz started shovelling the last of his grilled fish down his throat before struggling into his linen jacket, while cool Hermione seemed determined to be the last in the room to panic. *Whoop, whoop, whoop...Attention. Attention. Attention. An emergency has...*

Fuck that, it was time to panic. The room was on the move and so was she. *...been reported. All occupants walk to the nearest stairway and walk down to your assigned entry floor or main lobby. Do not use the elevators. Repeat; do not use the elevators. Walk to the nearest stairway. Attention. Attention. Attention. An emergency has been ...*

She made a b-line for the door, shoving her way past a gaggle of noisy diners pushing in their chairs, grabbing bags and like her, hurrying from the restaurant. Davey, Davey, she needed him. Don't panic, Constance. Don't panic, girl! But Theo was upstairs with Cyn. Seven floors up! She had to reach them! And Sapphie. Where was Sapphire?

Whoop, whoop, whoop...Attention. Attention. Attention... She dodged a cluster of waiters looking troubled about what to do with armfuls of plated food. Suddenly she felt a tap on her shoulder. It was the young Latino busboy holding out her embroidered shawl. ... *Attention. An emergency has been reported. All occupants walk to the nearest stairway and walk down to your assigned entry floor or main lobby. Do not use the elevators. Repeat; do not ...* Idiot! In her haste, she had left it draped across the back of her chair.

'Gracias, Mateo.' She put both hands to her heart. 'Gracias, gracias so much,' she said breathlessly as she took Granny Bray's heirloom from him and threw it around her bare shoulders.

'Is beautiful.'

'Sure is. Go! You should run! Thanks, again.' She looked back and saw the boy being hustled through the kitchen doors. Nice kid, she must mention him to Sapphie. *Whoop, whoop, whoop... Whoop, whoop, whoop... Whoop, whoop, whoop...* The bell goes, school's out and we're climbing over desks to be first out the door. That was how it struck her as she joined the frantic rush, bumping into guests hurrying through the lobby, being shepherded to the exit. No panicking. Just push through them until you reach the far end of the lobby, Constance, and make it around the corner to the fire stairs. Cyn will have the kids. Either Theo on his own, or Sapphie if she's back from wherever.

Whoop, whoop, whoop... Whoop, whoop, whoop...

'They've threatened to blow us up!' yelled a guy she and David had spoken to earlier this afternoon. She did a neat side-step past him, wishing she hadn't been so quick to put David on the plane. But that was unfair. Poor Niall. *Whoop, whoop, whoop...*

She pushed on for the fire stairs, past guests running the other way. Desperate to catch Cyn and Theo. And fingers crossed, Sapphire. *Attention. Attention. Attention. An emergency has been reported. All occupants walk to the nearest stairway and walk down to your assigned entry floor or main lobby...* Agitated guests were being directed by hotel staff to move outside to designated assembly points. She saw their man—the tall dark one who had informed them of the curfew and the food line-up. He was employing his brand of calm persuasion, ushering people out of his lobby and onto the front lawn.

Whoop, whoop, whoop...

'Can you believe it?' a woman carrying an armful of Louis Vuitton shouted at her, 'Some crazy guy says he'll pop off rich people if the government doesn't pay the welfare checks.'

'Pay the poor sods and we can all go home,' she yelled as she dodged the woman and hurried past the gaping mouths of four darkened elevators in her rush for the fire escape. A cattle-stampede. Guest tumbling down the stairs. She stood at the bottom, leaning against the wall, ready to catch Cynthia. Unless, of course, they had already made their escape. *Whoop, whoop, whoop...*

Seven floors up. She tried to estimate how long since she first heard the alarm go off. How long spent mopping up the spilled wine? Time wasted pushing bread rolls at the divine one. The Latino boy calling her back for the shawl. Enough that she should still be able to catch Cyn on her way down. Or maybe not. Depending. Had she grabbed Theo and made a run for it at the sound of the first alarm? If she had, given the woman's athleticism, she would be outside in the evacuation area by now. What should she do? Go up? Or go outside?

Attention. Attention. Attention. An emergency has been reported. All occupants walk to the nearest stairway and walk down to your assigned entry floor or main lobby... But what if Sapphie had returned and Cynthia had to go and get her from their suite? Another few minutes. She should wait another few minutes, then go check outside. Except, if they are outside then they are safe.

Whoop, whoop, whoop... Whoop, whoop, whoop... Whoop, whoop... She leant against the wall, out of the way of the traffic. A fire? A bomb, what was it? A madman with a gun, the woman said.

The hoodie! Suddenly she remembered the one in black shoving her aside as he leapt from behind the bushes over by the bungalows. In the elevator, too. His heavy bag. But not when he left the bushes. A bomb? She should tell someone. A hotel person was walking along the line of darkened elevators, sticking Out of Order signs on them. 'Excuse me. Hey? Excuse me.'

'M'am, it's that-away!'

'No! I need to talk to management. To the police. I might know something.'

36

SAPPHIRE

Disobedience is the true foundation of liberty.

Henry David Thoreau

Santa Monica, Los Angeles
Friday 1st May 1992

Waiting and waiting. Wanting them to charge her so she could get it over and go home, cop her mother's tantrum. Grounded young lady, grounded! She knew it was coming and knew she deserved it. Meanwhile, she'd had plenty of time to scrutinize and mentally record the scene: Colour of the walls (predictable); police posters (uncool); uniformed cops (some were ok, some were bullies); detectives (jerks); students (noisy, interesting). Like her fellow detainees, she was as bored as she was angry.

Too close. Too sweaty, the one who'd been sitting on her left. Thank god the doofus had started annoying someone else further along the bench. At least he was a fellow protester, so she'd given him a "G'day mate" to shut him up. He had boasted that he knew all the words to Men at Work. Down Under, she corrected. The song is called Down Under, maaayt. But he was okay. Helped pass the time, she supposed.

She was confident she could reliably describe the whole scene in her article. And for sure, she would never leave home in future without a reporter's notepad. She must be ready to record everything that happened to her. Even, she thought as bile rose in her stomach, the unthinkable. She had to move on, move past what they tried to do to her back at the library or that would mean they'd won. And they hadn't. No way. She had to think positive thoughts. It could have ended so badly. So really, really bad. Thanks to Gloria and Mr Olsen, it hadn't. But she hated them, the animals.

'I should have been back ages ago,' she said to Niesha through the cell bars that were keeping her friend from her. 'I'm in for it. My mother's going kill me.'

'But at least your godmother knows. The firefighter passed on the message. You're at a rally. Your mum is gonna understand.'

'You don't know my mum!'

The place was gradually emptying but she was still sitting on a long bench against the wall in their stupid cop shop being ignored, counting out her life in clank, clank, clanks as officers kept opening and shutting the metal doors of the crowded cells behind her. Kane—and a whole lot of others—had been taken away and processed. Ticketed and ordered to turn up in court next week. Kane had made a theatrical departure, hobbling out of the place complaining of a busted back and a bunch of bruises to go with his fine.

'No justice, no peace,' he'd yelled, flashing the fine above his head on his way out the door.

She put her hand to the side of her face where the brute had swiped her. She could feel it pulsing. Pulling a long swatch of hair over her cheek to cover the mark left her staring out of only one eye. Too bad. And other bits of her body felt wrong, as well but all for a good cause, she figured.

When they were pushing everyone up against the police cars outside and cuffing them, Niesha had assured her that they'd eventually have to release her without charges. They can't lay any of their shit on you, baby girl, her friend said. And because she was a minor, the police would be obliged to deliver her back to the hotel. And then they send your mummy and daddy a big fat invoice for the privilege, added Niesha.

Yeah, ok. So, if they do have to release me, when, she wondered? This whole business of cooling her heels in a cop shop in Los Angeles while in another life she'd be running around the netball court in Leura today was wild. Missing her Australian Saturday while rotting on a hard bench in her American Friday. Niesha's voice through the bars snapped her out of her trance.

'The buzz I'm picking up in here is that there's been some kind of heavy drama up at your hotel. Everyone's been evacuated.'

'What? A fire?' Her first thought: she should be with them. Her mother, her father, Theo. Goddy. She should be there!

'Not sure. They're saying it was some nutter ... with a gun. Wanted to talk to Clinton. They marshalled everyone out on the lawn.'

'Hey, back off!' Niesha said to the officer who opened the cell and took her by the elbow. 'Just hang on, officer. I'm talking to my little sister, do you mind. This is personal. And important.' Niesha tried to shake the woman off.

'What's important,' said the cop '...is that you do what I'm tellin' you Miss and git your ass over there. They ready for you, girl.'

The one pushing Niesha out of the cell, skin darker and duller than Niesha's, looked like a lot of them today, like they got off on throwing their weight around. And this one had a lot to throw around, squeezed into trousers so tight across humungous thighs and buttocks Sapphire expected to hear seams pop. But Niesha, after a shrug, went with the cop, allowing herself to be taken away for processing. Across the other side of the room, her friend's fuzzy head stood out. Niesha was bothering them. Heads were shaking. Busy, busy, busy. It was a madhouse. Police and students, all yelling and bullying. Niesha would be standing up for her rights, over there by the counter, that much she knew. She was about to ask permission to go to the bathroom when she saw him standing in the main doorway. He had come for her!

'Nick!' she yelled, jumping up from the bench, waving her arms

He was in silhouette, backlit by the flashing lights of the police cars outside, all jiggerly red and blue against the sunset haze. Goddy. Gloria told Goddy and Goddy somehow told Nick.

'Nick ... Dad ... over here!'

He spotted her through the crowd and waved. The celebrity, her handsome Californian Dad. American but born in Greece. And promising to take her there one day. She scanned the room for Niesha. She had to introduce her to her American father but there was no sign of her friend anywhere, anymore. And she needed to tell her it was all okay now, her dad would be taking her home.

She watched him head across the room to the counter. The officer he spoke with was like a cop out of a kid's cartoon. Chubby, red faced, droopy moustache and looking as if he was still in the uniform he had worn truckloads of hot dogs and mustard ago. His neck squeezed out of his collar like toothpaste. He said something to Nick before he turned and signalled a policewoman further down the long counter. The policewoman, young, slim, with pale blonde hair pulled back in a bun and scarlet lipstick saw her father, excused herself to a student she'd been dealing with and came hurrying around from behind the counter to join Nick. By her warm greeting and the way her father left his hand resting on the woman's arm while they spoke, she guessed the pair knew each other. Or at least, the young cop knew her dad. Lots did. He really was a celebrity since his last movie got everyone excited.

'Nick, over here!' she called, as her father and the woman made their way through to her bench. Was she in for it? 'Nick!'

'Baby. You, okay?' He hugged her.

'We were doing nothing wrong, Nick. Nothing. It's our First Amendment right.' She threw a look sideways to challenge the blonde officer. Only a raised eyebrow and the red lips curling into a half smile, hardly the reaction she'd hoped would greet her defiance.

'Wow. Listen to you. Angela Davis eat your heart out,' said Nick, not for the woman's benefit she hoped because if her father had shared a laugh, a smirk or so much as the hint of a smile with the cop she would disown him. But he hadn't. His smile was all for her.

'It's true! It's my right to be heard,' she added with less venom.

'It is true, honey and I'm proud of my gal. Now let's get you out of this joint. You've been here long enough, okay. I'm sorry I couldn't get here sooner but it's madness out there.' He turned to the officer. 'We good to go, officer Lovelace?'

The woman shrugged. 'Free to go, I guess, Mr Cristos.'

'But I'm not free to go, Nick. Not yet. They haven't even brought me up to the counter. All this time. I haven't been ticketed.' She looked to the policewoman. 'That's right, isn't it?'

'Because I called them,' said Nick. 'Sorry you had to wait, honey.' He touched the policewoman's arm again and nodded. 'Cheryl, here helped out on the set for a few days last year. Right, Cheryl?' he said to the cop who flashed a perfect row of white teeth. Ignoring the pat on her arm—which she did not welcome from a policewoman, even a pretty one who smelled like sandalwood soap—she stood on tiptoe trying to see if she could spot Niesha.

After minutes of listening to her father and the blonde swap movie set stories, she interrupted the pair, saying she needed the bathroom. At least it broke up the pow wow. She took a further pat on the arm, smiled graciously and watched as her father's pal muttered her farewells and walked back to attend to the detained student abandoned a few moments ago.

Niesha was nowhere to be seen among the dozens still noisily jamming the station.

'Nick, wait. I really do need to go to the bathroom. I need to find my friend, a girl I know.'

'Okay, *louloudi mou*. I'll wait out front.'

She loved all that funny Greek stuff. No one thought of her as their little flower back home. She hurried down to the bathrooms where they had earlier been taken by a different policewoman, a stout motherly type who'd smelled of pizzas. 'Niesh? It's me,' she called out as she came through the doors. 'You in here?' She wrapped on each door but no sign of her friend in the cubicles. No Niesha.

A student pointed her thumb towards the entrance. 'That girl, she gone, baby. They been shovin' us out that door quicker than you can say fuck d' pigs.'

'But ... ah, never mind. Thanks.' She left the bathroom and stood up on the bench, scanning the room for a glimpse of frizzy hair. No Niesha. And Nick was impatient to go. Outside on the boardwalk, she took Nick's hand and, this time, stood up on an abandoned milk crate to study the landscape. Possibly the same crate Niesha had used to address the crowd. The area was no longer crowded. Most of the protesters who hadn't been arrested had drifted away. 'One minute, hey? Just one more look? Promise.' She left Nick and ducked back inside.

'Did you see where she went?' she asked those along the benches and in the holding cells. A few shrugs. Heads shaken. No one seemed to know. Niesha had vanished. Gone.

Earlier this afternoon so much had happened and now only this empty feeling. Like a drizzly, rainy Sunday afternoon in Katoomba. Like walking out of the Mount Vic Flicks after an exciting ending, only to find you're back on boring old Harley Avenue. Like waking up from a good dream and finding it's really a school morning and Connie's yelling at you to get out of bed. And Jack's jumping on you and pulling your hair. It felt that lousy to know the tall, powerful student demonstrator who'd taken an awesome interest in her had vanished into the sunset. It was a lesson in how fleeting a friendship can be, she supposed. And how much she needed to grab and hold onto whatever was there while ever it was there.

Mateo, the same.

She left the police station and stood outside in the dimming light, trying not to inhale the dirty air. Living most of her life a million miles away in Australia and Niesha studying here in California, what hope had there ever been for a big sister kind of friendship? And Mateo? Well, he would be just some sweet boy she remembered when she was an old married woman, she supposed. Just a wildly handsome boy she'd fallen madly in love with because he was so different from all the other boys she knew. She caught up with Nick, letting him lead her to his SUV parked further up the Pier, while all the time swivelling her head around in the hope of catching sight of her friend.

'No luck, hey?' said Nick, his hand around her shoulder.

'I'll never see her again. She was so kind to me, Nick. Honestly.'

She booted a half-eaten apple along in front of her. Another couple of vicious kicks before she bent down and picked up a discarded water bottle. If there was one symbol that would always have her remembering this eventful day, it would be a stupid dumb plastic water bottle; the one Mateo brought to 'cleanse' her knee; the one the kindly old librarian offered; and the one she caught from the protester and hurled at the cops. And now this one she held in her hand; a sorry bit of trash left over from her first real political demo but a reminder of all that had happened to wake her up today.

Maybe the Katoomba High newsletter wasn't the best and only place for her L.A. story. Maybe there was a lot more to write about that Katoomba wouldn't get. Like the kindness of strangers who'd cared about her today. Gloria, for a start. And the old gentleman. They'd cared. So had Mateo and so had Niesha and some of the other kids. In truth, even Lovelace seemed half decent. For a cop. Interesting, at least.

What she had experienced this afternoon was one small person's day tucked inside a big, big day for America. On Nick's old Remington in his Redondo study tomorrow, away from all the noise, she would begin her story. Meeting Mateo, for a start. And the drunken idiots. No way was she finished with them, that was for sure.

No justice, no peace. If her run-in with the cops and Niesha's bravery had taught her anything today, it was that her personal freedoms were to be cherished. Not thrown away because she was worried about the consequences of reporting those who'd challenged them. One hundred-and-seventy-four stoned drunken imbeciles. SDI-174. She could have reported it to the cops who arrested her, here this afternoon but she hadn't. She wanted her mother with her. Her two fathers, too. And Goddy, as well. Gloria had spoken to Goddy, so she had witnesses; Gloria and Mr Olsen. She could start putting all these things down on paper but also write about how they made her feel inside. Especially about the way people can drift in and out of your world in such a short time but leave a big impression.

'I'll never forget her, Nick', she said.

'I want to hear all about it, believe me, Sapph. Let's get you home, first.'

She knew that no matter how many years from now, whenever she found herself here on the Santa Monica Pier, she would remember a girl called Niesha, remember her coming down 6th Avenue and how she took her by the arm and carried her along with her. Even when she was an old woman, she would remember the beautiful voice and how it thrilled her when Niesha called her "baby". How it made her skin tingle and fill her with pride when Niesha stood up on the crate and addressed the crowd through the megaphone. Knowing this was her friend talking, the tall skinny girl with the awesome Afro and skin like milk coffee. The grey UCLA sweatshirt and flared jeans with bright patches, images burned into her brain and there forever.

'Coming, you, old slowcoach?' said her father.

She took one last look around the boardwalk before catching up with her dad. She looked across at him and smiled. 'Lovelace? Honestly, that's her name, Nick?'

'Lovelace, yeah. Cute, hey?' He took her arm. 'C'mon, kiddo. Let's get you home.'

37

CYNTHIA

What is better than wisdom? Woman.
And what is better than a good woman? Nothing.
Geoffrey Chaucer—Canterbury Tales

Santa Monica, Los Angeles
Friday 1st May 1992

Attention. Attention. Attention. An emergency... Thankfully, there was no sign down below on the lawn that a tragedy had occurred. No fire engines or ambulances and no police yellow tape. But Theo was missing and only I had a key to my room.

'Hello?' A stranger's voice.

Turning from the patio railing, I saw her standing in the doorway, a Latino woman, middle-aged, in maid's uniform. *Attention. Attention. Attention. An emergency has been reported. All occupants walk to the nearest stairway and walk down to your assigned entry floor or main lobby. Do not use the elevators. Repeat; do not use the elevators. Walk to the nearest stairway. Attention. Attention. Attention. An emergency has been ...*

'Come,' said the woman, stepping into the room with outstretched arms 'Please, come. Hurry.'

'I can't,' I said, shaking my head and collapsing on the bed.

The maid took hold of my arm and tried standing me up.

'I just went to get his jars. That was all. A few minutes.' I tried to stand but my legs refused to do their duty. From the top of my head to my toes, I shook. When I tried to take in giant breathes to correct things, I felt the nausea rising. I left the woman and ran to the bathroom where I threw up. She followed me in. *Whoop, whoop, whoop ... whoop, whoop, whoop ... Attention ...*

'The baby is good, he is safe. Come,' she said, gently urging me towards the door.

Whoop, whoop, whoop ... whoop, whoop, whoop ...

'He's safe? But I—'

'My friend Juana. She went ahead with him. We'll find her outside. Come. Hurry please, we must go!'

Whoop, whoop, whoop ... whoop, whoop, whoop ... Gathering up my bag, I let myself be led out the door to join the trickle of humanity still dribbling towards the fire escape. Seconds ago, some part of me had been weighing fight or flight. Stay calm and investigate what happened to Theo, whether he had ... whatever ... a hotel person with a key who knew about Theo and was in league with the bomber ... a kidnapper? Or make a run for the border, disappear into thin air, never to be seen or heard of again, unable to face the parents because of my stupidity... lost ... allowed to fall to his ... kidnapped ... taken hostage by malignant forces.

Attention. Attention. Attention. An emergency has been reported. All occupants walk to the nearest stairway and walk down to your assigned entry floor or main lobby. Do not use the elevators. Repeat; do not use the elevators. Walk to the nearest stairway. Attention. Attention. Attention. An emergency has been ... It wasn't until the maid and I were almost at the ground floor, having raced down seven flights of stairs in a breathless rush—the maid surprisingly agile for a largish, middle-aged woman—that I began to focus on what I had coming to me: Connie's wrath. How to explain I hadn't meant to neglect Theo but to get the things I thought the little boy needed. *Whoop, whoop, whoop ... whoop, whoop ...*

'We were knocking. Juana and I,' said the woman, turning to me, taking my hand, as we continued down the fire escape. 'We thought we could leave our bags. But there was no answer. And then the alarm went off and—'

'And you heard him screaming?'

Whoop, whoop, whoop ... whoop, whoop, whoop ...

'Screaming, yes. Then soon his screams were right there ... behind the door. We knocked again and then we used our key. Juana squeezed through. Past the baby on the floor. The room was empty and he was so frightened, Ms Smart. My name is Rosa, by the way.'

'Cynthia.' We hurried past the gaping jaws of the darkened elevators and around into the main section of the crowded lobby where police and National Guards were still ushering guests outside. 'We put our bags in your cupboard,' said Rosa.

Whoop, whoop, whoop ... I took Rosa's hands and held them. And then I drew her into me and hugged her, hoping she understood how grateful I was. Relief is hardly a word to explain the emotions flooding through me, the sheer joy of finding I hadn't let Theo crawl out onto the patio and take a fatal fall. Or be kidnapped. 'I was petrified when I got back. When he wasn't—'

'Sshh.' I felt her warm hand on my back, the other cradling my head. 'You have a beautiful little boy,' she whispered in my ear. *Attention. Attention. Attention. An emergency has been reported. All occupants walk to the nearest stairway and walk down to your assigned entry floor or main lobby. Do not use the elevators. Repeat; do not use the elevators. Walk to the nearest stairway. Attention. Attention. Attention. An emergency has been ...*

'Oh no, Theo's my friend's baby, Rosa,' I said, standing back from her. 'I was minding him for her.' The words rang hollow. 'I'm so grateful, Rosa. So truly, truly grateful.'

'Let us find Juana. She has him. Come.'

The sirens had ceased. Thank god for small mercies.

It felt peculiarly quiet after the relentless afront of the alarm. And the barking orders.

I was about to follow the woman Rosa when, amidst the jungle of military and police uniforms, I spotted Connie. She stood over by the Reception Desk. In conversation with a policewoman. Theo was on her hip, gleefully playing with his mother's curls, twisting strands into dreadlocks and tugging on them. I stood for a moment watching as Connie good-naturedly kept taking his hand away and playfully smacking it while she went on talking.

The adored baby boy, the child I might have killed had it not been for the timely arrival of a couple of quick-thinking, god-sent women and the boy himself who had opted to crawl to the closed door rather than the open French ones. But good outcomes mean nothing. I was guilty of gross neglect.

And now it comes, I reasoned as I nodded to Rosa, excused myself and after watching her head outside to find her friend, made my way across to Connie and the cop. What are the charges? Leaving a baby unattended in a hotel room where the patio is accessible and the chairs and table close enough to the railing for a crawling, climbing baby to go over the top?

'Con? I can ex–'

'I know, love. Good thinking.'

'What?'

'You did the right thing; you gave him to the maid to evacuate him to safety while you went looking for Sapph around in the suite. But I take it she hasn't come in yet, right? She's still with Nick?'

'No. Yes. I mean yes, she's with Nick. It's cool. She's fine ... but ... Theo. I—'

'She's so sweet, your Mexican lady. She's outside. Gave me a fright, though. I was ready to crash tackle her when I saw her run past with Theo in her arms.' She bounced Theo for the cop lady's benefit. The child giggled and reached out for the policewoman's hair. 'I mean, God! A hotel maid running off with your kid?' Connie laughed as she untangled the tiny fingers and kissed them. 'I've been busy talking with the police but, thanks for the emergency management, Cyn.' She turned to the policewoman. 'This is my friend, officer. This is Cynthia.'

'Cynthia,' said the officer with a nod, seeming impatient to be on her way.

'They're holding the young man,' said Connie. 'They want to ask me questions. I reported him. Said I'd seen a guy in a black hoodie over by the bungalows earlier and thought he was acting strange. Looking suss.'

'He gave himself up,' said the policewoman. 'He's only seventeen and it was a bluff. But we—'

'They had me identify him,' Connie interrupted. 'He doesn't sound like a bad kid. Nothing in the bag but a load of rocks. He held up that hotel guy, you know the one you were making eyes at this afternoon, the tall dark one. The kid insisted he take him to see Bill Clinton, or he'd blow us all up. Thought he could get Clinton to open the Post Office down on Wiltshire. Start issuing the welfare cheques. His mother's an invalid and—'

'Connie? Stop. Please.'

'Okay, what is it?'

I had been given my get-out-of-jail card. But this was Connie. I couldn't lie to Connie. I'd spent my whole working life bullshitting to people, selling them what they wanted to hear. I turned my back on the officer and whispered. 'The truth is this; the reason the maid had Theo was because she and another maid—they are the two in my room tonight—they came to the door and heard him crying. I thought it would be okay to leave him in the room on his own while I went—'

'Ladies excuse me?' said the officer. 'Ms Labelle, I'll need to get some details. Please? This way.' She held out her hand to Connie.

'You what!' said Connie. 'You left him? On his own ... in your room?'

'Go do your thing with the police, Con. We'll talk when you're done. I can explain.'

'I bloody doubt it, Cynthia! You left him alone? Fucking Hell, what were you thinking? He's a baby, for fucksake. You left him on his own ... alarms going off? I thought you'd asked the Mexican woman to take him while you went for Sapphie? But you left him alone? Anything could have happened. What if it had been a fair dinkum bomb threat and you—'

'Stop it!' Harsh, but anything to stop the rest of the motherload Connie was ready to hurl at me. I turned to the stressed policewoman. 'Officer, did he get to speak with Mr Clinton, this kid who's worried about his mum's pension check?'

'Of course not.'

I reached into the side pocket of my bag and drew out Sarah Nowak's card. I studied it for a moment, committed the number to memory, and handed it to the cop. 'Might help things if he could. I'm thinking the Governor's communications director might be prepared to have a word with him. Calm things down a little. I hear they're lined up for miles at Post Offices across the city. Anyway, Clinton's here to listen to the people, so here's her card. Worth a try.'

The officer studied the card, looked at me as if I were a loony-toons, but eventually pocketed the card and nodded to Connie. 'Ms Labelle, this way, please,' she said to a confused Connie, who shot a look over her shoulder as she accompanied the policewoman into the office behind Reception. Connie would be stunned that a fool like me—one who could leave a crawling baby alone in a room while she went off to god knows where—could so confidently produce the business card of the American presidential candidate's senior staffer. I left her to her confusion and the law and headed outside in search of the two women I knew now to be Rosa and Juana.

The night was drawing in. The gloaming. The undark. The thought struck me, Mr Valentino! Oh, Connie my sister, my love, if only you knew the half of it. If only you knew. I am not just irresponsible; I am a truly, truly wicked woman.

I worked my way among the dawdlers, guests not yet ready to forego the camaraderie of a shared emergency, no doubt finding the chatty company out on the lawns a more amenable way to suffer the imposition of a curfew than to confine themselves to claustrophobic hotel rooms, even if the air they breathed out here was toxic.

Thick billowing clouds of smoke choked the skies, the fumes an irritant. The atmosphere wreaked of burning automobiles and PVC couches alight and spewing deadly chemicals. The sky wore a dark purple, post-twilight, apocalyptic haze, the area to the south glowing fiercely red as flames from torched buildings continued to rise into the sky and noises that sound eerily like gunshots but might have been crowd control bombs were exploding in the distance. All of it, a reminder of why we were under a curfew, tonight.

By now, the caffeine cravings were at Defcon Four. Where are they, my maidens? I scanned the evacuation area, now floodlit and eventually spotted the two women under the spreading canopy of the Australian fig. With gratitude bursting from every pore, I hurried towards them.

'This is Juana, Ms Smart,' said Rosa as I pulled up.

'I'm Cynthia. And Juana, thank you so much for what you did in there.' I hugged the young woman. 'Thank you, both. I should never have left him. It was only for a few minutes.' I turned to Rosa, 'I guess you filled her in?'

'Si,' said Rosa with a wink.

'Rosa,' said Juana, looking to her friend. 'She tell me. You went for his jars.' The younger woman was shy, the smile slow in coming but it was there.

'His jars, yes.' I gave a rueful smile myself and shook my head. Those bloody jars. If I never have to look at a jar of infant mash again, praise Heaven. 'Let's go get a coffee, shall we?' My invitation was met with palms pushed forward and heads shaken.

'No, no, no. Thank you Ms ... thank you, Cynthia,' protested Rosa. '...but we can go to our staff room. For coffee.'

'Bet it's not as good as what they serve in the café. Come on, girls, let's go.'

I gently ushered the shy pair through the lobby and out to the café by the pool, aware from the way they trailed behind they probably felt uncomfortable being invited to mingle with guests. But damn it, these two good souls deserved to be thanked and any hotel official who tried to give them a hard time would cop my tongue. Domestics or not, staff or not, they were my guests tonight and would be treated as such. And only fair the three of us should get to know each other before disrobing and brushing our teeth in the intimacy of Room 708.

A myriad of fairy lights strung in trees, a galaxy of electric stars blinking in a less than perfect evening sky illuminated the pool area. Except for the filthy smoke, I couldn't have dressed the scene better. To add to the Hollywood effect, the tourmaline water, lit from below, radiated a shimmering glow, flattering to faces now relaxed and reclining in chairs around the pool. Queue in soft breezes whispering through the palms, romantic music—Girl from Ipanema in the background—and you had the full production. Amazing how the universe, one minute upside down with shrill alarms going off, stampedes down fire escapes, uniform cops in bullet-proof vest toting rocket launches, sniffer dogs through the lobby ... and then suddenly, everything rights itself and there you have it; a sound-and-light show fit for Oscar.

I looked around for three empty chairs. 'Here we go,' I said, pointing to a lonely trio of Adirondacks over by the bamboo fencing under a canopy of overhanging palms Far enough away from the crowded area to afford some privacy. 'You take this one, Rosa. Juana, sit here, darling. I'll plop myself down in the middle.'

Before settling back, I caught the eye of a waiter. 'What can I get you two?' I said as the smiling girl came towards us. 'God knows, the moment calls for a celebration.' My body and mind were still buzzing. A blender stuck on whizz. Shock. I was in delayed shock. Or perhaps the malt. Who wouldn't be in shock? To think of it; a few moments more of waking up in an empty room with alarms going off and poor little terrified Theo might have given up on the beating his little fists at the closed door and crawled out the open French doors and up onto the table. It didn't pay to think about it. But I was. Thinking about it.

'Three coffees, please. Make mine double-strength if you don't mind.' Probably strong caffeine was the last thing I needed but I needed strong caffeine. I turned to Rosa and Juana, 'Have a cake, ladies. I hear they're delicious.'

We were interrupted when the person I was about to learn was Rosa's teenage son, alarmed at seeing his mother sitting among the hotel guests, came up to us. He was introduced as Mateo. I put it to the youth that he might know Sapphire. He needn't have answered. The smile said it all. And Sapphie had been right to swoon. This dreamboat of hers was certainly pleasant on the eye.

The other son, significantly older than Mateo and as good-looking, came across to join us.

'And this is my Javier,' said a beaming Rosa. 'Ms Smart.'

'Good evening, Ms Smart,' said Javier.

The brothers were polite and as affectionate towards Juana as they were to their mother, who did not look anywhere old enough to be Javier's mum.

Rosa Lopez, however, was sixty-two. We'd had this conversation while racing down seven floors of the fire escape. The woman looked sensational, especially now as she hugged her sons and shone her womanly light with a gleeful shimmy of her shoulders when I complimented her on her boys. Rosa had fewer spectacular features than the younger Juana with her abundant head of lustrous hair and the Penélope Cruz face, but Lopez had a vitality that made her look loose-limbed and up for a bit of mischief. Every inch Spanish. Exotic. When I teased Rosa that I could cast her in black stilettoes and red fantail dress and put her up on stage, clicking her castanets and dancing a moody flamingo, the joke was on me. Rosa danced the flamingo all the time, according to shy Juana whose sad eyes lit up when she spoke about some of the scandalous antics her fun-loving friend got up to when they were away from work.

All down to a love for this wonderful life we are given, the middle-aged Rosa said piously after her sons had left us. All down to—and at this point there was a wicked grin that left me in little doubt as to what kind of carnal thoughts the cheeky woman harboured—passion. All down to passion, said Rosa before leaning in to whisper the praises of hormone replacement therapy, urging me to give it a try when my time came.

Yes, I would, I assured her. When my time came.

I took hold of each woman's hand and smiled as the three of us leaned back in our chairs holding hands and peering up through the palms to where the natural stars should have been twinkling. Tonight, they weren't. On this night of chaos, Nature's glory was hidden behind a shroud of dark swirling smoke. But save for the tragedy of a rioting city and its brutal causes, I began to feel my juices stir. Forty? Yes, I guess I could face it.

I studied the amazing woman alongside me. If being sixty-two looked like Rosa Lopez, why wouldn't any woman take whatever she could get to get herself there? Like it's been said of praying; you'd be a fool if you didn't.

38

CYNTHIA

We often take for granted the very things
that most deserve our gratitude.
Cynthia Ozick

Santa Monica, Los Angeles
Friday 1st May 1992

Knowing Connie was fit to be tied, I was in no hurry to go upstairs and face the music. I remained sitting in my quiet corner.

It had been twenty minutes since I dispatched Juana and Rosa upstairs, telling them there was a bottle of Moet I'd opened but not touched this afternoon and hopefully with enough bubbles still there for them to enjoy it while they watched TV.

'Can I get you anything else, ma'am?' The waiter, probably wondering why I sat alone out here on such an exciting night.

'No thanks.' Let him wonder. L.A. was well into the curfew. On any ordinary night—not one of towering flames and putrid smoke consuming the city—I would have taken myself off for a run along the beach. Could I sneak past those kids dolled up in army fatigues with their AK-47s slung across their shoulders? Was Mayor Bradley for real. Would he charge me for breaking curfew? Hell, what a shit hole.

David flew out tonight to be with Niall. Once I'd allowed Connie to vent, I could invite myself to share the suite with mother and daughter, leaving Juana and Rosa in peace to enjoy Room 708. I guessed they were embarrassed about the arrangement anyway and would feel more comfortable having the room to themselves. Meanwhile, I caught the waiter's eye and apologized. I had changed my mind. 'A large tumbler of water, please.'

'Ice, madam?'

'Hold the ice.' What was it with Americans? They lived for ice. Ice and air con. Did they do it to set themselves apart from the Mexicans. From the rest of the South American continent. From the third world people who had no other choice but to suffer tepid water—if lucky enough to get water—and blistering heat. I sat back and reflected on tonight's conversation with Rosa and Juana. It had been an eye-opener; Rosa, for the menopause advice, a shining example of a post-menopausal woman who was still a vibrant and attractive femme fatale, according to the giggling pair. A woman who had little trouble getting men into the cot. And with the hilarity out of the way, Juana's secret revealed.

Rosa had explained Juana's quiet reserve. The poor soul was beside herself with worry, she said, holding Juana's hand. Juana lived in South Central, on Vermont where the worst of the rioting was happening. She lived there with her six-year-old daughter and the grandmother. Tonight, as the fires raged down in those parts and the guns went off, it terrified Juana to think of her daughter and the old lady being alone in the madness. And Juana knew about madness, said Rosa, having escaped El Salvador to come to America for hers and her daughter's safety. Her husband, Rosa explained, was one of the tens of thousands Disappeared by El Salvador's evil military junta.

With a protective arm around her friend, Rosa spoke of the suffering, the torture, the targeting of civilians and the sheer terror of living under the regime. Mexico was not good, Rosa said. She also had needed to leave to find a way to bring her family to America and away from the street gangs that preyed on them but added the gangs were nothing, compared to the cruelty dished out by El Salvador's rulers.

Tonight, I had been given a glimpse into the horror women like

Juana, and to a lesser extent Rosa, had suffered. We let them fetch and carry for us. Pick up after us. Have them make up our rooms. Collect our wet towels from the floor. Mop up our tea and coffee slops. And if they're lucky, we leave these proud and courageous women a lousy tip for their troubles. I felt a sense of shame, imagining all the domestic staff I'd taken for granted during my years of travel, instead of paying heed to their stories and who they really were beneath their uniforms.

It struck me I had missed dinner, apart from the crème brulees we three had devoured, thanks to an over-attentive Javier Lopez. Had Connie smuggled portable food up to her suite? Knowing Con, the answer would be yes. The woman had a history—going back to our teenage years—of surreptitiously sliding any plate of left-overs or smorgasbord offerings into napkins. Head held steady, eyes casing the room, sweating on the right moment to do the sly slide and then abracadabra, the disappearing trick! Off the lap and into the bag.

Often back in our student poverty days, the little packets of butter, Vegemite, peanut butter, sugar, raspberry jams, pepper and salt sachets and honeys melted or burst on the way home, causing irreparable damage to textbooks, clothes and whatever other cargo lay at the bottom of Connie's backpack. Bread rolls. My god, the stale rolls I had eaten because Con hated waste. Connie worked on the principle that food served—and not eaten—was food destined for the piggeries and she, being a higher level of sentient being than the pig, was duty-bound to rescue it from the grunters. I remembered Connie secreting a half-eaten hamburger into the pocket of her summer school blazer, only to find beetroot juice had leaked through the fabric. The paper napkin had not been up to the task. Con had gleefully eaten the hamburger remnants on the way to the principal's office for the reprimand, soggy lettuce, runny egg yolk and the offending beetroot, notwithstanding.

Not particularly hungry, I considered taking my evening walk within the hotel grounds before going upstairs. At least inside the confines of the Miramar's luxurious gardens it was still an elegant promenading kind of thing to do. I could jog across to the bungalows, swing down by the big gates and back. Then go upstairs and face the Gorgon's wrath. I left my palmy corner of the pool area and walked through into the lobby.

'Sapphire!' I called out, waving as I hurried across the room. They were about to head around to the elevators, she and Nick.

'Goddy, what are you doing downstairs?'

'What am I doing? I'm waiting for you, dear girl. I'm not exactly Numero Uno for allowing you out of this precinct on your bike. Hi, Nick.'

'Evening,' he said.

'Other stuff as well, Sapph. Anyway, your mum is on the warpath, believe me. Go ring her and let her know her little chic is safely penned, okay? Then we better get you fed.'

'She's been on the phone to me. Several times. She knows,' said Nick. 'Not happy about it but she knows the story.' He smiled at his daughter and indicated Reception.

With a monumental teenage-style despairing sigh, Sapphire left us and headed across the room to one of the hotel's guest phones. I looked back at Nick and caught him smiling. I did likewise and for the briefest moment, we shared a warm feeling. We were parent and godparent to an extraordinary young person. 'It's my fault the poor kid's about to cop it,' I said. 'I probably should have forbidden her to leave the grounds this afternoon but she was so excited that Bill Clinton was here ... upstairs ... She's no doubt told you about the school paper she wants to submit when she gets—'

'Cynthia?'

'Yes, Nick?' I was glad he stopped me. I was in confession mode tonight and might have spilled the beans, confessed I'd been too drunk to drive his daughter this afternoon.

'She put the hard word on me about your film,' said Nick. 'Did I know about it? Yes, I did know about it, I said. Then have I read it? Well, yes, I started to read it. Then, how much had I read? The first few scenes. Only the first few scenes? Yes, because I was rudely interrupted when I had to rescue my wayward daughter from the clutches of the law.' He looked across to Sapphire and grinned. 'You've got a fan there, Cynthia. She wants me to take a serious look at your project. And I intend to do just that.'

I was about to excuse the quality of the script I'd handed him at lunch—explain that I had what would eventually be a superior draft sitting upstairs—but then thought I shouldn't. It could sound a little too Mae West. 'I guess you've got offers pouring in?'

He shrugged. Took his time to answer. 'I'm thinking about heading down your way. Queensland Film's approached me. Am I interested in directing something for one of their writers? Possibly. The Film and Television School's offering me a residency so who knows? I could handle a Sydney sabbatical and Sapphie's tickled about the idea.'

'I'll go check her. She's probably getting her ear chewed off.'

'She's not eaten since lunchtime. I guess we better chase up some chow for her,' he said as I hurried off.

'Rooms 746 and 708, thank you,' I said at the restaurant desk. I had my ticket. The other two didn't. But then neither David Labelle nor Sapphire Labelle of Room 746 had used their tickets tonight, as the record showed. Nick was David Labelle. Sapphire, his daughter. We used a twisted truth to say father and daughter had been locked away with the police, giving evidence about the suspected bomb culprit. I had not turned up on time because I had been frantically looking for them. Dragon Lady at the desk took one look at Sapphie's torn tights and reluctantly bought the lie, letting us in, three apologetic late comers to a buffet whose tired leftovers were already being cleared away. The torn tights were collateral damage from the demo, I presumed. I tried to tease the mop of straggly hair away from her eyes but her hand flew up to grab mine. Okay, I figured. We'll go with the contrived look.

Save for the company, the dinner experience was abysmal. We ate little of what was on offer, hurrying through the meal. Sapphire seemed tired and after hearing some of what had gone on at the rally, I felt it was little wonder. Remembering Ms Martinez's words, I sensed there was more to it but had no intention of pushing her. We discussed the troubled youth responsible for the evacuation, the problems at the Post Offices and the poor wretched citizens deprived of their welfare cheques. The three of us also took a stab at George Bush, complaining about how pathetic his attempt were to end the riots.

Sapphire chipped in with her opinions but mainly, I sensed she was preoccupied. I occasionally caught her staring into space. When Sapphie left us to go to the buffet counter, Nick explained her mood. She was sad about the friend she had made and lost this afternoon.

'Poor girl.'

'Can you ask her about the bruise on her face, Cynthia? I'd like to know who did that to her.'

'I noticed it. She keeps pulling her hair across it. I'll wait until I get her on her own upstairs, hey?'

'Sure. But let me know.'

Even though we tore George Bush apart, I made no mention of the Clinton people or their readiness to embrace the junior reporter. That opportunity had passed and no sense in disappointing the girl by telling her about it. Her day had been traumatic enough, I figured. It would have broken her young heart to know she'd missed the best scoop of all time because she'd taken part in a righteous protest rally. Too much for her to have to think about on what was supposed to be her annual holiday with Nick. I would call Ms Nowak later and explain.

'Better you went around there when he was still asleep, than wait till he was awake,' said Nick when I ventured to speak of my unforgivable babysitting sin.

'Well ... he was stirring. I suppose I could have taken ... I thought—'

'Forget it,' said Sapphire. 'She's neurotic. You know that Goddy.'

'She's cut from the finest mother cloth, Sapphie. I'm the one who goofed. And it could have ended in tragedy.'

'She likes to play the martyr thing if you ask me,' she said, sulkily.

'That's enough, Sapph.' Nick pressed her shoulder. 'You kids are her life. Don't forget it.'

Sapphire took her father's rebuke and changed the subject, telling me all about the black girl Niesha, a brave and apparently beautiful UCLA student radical. Friend, but a friend in passing, Sapphie said with a forlorn look. Nick and I, simultaneously, reached across and took her hands. Nick hugged his beautiful, sentimental, brave daughter. I felt like doing the same but left it as a father and daughter moment. Sapphire's other find of the day, Mateo, also came up for discussion. This brought a smile to her face as she spilled her heart about Mateo and I was able to tell her I agreed, he was 'divine' and I had spoken with him.

'What? Goddy, no!'

'Yes,' I said. 'His mum is sleeping in my room tonight, what's more. Rosa Lopez is one of the maids sharing Room 708. I've met Mateo's big brother, Javier, too.'

Our conversation was cut short when the waiter called time on us. The room had completely emptied of guests by now. 'Let's go face the music,' I said as I took my goddaughter by the arm and led her out to the lobby.

Nick looked puzzled. 'What do I do? Should I go up with you, Sapphire?'

'Please?' she said.

39

CYNTHIA

You can knock on a deaf man's door forever.

Nikos Kazantzakis: Zorba the Greek

Santa Monica, Los Angeles

Friday 1st May 1992

'You're breaking curfew, driving back to Redondo, tonight,' said Connie, pacing the room with a squawking Theo.

'Uh-uh. They gave me a pass. Deliver her here, they said, then beat it home. And if I'm pulled over, I give the number they gave me. I'm on my way.'

'At least *you* got her home.'

I caught the inference. Who wouldn't?

'She's here and she's safe, Connie,' said Nick, waving over his shoulder as he made his way to the door.

'There was a bloody curfew coming, Nick!' said Connie, whose cold blue eyes had me fixed.

'The streets were dangerous,' said the furious woman as she kept pacing the floor, whacking Theo's back and jigging the poor creature. 'Sshh, sshh, there we go, bubba,' she clucked. 'If she hadn't been allowed out Nick, she would never have been at that stupid fucking rally, would she? Never got herself arrested. Christ, don't you see; anything could have happened!'

'Like what, Con?'

'Like she might have ... I don't know ... copped a criminal record, for one thing? Meaning she'd never be allowed back in the States.'

Nick stopped in his tracks and turned to the room. He shot a glance his daughter's way. We were flying at thirty-thousand-feet. Atmospheric turbulence. Oxygen masks, someone. Nobody spoke. Until Connie did.

'Like never being able to visit you again?' said Connie, crash-landing the plane.

'Stop it! Just stop it. I'm an American,' said Sapphire belligerently, from her corner. 'Born here, remember?'

'No more lip from you, young lady. You hear me?'

'The whole of the seventh floor can hear you.'

'You've been grounded. Seen and not heard, remember? Meaning, no Malibu for you tomorrow. That'll teach you to—'

'Okay. Stop it, both of you!' I'd heard enough. I tossed my bag onto the lounge and strode to the door and pulled Nick back into the room. 'Stay. Just for a moment, Nick. You need to hear this. You too, Sapphire. You're not a child.' I shut the door and turned to face Connie.

'Mia culpa ... mia culpa ... mia culpa,' I said, beating my chest and bracing myself for the moment of truth.

I strode up to Connie and stood inches from her face so that she was forced to stop jigging the child. 'I am a worthless piece of shit, Con. Sorry, Nick. Sorry Sapphire. You are right to be angry ... with me ... not your daughter. Letting Sapphie go to the library ... and not telling you ... isn't the only thing I did wrong today. Is it?'

I took Theo from her and placed him on the floor, tossing his blue teddy across the room. He immediately took off on hands and knees in pursuit of it. The child was making my point. 'I get it, Con. Get why you're angry. I am totally, totally unfit to be a mother and you and David were—'

'I'm ... Cyn?'

'No, I left a baby I had been told only last week was a crawling baby. I left him alone in a room seven floors up with patio doors open. Didn't I? So, on just these two transgressions today—' I threw out my arms and faced the rest of my stunned audience. 'Totally, totally unfit to be a mother. And so, yes, it's great that you didn't succumb to my madness last week. Because it was madness, Con. Absolutely. And insulting, to boot. I should never—'

'Cyn. Stop it. Right now. Don't go—'

'No. Listen to me. I should never be left alone with children—babies or teenagers—let alone have one of my own. You want to know the truth? I was too pissed when Sapphire came to my room this afternoon.' I pointed to my goddaughter. 'And that girl over there has been too decent to mention it.'

I turned around to face Nick. 'Yes, Nick. Too pissed to be trusted to do the right thing by your daughter. Too much of a lush to offer her a lift to the library when she came to me, came looking for me to drive her there. I didn't tell you that when I rang you, did I, Nick?'

He put his hand up in a blocking manner.

'The poor girl,' I said, going across to Sapphie and putting an arm around her. 'She came to me, her godmother, to run her around to the library. Fair enough. Problem was, her godmother was in the throes of getting wasted, wiping herself out. Why? Because I hate myself. That's why. I hate who I've become. Today I imploded. I fucking imploded ... in a mire of self-pity.' I looked around at the shocked faces. 'I'm imploding now, right? I'm turning Forty and I'm already washed up.' I was breathing hard. The baby was whimpering ... frightened of the mad woman in the house, I guessed. I took a break. Breathed in and breathed out again. 'Washed up,' I finally muttered as I grabbed my bag and made for the door.

'Because one lousy guy at Goldwyn's turned you down? For God's sake, Cynthia.' Connie yanked Theo up into her arms and looking between me and Nick, shrugged. 'I told you what you needed to—'

'Oh god, Connie!' I spun around to face her. 'Do you honestly think that stupid screenplay is all that's going on in my pathetic little life?'

I strode up to her, stood inches from her face. 'What am I, Con? Who am I? I'm nothing, that's what. Look at you. David adores you. Your kids adore you. And they are superb kids, by the way. You're a real woman, Connie Labelle, a real fucking woman with a real fucking family. Not like—'

'Stop it! All of you just stop it, will you!' shouted Sapphire as she put her hands over her ears and ran to me. 'I love you to death, Goddy. I love everything about you.' She hugged me around my waist, her head buried deep into my midriff. 'Love you to death,' she said, looking up at me.

She turned to her mother, tears streaming down her cheek. 'Nothing would have stopped me going to the library today, Mum. Or to the Pier. Nothing, do you understand? Not you, not Goddy. Daddy, Nick. No one. It's my life. Get out of it!' She ran from the room, into the bedroom, throwing herself face down across her parents' bed.

Leaving the others still absorbing the bomb the teenager had thrown, I followed her in and stood beside the sobbing girl, my hand resting gently on her head.

'I know about it, Goddy,' she said, turning to look up at me. 'Last week?' she took my hand and pulled me down. Her voice was soft. 'At home? 'When you were all out on the veranda?'

Dumbfounded, I could think of nothing else to do but lay beside her, face to face.

'I didn't go to my room straight away—'

'And so, you heard us?'

'I know it was wrong. But I was curious. I shouldn't have but I did, I listened. And last night, when I was in your room watching TV and you were taking a shower and the bathroom door was closed?'

'Yes?'

'I saw that big envelope on the end of your bed.'

'Sapphie.' I smoothed her cheek and dreaded what was coming.

'I read that stuff, Goddy. It was so wrong of me but I read it. About your hormones and things. And those images.' She sat up and brushed wet tendrils from her eyes, turning to fix me in a penetrating gaze. 'They were cruel to you last week,' she finally said. 'So cruel, Goddy. I can't believe it. I can't!'

'No, Sapphie. They weren't. They weren't cruel, my precious. Not at all. Your mum and dad were right. It was too big of an ask. I hurt your mother's feelings. She's been hiding it—'

'Until now!'

'I hurt her, Sapphie. It was insulting. I had no right to ask. No right at all.' I sat up and hugged her, cradling her head to my chest. 'I have you, and I love you, my darling girl,' I whispered as I ran my fingers through her sweaty hair, pulling it away from her cheek. It was apparent she had been trying to hide the hand imprint by dropping a thick fall of hair across one eye. An ugly red blotch on her cheek. With our faces together, I whispered, even softer this time, my eye going to the open bedroom door where Nick and Connie were in conversation in the living room. 'Tell me about it, sweetheart?'

'About this?'

'About that, yes. Who hurt you, Sapph? I know something happened at the library this afternoon. Gloria Martinez was about to tell me when she seemed to think better of it. Maybe you told her not too. But I figured something happened. Do you want to get your mum in here?'

'Please. And Nick, too.'

I left Sapphire soaking in a hot bath, with Connie and Nick making plans to gather the evidence from the firefighter and the librarian. They would report the attack to Officer Lovelace in the morning. It was Sapphire's decision, hers alone. Her attackers should be made to answer for what they did to try and damage her sense of self. Other girls shouldn't be treated the way they had treated her.

We heard her out in silence, letting her vent the anger and the indignation she felt at the way the louts in the red convertible had violated her rights.

It was her own, well-considered decision to report the attack.

And after hearing what had happened to her daughter, the goddaughter I had so shockingly abandoned, I waited for the eruption.

It didn't happen. Connie's anger was palpable but the loving mother's way of handling the atrocity that had befallen Sapphire was to fuss, enough that the level-headed teenager seemed the one in control. Even to providing Nick with the exact time, place and the red convertible's registration number. 174 SDI. And a full physical description of her three attackers. And details of two her witnesses.

Now I sat alone on the beach out front of the Miramar, staring out at a murky horizon.

Dark columns of smoke rose over the worst of the afflicted areas. Flames licked the sky. I could hear sirens and rotor blades chopping the air above. A young National Guard—who at first had challenged my right to be out after curfew, before considering the Aussie visitor harmless enough—stood a short way off from me. In his camouflage gear and heavy ammo, he reminded me of the youths who fought in Vietnam twenty years ago. It was reflected here on the streets, tonight.

Gunshots, tanks, helicopters, fire, dread.

This was how it must have been for Jesse.

In his letters home he had never reached far enough into his soul to talk about his fears, no doubt censoring himself ahead of the brass who checked letters before they went out. In Mosman we often sat late into the night contemplating philosophical issues, discussing our deepest feelings about religion and politics, about death and how we would face it when it came but Jesse hadn't wanted to frighten me about his war. Wouldn't have me worry about him up there in the jungle. But it must have been horrific, a nightmare. Especially for one as naturally placid and gentle as Jesse McKenzie.

It had all come out, the truth of the carnage. Thanks to the cameras and fearless reporting, the world had learned about the savagery of Vietnam. The duplicity of politicians. The slaughter. I picked up a handful of sand and watched it drift through my fingers.

What parts of him were left behind in the jungle when they were ambushed, I wondered? When the grenade blew up? His precious blood? Bits of his brain tissue? Half an arm, part of his leg? They never told me how he died, from what wounds. I was too young, they said. It didn't matter, anyway. Jesse wasn't coming home. They never knew how close we really were to each other. I was just the girlfriend, young and able to get on with my life.

I thought about the letter I had written to him, my last letter, about my missed period.

Written but never sent.

I toured the University grounds on Open Day, the letter in my bag, stamped and ready to post. I joined some campus clubs, the Labor Club and a women's group. I made my decision. On that day, I was certain I wanted a Sydney University education more than I wanted our baby. I tore the envelope into small pieces, tossed it in the nearest bin and went off to find the address in Bondi of the Curlewis Clinic.

Had I listened to Connie, not been afraid of shaming my family, told a sanctimonious society to get fucked and sent that letter to Jesse with the happy news of the pregnancy, might the father-to-be have been less heroic in going out ahead of his mates? Could my letter have saved his life? I will never know.

Unforgivably, I had been too pig-headed to take counsel from Connie. Too ready to want it all behind me. Had I not succeeded in pushing Connie away that day at the clinic—not walked into that Bondi surgery, got up on the table, put my feet in their stirrups and in ten lethal minutes of suction and small-talk ended the inconvenience threatening my brilliant career—might he be alive? In truth, there was nothing I could have done to save Jesse from that grenade but today, there would be his child to tell of his bravery, a child to carry on a father's story. A new life to fight back against the nihilism of war.

To have given birth to Jesse's child, to greet him at the dock at the end of his tour of duty with our baby strapped to my chest—as Sapphie had been strapped to Connie's. One unforgivable decision as prologue to haunt my days. If only I'd had the courage to put it to Fiona and Gus McKenzie, a couple whose only child was fighting up in the jungles of Vietnam. Asked them if they'd accept the pregnancy, albeit that we were young and not yet married. If I'd let them know their son's baby was on the way, Jesse's baby. Earnest Presbyterians but wouldn't they have stood by me, even back in those days?

But I hadn't asked. And I'd already secretly aborted three days before the McKenzies received the dreaded telegram and visited the Smarts to inform us of the tragedy. Three days. Three days I could never reclaim.

Jesse's baby would have eased their loss, given them a grandchild to cherish. All the medals and ribbons in the world could never compensate even the patriotic McKenzies for the loss of their soldier son but a grandson or granddaughter might have eased their pain a little. As it was, grief pursued them to their graves.

And Paddy and Moira. Too ashamed to tell them their eighteen-year-old unmarried daughter had ignored all the advice and warnings, committed the unforgivable sin and got herself knocked-up. Even as the two grieving families sat in the McKenzie's dimly lit living room after the funeral, trying bravely to tell Jesse stories to keep him alive, there'd been no admission from me that I had just cost them the only chance they were ever going to have to hold on to something of Jesse other than the stories and the memories.

The National Guard soldier wandered across to me and offered to light the cigarette I'd been nursing. 'Thanks,' I said, passing it up to him once it was lit. 'I'm trying to quit. Old habit,' I laughed. He took the cigarette, buried it in the sand, pointed to his watch and with a smile and a salute walked back to his post. I watched him go.

Our child would be about the same age. And the same age as Jesse the day at the docks when I kissed him goodbye. A grey, rainy, sad Sydney morning lost in the mists of long ago, the morning he hugged me and kissed the gold Claddagh ring before slipping it on my finger.

I'll always be with you, aways a part of you, he whispered that day.

Promises made in the rain. Echoes across empty chasms. Regrets and self-reproach.

Self-loathing was territory I knew intimately, having circled the wagons so often, so relentlessly. I had betrayed the McKenzies. Betrayed my parents. Betrayed loyal Connie who had promised to stand by me and the baby, even trying to drag me out of the clinic, right up to moment before the procedure. All of them, I had betrayed them all, robbed them of so much.

Jesse. Vietnam. Nui Dat. Words that chilled me.

I closed my eyes, not to forget but to remember.

Bright echoes, Professor Wadsworth called them; distinct images of the six tiny bones imbedded in the walls of my uterus—the foetal remains of a botched abortion two decades ago.

Last week, in the scans. Tiny limbs showing up. Bright echoes, the name the medicos give the shadowy images. Rare but not unknown. Intrauterine remains embedded. A small part of Jesse's DNA. The tiny bones of our never-to-be child. Our joined chromosomes. Proof I had not been just the girlfriend. We had loved each other and had planned to spend the rest of our lives together.

The probable cause of my infertility all these years. The barren wife. Acting like an IUD, said the esteemed professor of gynaecology. A hysteroscopy is the gold standard for the removal of these bony fragments and provides a complete resolution of symptoms, a minor procedure, Wadsworth assured me as he turned from his x-ray wall. Even now, were we to remove the retained foetal bones, he said in his avuncular tone, reclaiming his chair behind the big brown desk, there is a chance … a slim chance at this stage ... that you could conceive. He cited international case studies. At any rate, they should be removed, he concluded.

I'll always be a part of you, promise? Whatever happens, you and your Jesse? A summer's night in Mosman. The night of jasmine, gardenias and scented roses.

And the same promise that went with the Claddagh ring one sad, rainy morning by the Woolloomooloo docks. How could I let them trash the last of him? I had promised him. Always a part of me.

'Can anyone join the party?' It was Nick walking out of the darkness as he came along the beach towards me with the young soldier in the rear. I leapt up and brushed the sand away, guilty at having overstayed my time, caught in another world. The world where I had to leave Jesse in a foreign jungle, broken into a thousand pieces I could never put back together again.

'Connie thinks she might have gone a little overboard.'

'You reckon?'

He gave a gentle laugh, not unkind, a sympathetic laugh. 'She sent me to bring you home, Cyn.'

'It's been a tough day, Nick.'

'I think so. A tough day, especially for some poor suckers who won't wake up tomorrow. Even those who do, they'll wake up and realize their world is in a mess.'

'Their whole country's in a mess.'

As we walked back across the sand, Nick propped. I turned to see what had stopped his progress. 'She possibly shouldn't have told me,' he said. 'But well, heck, she did, Cyn. You know Connie. She told me about the visit to the Blue Mountains last week.'

'Oh, for fucksake!'

'She told me out of real concern for you, Cyn. Honestly. She probably thought I'd understand you better.' He took my hands and held them as he stared into my eyes. 'It seems that's what the old girl wants, for me to understand you. She loves you.'

'It was a slap in the face at first but I'm over it.'

'No hard feelings about the refusal?'

I took my time to answer. 'Uh-huh. No hard feelings. She's my sister, isn't she? My soul sister? I love her. That's it. I love her. End of story.' I released myself from his grip, picked up my pace and walked ahead of him. I could see the moon through the clouds. Faintly. Could see a few dim stars trying their hardest to break through the gloom. The riots would go on for days, people would get shot and killed. Buildings would burn. And the Korean shopkeepers would clean up the wreckage and start all over again.

I turned to Nick. 'Have you ever danced on a beach at midnight, Mr Cristos?'

At first, he looked puzzled. And then he signalled the soldier across to him.

Putting his arm around the surprised younger man's shoulder, Nick eyed him, smiled, and began to hum the well-recognized theme song as his foot stepped out on the sand.

The youth shot me a wink, shrugged and slinging his rifle around his back, fell in with the slow-stepping folk dancer, the two men, shoulder to shoulder, stepping out the rhythmical Greek folkdance accompanied by Nick's musical beat.

Deliberately, unhurriedly at first, then gradually their rhythmical movements picking up until faster and faster, both smiling, they moved to the tinkling of bouzouki and mandolins. Zorba's legendary dance. The dance of the philosopher who said a person must keep moving. Stagnation is death. On a slope, even a stone comes to life. All that can be enjoyed must be enjoyed here and now.

And perhaps, that was the best strategy after all. Move on. Treasure the past but know it can't be changed. Don't dwell there. Enjoy the here and now and like Zorba, like Rosa. Find the passion, let yesterday go and tomorrow take care of itself.

I left the dancing pair laughing and high fiving each other, lighting cigarettes and looking out on the troubled horizon.

I crossed Ocean Avenue, heading for the Miramar Hotel and Suite 746.

40

CYNTHIA

Cnr Florence & Normandie
South Central, Los Angeles
Saturday 2nd May 1992

Ignoring this morning's Icelandic conditions at the uber air-conditioned Miramar, I'd chosen for the march a pair of denim shorts, a soft embroidered muslin shirt and my white espadrilles. Rosa reminded me to apply sunscreen and Juana, to take a hat. Thankfully the Indian shirt was letting in what little breeze there was in downtown Los Angeles on this scorcher of a day.

'Hi, I'm Cynthia. From Australia,' I said as I approached the man. He was tall, ebony and athletic. I pinned him for a basketball player.

'Leon,' he said, adding with a cheeky grin, 'G'day, maaayt'

'Yeah, g'day to you, too, Leon.' We shook hands and I thought; there you go, Mick Dundee again, my penance for sharing my country with the celluloid larrikin. 'They sent us over here. We convinced them we could swing a boom.'

'From Oz, hey? Appreciate your help, sister. ' He turned and signaled to the woman standing a little way off from him who held the hand of a small child, the little girl's torturously tight pigtails tied off in red bows stuck out at right angles from her skull. 'C'mon over here you guys. Say hi to Cynthia.' He turned back to me. 'You said Cynthia, right?'

'Right. Or Cyn,' I said with a shrug. 'Friends call me Cyn.'

He met the comment with a wink. 'Cool. Cyn's from Down Under, guys. And she's a good sister. She wants to help.'

'Here comes my friend,' I said as Connie approached us. 'She's also handy with a broom.'

'You guys come from the march, right?'

'Yes,' said Connie. 'Hello,' she said to the woman. 'I'm so sorry.' Connie cast her arms wide to encompass the ugliness around us. 'For all this.' She bent down and attempted to engage with the shy little girl but lids came down slowly over beautiful big brown eyes before the child ducked behind her mother's leg.

The basketball player took the broom the woman held out to him and passed it to Connie. He moved a short way off and grabbed a second broom that had been leaning against the wall, possibly his own. 'Here you go, Cyn, take this.'

'So,' I said, looking at Connie down on her haunches. 'What should we be doing apart from frightening this poor pet and getting in your way?'

He laughed.

'Where should we start?'

'Say. Y'wanna sweep some of that mess over there into piles. Be great.' He pointed to a trashed area across the road. 'Don't go near the big stuff. And stay clear of the window glass, of course. Just if y'all can make piles, right? Some dude's gonna come behind and bag it. Y'all okay with that?'

'Sure. Whatever.'

'Right-oh, maaayts,' he said.

'Mick Dundee's got a lot to answer for, hasn't he?' said Connie. 'I guess you saw the movie.' She was looking up at him from where she was still squatting, still trying to engage a poor little kid that any sane adult could see wasn't coming out from behind the mother's leg anytime soon.

Leon pantomimed pulling out his big crocodile knife. 'That's not a knife. This is a knife.'

The mum nudged him. He saluted and quickly dug into a large sports bag sitting against the wall. 'Here you go then, cobbers. One each for y'troubles.' He handed us a white t-shirt each.

'Thank you.' I took the t-shirt from him, studied it and smiled at the couple then tucked it into the canvas bag slung across my chest. Connie battled to slip hers over her boobs. The woman took it from her and swapped it for a larger size. We all laughed as Connie, not intending to be twice embarrassed, sheepishly stowed it in her knapsack.

'Take 'em home with you, ladies,' said Leon. 'And remember us. All the way Down Under. Remember us back here in L.A.'

'Thank you. I shall,' said Connie. 'As if any of us could possibly—'

'Forget you,' I said, yanking Connie by the arm. 'Let's go.'

'What did you guys think of the march?' he called after us as he stood, his feet apart, hands on hips. The little girl, by now, was tugging at her mother's jeans, no doubt impatient for this stranger interlude to be done with. The mother looked impatient as well. It was hardly the right time and place for a pow-pow but the friendly young man seemed as ready to prolong the meeting as Connie. I simply wanted to be useful. Otherwise, we might as well have stayed in the march.

'It felt right ... to march,' said Connie. 'But we figured we might be more of a help doing something practical like this. There're enough of them marching. Plenty of celebrities in there too. Hollywood to the rescue,' she said with a laugh. 'We stepped out of it back there a bit and here we are.'

'And we sure appreciate it, sis. Sure do.'

'Let's go, Con. C'mon.' I waved the couple off with a salute and dragging Connie in my wake, headed across to the other side of the road, stepping gingerly around smoking debris, piles of ash and shattered glass, aware the Jody Boffas were copping a hiding.

The tail-end of the marchers had been and gone and more than an hour of sweeping and picking up had passed before the Clinton entourage hit Normandie. Towering above the heads of most who were gathered around him—politicians, journalist, municipal dignitaries and those with their stories to tell—I saw the famous head bent in earnest conversation with an animated black man. Bill Clinton was a man who listened.

'Con,' I called to her. Connie was further down the pavement, going at it like she was tasked with cleaning up the whole of Los Angeles by nightfall. 'They're here. They've arrived.'

We stopped sweeping and leaned our chins on our brooms while we watched the crowd gathering around the candidate. I picked out Agent Maloney—dark suit, dark glasses, hovering near Clinton—and pointed him out to Connie.

'A bit of hunk, hey?' she said.

Amid the turmoil, I spotted Sapphire—blue jeans, white t-shirt, black Yankee's cap, hair pulled back with a band. She was speaking to a teenager of similar age to herself. Notebook in hand and studiously recording the interview. Any moment, I expected my goddaughter to look across and be surprised to see us.

I scouted the crowd for Nick and found him in conversation with Sarah Nowak. Late last night when I figured the Clinton party would have returned from their campaign meetings, I made the call to Sarah, a second go at setting up Sapphie's interview. I had never imagined she'd be so wholeheartedly embraced by them.

Given what I explained had happened to the brave girl in her pursuit of interviewing her hero, including not only the attack but later being arrested at the protest rally, Nowak was lapping up my hard sell when the great man himself came on the line. The Arkansas southern drawl was thrilling to hear. I was speaking to the man who I knew beyond doubt would soon be leading the free world. I'd had trouble staying on my feet. My knees had wobbled. I'd felt sixteen all over again.

Of course, he would love to give Sapphire the interview, he said in his unmistakable Arkansas drawl. He had read her note. If you can have her ready at her door by seven-thirty, why not let her come down to breakfast with us and let's do the interview over bagels.

I was already feeling excited enough about telling Sapphire she was getting her scoop when he topped the pie with a cherry. He was inviting Sapphire to accompany his party on the meet-and-greet down in South Central. Providing, he cautioned, it was okay with her parents and one of them accompanied her. When I mentioned Nick Cristos, Clinton went into a rave about a particular scene in Cristos's *A Given*, the much talked-about hit at Venice last year.

I replaced the receiver feeling I'd just returned from an outer galaxy.

'Are you as proud of her as I am?' said Connie, stopping her frenetic sweeping to look at the scene being played out across the road. 'What a kid! Let's get over there. Surprise her.'

'Uh-huh. Wouldn't look professional. It'd embarrass her, Con.'

Nick was the first to spot us. He checked the situation before peeling off to come across. 'She's amazing, that girl,' he said. 'I tell you; she had more questions than that guy had answers. Yeah, honestly. My god, does she know her American politics.'

He took my face between his hands and planted a kiss on my lips, a quick and wholesome one but a kiss, for all that. I shot Connie a sheepish look. She grinned.

'How was it, breakfast I mean?' I said, still looking over to the Clinton crowd but aware I was putting a finger softly to my lips.

'By all accounts, it was a hoot. I got there at the tail-end but I loved watching her in action, Cyn. She's so dammed mature. No gushing, no shyness. I reckon Clinton saw some kudos for himself in giving her the exclusive. She came away with a great pic of Chelsea he autographed for her and gave permission for it to be used in her article.'

Nick patted us both on the shoulder and hurried off again to be with his charge.

Connie watched him go before turning her gaze on me. She shrugged, smiled and picked up her broom.

Diving into my bag, I retrieved my water bottle and a couple of the health bars Rosa had packed for us from her guest supplies trolly. The white t-shirt was on top. I dragged it out and held it up.

What's black, what's white, it read on the front. I turned it over. ... *when everything turns to ash?*

I showed it to Connie. 'What's black, what's white when everything turns to ash? Kind of true, no?'

I waited for her reply.

Despite Con appreciating the fact I'd secured the Clinton deal for Sapphie, and despite Nick assuring me she harboured no grudge against me for my bad mothering yesterday, there had still been whisps of icy winds blowing through the sister-love this morning.

But my heart was warm and my arms were ready. It was up to Connie. Nothing is black and white, black or white. Who's right? Who's wrong? It's all a matter of degrees. And no way can our friendship turn to ashes because Connie's got it in her head that I consider her only good for breeding. Or for my part, that I was hurt by her refusal to hatch me a baby.

Connie examined the shirt's logo. She looked across to where Sapphire was introducing a tall, thin black girl with an Afro to the candidate. Connie spread her arms. 'Do you forgive me, Cyn?'

I dropped the shirt back in the bag. Connie's blue eyes were filling up with tears. 'Oh, Con. Forgive you? I love you, girl. I just want us to get back to being like we—'

'I've been a lousy sister, haven't I?' Connie said. 'I mean, come on. You were given really shitty news and what did I do but turn—'

'I was way out of line, Con. I had no right asking such an outlandish favour from you. Or David. Absolutely no right. I don't think of you that way. Honestly, darling. I don't.'

'Maybe sometimes.' She shrugged. 'But nothing's black or white, is it?' She was smiling now.

'You had a right to resent me, Con, it was a brutal ask. I never intended to imply—'

'You've got *her,* Cyn,' said Connie, nodding across the road to the girl we both cherished. 'You always will. Always.'

'I've got our girl, you're right. I'm fixed for life, Con.'

'You bloody-well deserve her,' she laughed. 'And all the teenage angst that comes with her,' she said, pulling a face.

'We'll get her through it. We'll manage.'

I looked around at the destruction in the neighbourhood. The buildings still smouldering; the overturned vehicles; the smashed store windows; the sorry remnants of loot dropped and left behind in the mob's god-awful rush to ransack their neighbourhood. 'How do these poor buggers move past this?'

'It kinda makes our piddly little squabbles amount to nothing but a hill of beans,' said Connie, grinning, aware of the Hollywood cliché.

I whacked her on the backside with my broom.

'Ouch. That hurt!"

We laughed, knocked brooms together then waved them in the air to attract Sapphire's attention and were rewarded when the teenage reporter, with notebook tucked under her arm and pencil sideways in her mouth, acknowledged our presence with a passing wave.

'By the way,' said Connie, resuming her broom work. 'Happy Birthday, sis.'

BOOK CLUB QUESTIONS

1. Did you feel the three different Points of View worked for you?
2. To which character did you most relate and why?
3. Were you familiar with the 1992 L.A. riots before reading *Bright Echoes*?
4. Did you see a connection between those riots and recent ones in the U.S.?
5. Is current relevance in a story important to you or not?
6. Was there too much about the riots?
7. Did the author's use of interiority for her three main characters help you relate better to them?
8. Discuss the novel's pace. Did it lag; if so, where?
9. Were you keen to discover the secret in the big white radiologist's envelope?
10. Did the revelation shock/disgust/prove interesting?
11. Did you get the dual purpose of the book's title (echoes of the 1992 flames, as well as the ultrasound medical name)?
12. Would you recommend *Bright Echoes*?

CPSIA information can be obtained
at www.ICGtesting.com
Printed in the USA
LVHW050113010522
717630LV00004BA/333

9 780648 000297